Paul Gerhardt as a Hymn Writer and his Influence on English Hymnody

By

Theodore Brown Hewitt, Ph.D.

Assistant Professor of German
Williams College

New Haven
Yale University Press
London: Humphrey Milford
Oxford University Press
Mdccccxviii

Library of Congress Cataloging in Publication Data

Hewitt, Theodore Brown, 1881—
    Paul Gerhardt as a hymn writer and his influence on English hymnody.

    "Second edition."
    Originally presented as the author's thesis, Yale, 1917.
    Reprint of the 1918 ed. published by Yale University Press, New Haven; with new afterword and updated bibliography.
    Bibliography: p. 171
    Includes index.
    1. Gerhardt, Paulus, 1607—1676. 2. Hymns, English—History and criticism. 3. Literature, Comparative—German and English. 4. Literature, Comparative—English and German. I. Title.
BV330.G4H4 1976 245'.31'0924 [B] 76-13913
ISBN 0-570-01313-5

A portion of the expense of printing this thesis has been borne by the Modern Language Club of Yale University from funds placed at its disposal by the generosity of Mr. George E. Dimock, of Elizabeth, N. J., a graduate of Yale in the class of 1874.

TO

B. A. F. H.

PREFACE

Das deutsche Lied ist einzig,
Ein Schatz für Geist und Herz,
Gehoben aus den Tiefen,
Wo Freude wohnt und Schmerz.
Kein andres Volk auf Erden
Genosz des Schicksals Gunst,
Solch einen Schatz zu sammeln,
Reich an Natur und Kunst.*

So far as is known to the writer of this thesis there has appeared hitherto no attempt to treat comprehensively and in detail the subject of the direct and indirect influence of Paul Gerhardt's hymns upon English and American sacred song. That there exists a very real influence is universally known, but how widely it has made itself felt is apparently a matter of little concern on the part of many, because we often find hymnals accrediting a hymn to the English translator with no mention of its original author. The present dissertation has been prompted by a desire to make some contribution to the subject of the relation of English and German hymnody in general, and in particular to show the great debt which the hymnody of England and America owes to the poetry of Paul Gerhardt. It was presented to the Faculty of the Graduate School of Yale University in candidacy for the degree of Doctor of Philosophy in June, 1917.

For great assistance rendered to me by way of suggestion of sources I am under obligation to Dr. Bernard C. Steiner of the Enoch Pratt Free Library of Baltimore, Professor Gustav Gruener of Yale University, Professor Waldo S. Pratt of the Hartford Theological Seminary, Professor H. C. G. von Jagemann of Harvard University and to Professor John G. Robertson of the University of London; for help not only in this phase

---

* Stanza 1 of *Das Deutsche Lied,* a poem of six stanzas by Professor A. H. Palmer, 1915.

of the work but also in the general treatment of the subject I am deeply indebted to the counsel of my father, Professor Emeritus John H. Hewitt of Williams College and to Professor Arthur H. Palmer of Yale University.

New Haven, Connecticut,
        April 9, 1918.

CONTENTS

                                                                   PAGE

Bibliography xi

PART I

CHAPTER

I   Gerhardt's Life and Times 1

II   Gerhardt's Relation to Earlier Hymnody of Germany 6

III   Characteristics of Gerhardt as a Hymn Writer 13

PART II

I   History of English Hymnody and the German Influence upon English Hymn writing from the Early XVIth through the XIXth Century 27

II   English Versions of Gerhardt's Hymns 35

APPENDIX

1. Biographical Sketches of Translators 144

2. Tabulation of Alliteration, Assonance, etc. 149

3. Index by Subjects 158

4. Index of English Versions 160

5. Index of Gerhardt's Hymns 167

6. Afterword 170

7. Bibliography 171

BIBLIOGRAPHY[1]

Allg. deutsche Biographje, 1875 ff: article by Berthau.

Bachmann, D. J. F.: Paul Gerhardt. Vortrag im Evangel. Verein für kirchliche Zwecke. Nebst 18 Liedern v. P. Gerhardt. Berlin, Schlawitz, 1863.

Bachmann, J. F.: Gerhardts Gedichte: Historisch-kritische Ausgabe. Berlin, 1866, 1886.

Benson, L. F.: The English Hymn. New York, 1915.

Blätter für Hymnologie: A. F. W. Fischer and J. Linke, 1883-1889.

Bode, Wilhelm: Quellennachweis über die Lieder des hannoverschen und des lüneburgischen Gesangbuches, samt den dazu gehörigen Singweisen. Hannover, 1881.

Bötticher, G.: Die Literatur d. 17. Jh. Angew. u. erläutert, 3 verb. Auflage. (Denkmäler e. älteren dtsch. Lit. IV, 1.)

Bunsen, Chr. Karl Josias, Freiherr von: Versuch eines allgemeinen Gesang- u. Gebetbuchs. Hamburg, 1833. Allgemeines evang. Gesang- u. Gebetbuch. Hamburg, 1846.

Burdach, A.: A monograph, in *Deutsch-Evangelische Blätter* 32. pp. 179-84 (giving reasons for fixing May 27, 1676, as the date of Gerhardt's death).

Crüger, Johann: Geistliche Kirchenmelodien, 1649.
"   "   : Praxis Pietatis Melica, 1648 etc.
"   "   : Geistliche Andachten, pub. by Ebeling, 1666-1667.

Cunz: Geschichte des Kirchenliedes. Leipzig, 1855.

Deutsche Nationallitteratur by J. Kürschner: Vol. 31,—Das deutsche Kirchenlied des 16. u. 17. Jahrhunderts.

Dietz: Tabellarische Nachweisung des Liederbestandes. Marburg, 1904.

Ebeling, J. G.: Pauli Gerhardi Geistliche Andachten. Berlin, 1667 etc.

Eckart, R.: P. Gerhardt—Bibliographie.
"   "   : Stimmen u. Schriften über P. Gerhardt.
"   "   : Ein Nachklang z. Jubiläumsjahr, 1907.

Feustking, Joh. Heinr.: Gerhardts Geistreiche Haus- und Kirchenlieder. Zerbst, 1707.

Fischer-Tümpel: Das deutsche evangel. Kirchenlied des 17. Jahrh. Gütersloh, 1906.

Gerok, Karl: Gedichte von P. Gerhardt, mit Einleitung u. Lebensabrisz. 6. Auflage. Leipzig, 1907.

Gervinus, G. G.: Geschichte der deutschen Nationalliteratur. ed. 1842, pt. III, p. 366.
"   "   : Geschichte der deutschen Dichtung, 1871, vol. III, p. 460 ff.

Geyer, P.: Paul Gerhardts Geistliche Lieder, in *Neue Kirchliche Zeitschrift* 18, pp. 177-199. 1907.

---

[1] Owing to the European war it has been impossible to extend this bibliography beyond the year 1913.

Goedeke, Karl: Gedichte von Paul Gerhardt mit Einleitung und Anmerkungen, in *Deutsche Dichter des 17. Jahrhunderts,* vol. XII. Leipzig, 1877.

"   "   : Zur Geschichte der deutschen Dichtung III, p. 182. Dresden.

"   "   : Grundrisz zur Geschichte der deutschen Dichtung, vol. II, III. Dresden, 1884, 1887.

Günther, R.: Über Deutung und Änderung einiger Stellen in Paul Gerhardts Liedern, in *Monatsschrift für Gottesdienst und Kunst* 11, pp. 343-348.

Hahne, F.: P. Gerhardt u. A. Buchner, in *Euphorion* 15, pp. 19-34. 1907. (A good article on Gerhardt's metre.)

Haupt, E.: Der Konflikt zwischen P. Gerhardt u. d. Groszen Kurfürsten, in *Deutsch-Evangelische Blätter,* 32, pp. 80-98.

Herford, C. H.: Studies in the literary relations of England and Germany in the sixteenth century. Cambridge, 1886.

Herrmann, P.: Deutsche Dichter u. Gedichte auf Island, in *Unterhaltungsbeilage der Täglichen Rundschau.* Berlin, 1907, N. 147-8. (Das Lied v. Kaiser Friedrich Rotbart—Paul Gerhardt—F. de la Motte-Fouqué.)

Jahresberichte für neuere deutsche Literaturgeschichte. Stuttgart, Leipzig, Berlin, 1890 ff.

Julian, J.: Dictionary of Hymnology. Scribners, New York, 1892.

Kaiser, Her. v. P.: Paul Gerhardts sämtl. Lieder. (Hessische Volksbücherei, vol. 339-345.)

Kawerau, G.: Paul Gerhardt: ein Erinnerungsblatt, in *Schriften des Vereins für Reformationsgeschichte,* pp. 92-97. Halle, 1907.

Kelly, J.: Paul Gerhardt's Spiritual Songs. London, 1867.

Kirchner, J.: Die Lieder P. Gerhardts, in *Evangelisches Schulblatt* 55, pp. 31 ff.

"   "   : P. Gerhardts Gattin und Sohn: ib. pp. 236-242. (Anna Maria geb. Berthold u. Paul Friedrich Gerhardt.)

"   "   : Gerhardt inmitten seiner Leidensgenossen. In *Studierstube* 5, pp. 184-193.

"   "   : P. Gerhardt. In *Beiträge zur Literaturgeschichte,* Heft 51. Leipzig, 1907.

Knipfer, P.: Paul Gerhardt. Leipzig, 1906.

Koch, E. E.: Geschichte des Kirchenliedes und Kirchengesangs der christlichen insbesondere der deutschen evangelischen Kirche. 1847, 1852, 1866-9.

Kraft: an article in Ersch u. Gruber's *Allg. Enzyklopädie.* 1855.

Krapp, L.: a monograph in *Gottesminne* 5, pp. 540-560.

Krummacher, F. W.: an article in Piper's *Evangelische Kalender,* pp. 204 ff. Berlin, 1866.

Kübler, Theodore: Historical Notes to the Lyra Germanica. London, 1865.

Langbecker, E. Chr. C.: Leben und Lieder von Paulus Gerhardt. Berlin, 1842.

Lippelt, W.: Ein eigenhändiger Brief P. Gerhardts nach Lübben im Autographenhandel. Niederlausitz Mitt. 10, pp. 61-62.

Massie, R.: Lyra Domestica. London, 1860, 1864.

Monatsschrift für Gottesdienst und Kunst. (Paul Gerhardt Heft.) 1907, 12. N. 3. (Monographs on the relation of composers and artists to Gerhardt.)

Nelle, W.: Gerhardt, Rist, Tersteegen, Gellert in unseren heutigen Gesangbüchern, in *Monatsschrift für Gottesdienst und Kunst* 10, pp. 141-151; 189-191; 250.

Niebeling, F.: Paul Gerhardt u. seine Lieder nach Text u. Melodie, in *Deutsch-evangelische Rundschau,* 1907.

Pachaly, P.: Die Form der Gerhardtschen Lyrik. In *Euphorion* 14, pp. 502-506. 1907.

Pahnke, K. H.: Paul Gerhardt, ein Idealist des Glaubens, in *Idealisten u. Idealismus des Christentums,* pp. 100-128. Tübingen, 1903.

Petrich, Hermann: Paul Gerhardt, seine Lieder u. seine Zeit. Gütersloh, 1907.
"   "   : Der Dichter u. seine Kunst. Gütersloh, Bertelsmann, pp. 267-304.
"   "   : Paul Gerhardt. Ein Beitrag z. Gesch. d. deutschen Geistes. Gütersloh, Bertelsmann XIV, 360 p.

Pick, B.: Lyra Gerhardti; or selection of P. Gerhardt's spiritual songs: a memorial leaf. Burlington, Iowa, German Literary Board, 12°, 1907.

Reclam, Ph.: Gerhardts Gedichte, in the "Universal-Bibliothek."

Ritschl, A.: Geschichte des Pietismus. Bonn, 1880, 1884, 1885.

Rogge, B.: P. Gerhardt, der christl. Liederdichter. In *Deutsch-evangel. Charakterbilder.* 2. Aufl. Altenburg, 1903, pp. 151-160.

Roth, E. G.: P. Gerhardt, nach seinem Leben und Wirken. Leipzig, 1829.

Schaff-Gilman: Library of Religious Poetry. 1881.

Schaff-Herzog: Encycl. of Religious Knowledge. New York, 1894.

Scherer, Wilhelm: Geschichte der deutschen Literatur. Berlin, 1899.

Schirks, W.: Paul Gerhardt, ein Lebens- und Charakterbild. In *Theol. Stud. u. Kritik,* 1855.

Schmidt, Friedrich: Paul Gerhardts Geistliche Lieder. Leipzig, Reclam, 1884.

Schultze, O.: Paul Gerhardt und der grosze Kurfürst. Berlin, 1840.
"   " : Paul Gerhardts Geistliche Andachten. Berlin, 1842.

Smend, J.: Paul Gerhardt u. das evangelische Kirchenlied. In *Der Protestantismus am Ende des 19. Jahrh.* I, p. 301 ff.

Spitta, F.: Paul Gerhardt und S. Bach, in *Monatsschrift für Pastoraltheologie.*

Steinhausen, H.: P. Gerhardt u. sein Denkmal, in *Kunstwart* 161, pp. 538-541.

Trepte, E. W. H.: Paul Gerhardt: Eine biographische Skizze. Delitzsch, 1829.

Wackernagel, Philipp: Paul Gerhardts Geistliche Lieder, herausgegeben von Ph. Wackernagel. Stuttgart, 1843. (9. Aufl. herausg. v. W. Tümpel. Gütersloh, 1907.)

Wackernagel, Ph.: Das deutsche Kirchenlied von der ältesten Zeit bis zu Anfang des XVII Jahrhunderts. Leipzig, 1864-1877.

Wackernagel, Wilhelm: Geschichte d. deutschen Litteratur. Basel, 1894.

Waldberg, M. F.: Renaissance-Lyrik. Heidelberg, 1888.

Wernle, P.: Paulus Gerhardt, in *Religionsgeschichtl. Volksbücher* IV, Heft 2. Tübingen, 1907.

Wildenhahn, K. A.: Paul Gerhardt, Kirchengeschichtliches Lebensbild aus der Zeit des groszen Kurfürsten. 1845. (This has been translated by Mrs. Stanley Carr, 1856.)

Wimmer, C.: Gerhardts Leben. Altenburg, 1723.

Winkworth, Catherine: Lyra Germanica. First Series, 1855. Second Series, 1858.
"   "   : Chorale Book for England, 1863.
"   "   : Christian Singers of Germany. Macmillan, 1869.

Zschnarack: Paul Gerhardt, in *Religion in Geschichte und Gegenwart 2*, pp. 1314-1317.

For a complete list of the biographical sketches, monographs, etc., which appeared in 1907 on the occasion of the 300th anniversary of Gerhardt's birth, cf. *Jahresberichte für neuere deutsche Literaturgeschichte,* Vols. XVI-XVII, 1906-1907.

MUSICAL SETTINGS[1]

Paul Gerhardts Geistliche Lieder in neuen Weisen von Fr. Mergner. 30 ausgewählte Lieder von Karl Schmidt. Leipzig, C. Deichert, 1907.

---

[1] Cf. also p. 21.

CHRONOLOGICAL TABLE

1607 (Mar. 12) Paul Gerhardt born at Gräfenhainichen near Wittenberg.

1622–1627 At school at Grimma.

1628–1642(?) Student at Wittenberg. Teachers: Röber, Martini.

1637 Gräfenhainichen set on fire by Swedish soldiers.

1642–1651(?) At Berlin; where he wrote Gelegenheitsgedichte, 18 of which
Crüger published in his "Praxis pietatis melica."

1651 Proposed as minister at Mittenwalde.

1651 (Nov.) Ordained as *Probst* at Mittenwalde.

1655 (Feb. 11) Marriage with Anna Maria Barthold.

1656 (Oct.) Called to Berlin to the Nicolaikirche.

1657 (Summer) Entered upon work in Berlin.

1662 Elector issues edict.

1666 (Feb. 6th or 16th) Summoned to Consistory and threatened with
deposition.

1668 (Mar. 5) Death of wife.

1668 (Autumn) Called to Lübben.

1676 (May 27?) Death at Lübben.

PART ONE

. .

CHAPTER I.

GERHARDT'S LIFE AND TIMES.

ALTHOUGH Paul Gerhardt's poems have been so great a power in the world, nevertheless facts concerning his own life are few. A fire set by the Swedish soldiers in 1637[1] destroyed all records which might enlighten us, yet from indirect sources and from his poems, we are certain of some facts of his biography.

He was born in Gräfenhainichen a few miles southwest of Wittenberg in the direction of Halle on March 12th in the year 1607 probably. In this small town, of the electorate of Saxony, which was surrounded by a high mediaeval wall, Paul Gerhardt spent the first fifteen years of his life. His father, Christian Gerhardt, was burgomaster of Gräfenhainichen where the citizens earned their living by cattle-raising, agriculture and hopgrowing. His mother was Dorothea Starke, granddaughter of Gallas Döbler, a Lutheran pastor. Both of his parents died probably when he was very young; and of his many brothers and sisters little is known.

At the age of fifteen having passed the examinations and being especially well prepared in Latin Gerhardt entered the Fürstenschule at Grimma. The school was noted for its pious atmosphere and stern discipline: its chief aim was to inculcate in the pupils "Gottesfurcht und gute Sitte."

It is natural that Gerhardt on completing his course at Grimma in 1627 should choose Wittenberg as his university, for it was situated almost at the gates of his native town. Furthermore since this was the place where Luther and Melanchthon had worked, the Protestant world looked toward Wittenberg with great hopes. He entered the university in 1628. Two of the teachers in particular had great influence on him, Paul Röber and Jacob Martini. These men were guardians of Lutheranism, and Röber besides composing hymns wrote many Latin disputations and polemics against Rome and Calvinism; in his sermons he often took his text, not from the Bible but from some religious poem, preaching for example on "Was mein Gott will, das gescheh allzeit." In this way Gerhardt was taught the

---

[1] Cf. pp. 2 and 3.

full use and purpose of hymn writing.   Beside Röber and Martini another Wittenberg professor was of influence on Gerhardt, the philologist August Buchner, one of the most esteemed members of the faculty.   He had intimate friendship with Opitz and had warmly advocated the latter's *Von der Deutschen Poeterei* and had himself written *Anleitung zur deutschen Poeterey*.   As this book was easily copied[2] by many of the students, it is reasonable to assume that this effort toward spreading Opitz' rules for rhythmic measure had its due influence on Gerhardt.

More is not known concerning his university career.   A Latin epigram of the year 1642 points to the probability of his being still at Wittenberg, while the certainty of his being in Berlin the next year 1643 is proved by a *Hochzeitsode*.[3]   Gerhardt was undoubtedly tutor in the house of Andreas Barthold then "Kammergerichtsadvokat," whose daughter wedded Joachim Fromme, the archdeacon of the Nicolaikirche in Berlin; this wedding was the occasion of the congratulatory *Hochzeitsode*.   During this period in Berlin from his thirty-seventh to his forty-sixth year he wrote a number of "Gelegenheitsgedichte" which show us Gerhardt as quite at home moving in a circle of educators and clergymen.   Among his friends was the well known choirmaster of the Nicolaikirche, Johann Crüger, who first introduced Gerhardt's hymns into common worship by publishing eighteen[4] of them with other poems in his *Praxis pietatis melica*.   In these early poems Gerhardt's depth of feeling and natural warmth of character are present. Since his twelfth year the Thirty Years' War, a period of destruction unparalleled in Germany history, had been going on.   The horrors of the epoch made deep impression upon his imaginative mind, and the strife, the struggle for freedom of the conscience enlisted his sympathy and strengthened his determined resistance to all religious compulsion.   The hope and joy in this life were taken away and confidence in another world was needed. Gerhardt even in these early hymns gave fully that deep assurance in the guidance of God.

He himself had suffered individual loss.   The Swedes in 1637 determined to punish Johann Georg, the Elector of Saxony, because he, in spite of a signed contract with them, had deserted the Protestant cause, and in their ravages they appeared before Gräfenhainichen and demanded a war tax of 3000 Gulden.   It was paid, but notwithstanding the payment the Swedish

---

[2] In 1665 there was published an authentic edition.
[3] Cf. *Goed.* 10: "Der aller Herz und Willen lenkt."
[4] Among these 18 were:

> "Ein Lämmlein geht und trägt die Schuld" *Goed.* 68.
> "O du allersüszte Freude" *Goed.* 76.
> "O Welt sieh hier dein Leben" *Goed.* 71.
> "Wach auf, mein Herz, und singe" *Goed.* 59.

soldiers set fire to the town. The Gerhardt house and the church with its many records were among the four hundred buildings destroyed.

Whether Gerhardt felt the pinch of distress of the war, or hesitated to enter a field already crowded with a superabundance of young clergymen, or for what reason he stayed so long in Berlin as tutor is not known, but he was already forty-five years old when he began his first church work. In a letter of the clerical cabinet ("Geistliches Ministerium") of Berlin to the magistrate of Mittenwalde (Sept. 1651) Gerhardt was proposed as minister and he is characterized as being of "well known diligence and scholarship, of peace loving disposition and blameless life, besides being loved and esteemed by both high and low in Berlin." Upon the successful outcome of this recommendation Gerhardt was ordained "Propst"[5] of Mittenwalde on the 18th of November, 1651, entering his new office in December of that year. At his ordination he pledged his support especially of the Lutheran Book of Concord (*Concordienformel*).

The community of Mittenwalde had suffered severely in 1637 as had Gräfenhainichen from the Swedish marauders and attacks of pestilence, and Paul Gerhardt undertook his duties here with full understanding of this universal suffering, and fulfilled them with all his strength. The poems which he wrote at this time give evidence of a tender, yet strong pastoral care. He was a spiritual guide and comforter, yet in spite of his ardent work in Mittenwalde he apparently yearned for Berlin, and often returned thither to visit. On February 11th, 1655, at the age of forty-eight he married Anna Maria Barthold, daughter of Andreas Barthold and sister of Frau Fromme.[6] Their first child, born to them in 1656, died in infancy and a memorial tablet in the church in Mittenwalde shows their grief. That same year Gerhardt accepted the deaconry at the Nicolaikirche in Berlin, and began his work in the summer of 1657. He seems to have had some hesitation about leaving Mittenwalde, because it was only "after fervent prayer and mature deliberation," that he accepted the call to Berlin. However, without doubt he and Frau Gerhardt were glad to be again among such friends as Georg Lilius and Michael Schirmer whose tastes were so similar to their own.

When Gerhardt came to Berlin he entered a city full of sharp strife between the Lutheran and the Reformed clergy; the Great Elector was by inheritance and by education in the Netherlands where he spent four years strongly in favor of the Reformed Church. Gerhardt on the other hand

---

[5] In Mittenwalde, 9 English miles south of Berlin, there were in the church two clerical positions, the first of which was known as the "Propstei," since its occupant was entrusted with the supervision of the clergy of the vicinity. Propst (or Probst) is from the Latin *propositus*.

[6] Cf. p. 2.

held the security of the Lutheran faith very dear. When hostilities between the clergy began to disturb the peace, the Elector issued on the 2d of June, 1662, an edict[7] the purpose of which was to maintain harmony between Reformed and Lutheran clergymen. Its only effect was, however, to fan the flames of the very conflagration he sought so hard to quench. The unconciliatory spirit was encouraged from Wittenberg, too, where Theology of Controversy had reached its highest pitch through Calovius, whose advice and judgment Gerhardt prized. His inclination toward Wittenberg is seen also in various Latin poems for special occasions.

Gerhardt did not seek the quarrel, but was drawn forcibly into it; he was concerned throughout the controversy in keeping a clear conscience and preserving the confession of the Lutheran Church. In all the documents that were issued in this period between the Magistrate, the "Stände" and the Elector it is said of him that he was always pacific and conciliatory. Being a strong adherent of all the symbolic books, including the Book of Concord, he could not conscientiously sign the edict. He was accordingly dismissed. The citizens of Berlin espoused his cause and appealed to the Magistrate who testified that Gerhardt had never "scorned nor rebuked the faith of the Elector." Also his influential patron, Mayor Zarlang, tried to reinstate him, but Gerhardt could not renounce his adherence to the *Concordienformel*, so in 1666 his position was filled by another. Nor on the other hand can the Elector be blamed for his stand; he wished only to have peace between the adherents of the two beliefs, and was sincere in the thought that the *Concordienformel* merely fomented strife.

For some years Gerhardt lived in Berlin without any position, supported by his friends in his congregation. He was, however, the victim of inevitable circumstances, for although within a few months of his resignation the edict was withdrawn, his patroness, Electress Luise Henriette, had died. All of his children had died in infancy except Paul Friedrich who survived him, and in March, 1668, his wife died who had been as strong a follower of the Lutheran Faith as he, and had encouraged him in his stand of not signing the edict.[8] Her death was the fulfillment of a wish that "the dear Lord might soon come and release her."

Gerhardt took into his home as housekeeper the widow of his brother-in-law Fromme.[9] His household was reasonably large for one in his condition,

---

[7] This mandate was a renewal of the edict issued by his grandfather on Feb. 24, 1614, demanding "moderation and modesty in the pulpit."

[8] The attitude of the women in this time of religious strife who urged their husbands to sign the edict is satirized in the following lines:

> Schreibt, liebei Herre, schreibt,
> dasz Ihr in der Pfarre bleibt.

[9] Cf. pp. 2 and 3.

a preacher without office; he speaks of three, or even of four servants, and mentions at times some business matters in Berlin that seem to be of moment. Although he must also have had pupils whom he tutored during these years, he evidently wished for some definite occupation, and it came. On the 14th of October, 1668, Paul Gerhardt preached a trial sermon ("Gastpredigt") in Lübben. The city council the following day with the unanimous consent of the citizens offered him the vacant charge and Gerhardt accepted it as a divine gift. The formal call under date of October 29th was sent to him at Berlin. Owing to various circumstances, such as the delay incident to necessary repairs on the parsonage, and also the serious illness of his son, Paul Friedrich, he did not enter his duties till Trinity Sunday, 1669. He was at this time sixty-three years old, and for seven years he worked faithfully in this new field.

Gerhardt died the 27th of May, 1676, with the prayer on his lips:

> Kann uns doch kein Tod nicht tödten,
> Sondern reiszt unsern Geist
> Aus viel tausend Nöten;
> Schleuszt das Thor der bittern Leiden
> Und macht Bahn, Da man kann
> Gehn zur Himmelsfreuden.[10]

He was buried in the vault of the Lübben church.

Shortly before his death, in his seventieth year, he composed a sort of testament or will of a moral nature for his own Paul in which he hoped to leave little of this world's goods, but an honorable name of which his son might not be ashamed. He commends to the boy the study of theology at reputable universities and also the avoidance of the Syncretists,[11] on the ground that they aimed at temporal things and were loyal to neither God nor man.

In a memorial service to Gerhardt in 1876, a tablet was put up on the north wall of the chancel of the church at Lübben; and his portrait hung there bears this inscription:

Theologus in cribro Satanae versatus.[12]

The Nicolaikirche in Berlin and the other churches where he held charge have portraits of Gerhardt on their walls. Also among the many memorials to him are charitable foundations in Mittenwalde, Wittenberg and Berlin bearing his name. To these tributes the present generation, now, three centuries later, adds its praise and gratitude.

---

[10] This is stanza VIII of his poem:
          "Warum sollt ich mich denn grämen" (cf. *Goed.* 122).

[11] The Syncretists sought to effect an agreement between the Reformed and Lutheran doctrines.

[12] "A divine sifted in Satan's sieve." Cf. *St. Luke* XXII, 31.

CHAPTER II.

GERHARDT'S RELATION TO EARLIER HYMNODY OF GERMANY.

The Mediaeval Period.

THE history of hymnody in Germany up to the time of Gerhardt falls naturally into two periods which might be called the Mediaeval Period, extending from the beginning of the eighth century to the end of the fifteenth century, and the Reformation Period covering the sixteenth and the first half of the seventeenth centuries.

The Hymns used in the services of the early church in Germany were, for obvious reasons, Latin hymns, for St. Boniface, the Apostle of Germany, though of English birth, entered Germany by the way of Rome. It was a Latin Christianity which he preached and the church services were, of course, those of the Mother Church. While the general use of the Latin language was favorable to preserving the unity of the Church and facilitated literary intercourse among scholars, this circumstance prevented for a long time the free and full development of a hymnody in the vernacular. The innate love of poetry, however, produced many sacred lyrics for private devotion and caused to be made metrical translations of Latin hymns and portions of the Psalter. In the consideration of the earlier period of hymnody reference will be made to a few Latin hymns, which though not of German authorship were yet used in the religious services of the Germans and had some influence in the development of the German vernacular hymnody. And in this consideration of hymns and hymn writers it will be convenient in the main to follow the chronological order.

Probably it cannot be known what and when Latin hymns were first translated into modern languages. If the statement made by Dean Milman in a footnote of his *Latin Christianity,* that the hymns of Ambrose were translated into German in the ninth century, is well founded, then probably the "Deus Creator omnium" and "Aeterne rerum Conditor," which are undoubtedly by Ambrose, were among the earliest of Latin poems to be so translated.

The oldest German poet is the Benedictine monk, Otfrid of Weissenburg, who was born about the beginning of the ninth century, according to some authorities in Franconia, according to others near the Lake of Constance.

He settled as a monk and priest at Weissenburg, where he wrote and completed (about 865) his *Evangelienbuch,* a versified gospel history, and a most interesting work from a philological as well as a hymnological point of view. This is the earliest example of a long German poem in rhyme. Of the rhymed prayers which some on doubtful authority have ascribed to him two have been translated by Miss Winkworth, "Du himlisco trohtin" ("Thou Heavenly Lord of Light") and "Got thir eigenhaf ist" ("God, it is thy property").[1]

A celebrated Latin hymn of early date, which is known to have been used as early as 898, is the "Veni Creator Spiritus"; it has been constantly sung throughout Christendom at the consecration of kings and at great ecclesiastical solemnities. It has been ascribed to Charlemagne, Charles the Bald, Gregory the Great and various others.[2]

To this early period belongs Notker of St. Gall, called Balbulus, the "Stammerer," who was born in Switzerland about 840 and died in 912. He wrote in Latin and was the originator of a form of Latin hymnody called "sequentia" or "prosa," which, when translated into German, gave rise to the earliest German hymns with which we are acquainted. Whenever in the eucharistic service a "Hallelujah" was introduced it had been customary to prolong the last syllable and to sing on the vowel "ah" a series of elaborate passages to represent an outburst of jubilant feeling. These were termed "sequences" because they followed the "Hallelujah" and repeated its notes. They were of course without words and what Notker did was to write words for them. Notker was characterized as a man of gentle, contemplative nature and "accustomed to find spiritual and poetical suggestions in common sights and sounds." One of the most remarkable of his sequences, "Media vita in morte sumus," is said to have been suggested to him while observing some workmen constructing a bridge in a precipitous and most dangerous place. This sequence was long used as a battle-song; one of Luther's funeral hymns, "Mitten wir im Leben sind," is a translation of it and portions of the Burial Service of the Church of England are taken from it. St. Gall, which was for a long time the especial seat of German religious literature, produced besides Notker several distinguished sequence-writers, presumably his pupils, Hartmann, Hermann, and Gottschalk. To Gottschalk has been ascribed the "Alleluiatic Sequence ("Cantemus cuncti") well known in England by the translation, "The strain upraise of joy and praise."

---

[1] This latter is regarded by some authorities as from the pen of St. Gregory the Great.

[2] For a scholarly discussion of the authorship of this famous hymn cf. Julian: *Dictionary of Hymnology,* p. 1206 ff.

An early example of the change of sequences from a rhythmical to a metrical form is seen in the so-called "Golden Sequence," "Veni Sancte Spiritus," called by Archbishop Trench "the loveliest of all the hymns in the whole circle of Latin sacred poetry." Tradition assigns its authorship to Robert II, King of France (997-1031). Its merit is attested by the many translations made of it into German, English and other languages.

By the beginning of the tenth century the impulse given to the arts by Charlemagne had gradually died out and the state of society had become so disorganized that for two centuries after the time of Notker the field of literature was comparatively barren. The twelfth and thirteenth centuries, however, mark a great change and form an era of rapid growth. Germany was now ruled by the Hohenstauffens, whose dream it was to prove themselves true heirs of Charlemagne by re-establishing the Empire of the West. As a result of their participation in the common life of Christendom, very largely through the influence of the crusades, came the development of chivalry and a national literature, the first great outburst of German poetry and song. A large class (more than two hundred) of minnesingers sprang up who glorified earthly and heavenly love and the Virgin Mary as the type of pure womanhood. In the church too the voice of native song now made itself heard. The "Kyrie eleison" and "Christe eleison" which passed from the Greek church into the Latin, as a response of the people, to be repeated over and over again, especially on the high festivals, were popularly enlarged, and these brief poems were called from the refrain "Kirleison" or "Leisen," also "Leichen."[3] These sequences, for such they were, were the first specimens of German hymns which were sung by the people. The oldest dates from the end of the ninth century and is called the "Leich vom heiligen Petrus." It has three stanzas, of which the first reads:

> Unser trohtin hat farsalt
> sancte Petre giwalt
> Daz er mag ginerjan
> zeimo dingenten man.
> Kyrie eleyson! Christe eleison.

The twelfth century produced the "Salve Caput cruentatum" of Bernard of Clairvaux,—a hymn which has come to us by Paul Gerhardt,[5] whose own hymn writing is wonderfully affected by Bernard.

---

[3] It is possible that instead of being a corruption of the Greek phrase the word may have denoted at first a certain dance measure. Cf. Grimm: *Deutsches Wörterbuch*, Vol. VI.

[4] "Our Lord hath given St. Peter power that he may preserve the man who hopes in him."

[5] Cf. p. 86 and note.

In the following century appeared two widely celebrated compositions, the "Dies irae" and the "Stabat Mater dolorosa." These, as well as many others of the best Latin hymns, such as the "Te Deum" and the "Gloria in excelsis," were repeatedly translated. Occasionally words of the original Latin were introduced into the vernacular as in the Christmas hymn:

> *In dulci jubilo*
> Nu singet und seyt fro!
> Unsres Herzens Wonne
> Leyt *in presipio*
> Und leuchtet *in gremio.*
> *Alpha es et O.*

The mystic school of Tauler, in the fourteenth century produced a number of hymns full of glowing love to God. Tauler is the author of the Christmas poem, "Uns kommt ein Schiff geladen" and the hymn of Self Renunciation, "Ich musz die Creaturen fliehen," both of which have passed into English, the best versions being those of Miss Winkworth.[6]

Of unusual sweetness and abiding worth are the hymns of Heinrich von Laufenburg, the most important and prolific hymn writer of the fifteenth century. Many are in intricate metres, while others are transformations of secular songs into religious songs. His cradle hymn, "Ach lieber Herre Jesu Christ," is a beautiful prayer of a mother for her infant child, and has become well known in England through Miss Winkworth's translation.

German hymnody of the Middle Ages is, like the Latin, overflowing with the worship of the saints and the Virgin who is even clothed with divine attributes and is virtually accorded the place of Christ as the fountain of grace. In characterizing the period Wackernagel says[7]

"Through all the centuries from Otfrid to Luther we meet with the idolatrous worship of the Virgin Mary. There are hymns which teach that she pre-existed with God at the creation, that all things are created in her and for her and that God rested in her on the seventh day."

One of the favorite hymns to the Virgin, "Dich Frau von Himmel, ruf ich an," Hans Sachs subsequently changed into "Christum vom Himmel ruf ich an," a change strikingly characteristic of the effect which the Reformation exerted upon the worship of the Virgin Mary. It substituted for it the worship of Christ as the sole Mediator through whom men attain eternal life.

THE REFORMATION PERIOD, 1500-1648.

Guizot in his *History of European Civilization* calls the Reformation an insurrection of the human mind against the absolute power of spiritual

---

[6] Cf. *Christian Singers of Germany.*
[7] *Das deutsche Kirchenlied,* II, p. 13.

order. In the changes that then occurred few things are more noteworthy than the new privileges granted to the individual worshipper. There was revived the primitive idea of the priesthood of all believers. Instead of the Latin Mass, the Reformation introduced a sermon in the vernacular, and for the chanting of priests and choirs it substituted congregational singing. Among the means which contributed to the large benefits which then came to the church the writing of hymns was not the least important. It is interesting to note that the leader of the Reformation was also the first evangelical hymnist.[8] To Luther belongs the extraordinary merit of having given to his people in their own language not only the Bible and the Catechism, but also the hymn book, so that they might directly answer the word of God in their songs. No sooner had there been felt the want of German psalms and hymns to take the place of the Latin hymns and sequences than Luther set about to supply the want. He was intensely fond of poetry and song and was himself a poet by nature. His estimate of the value of music is revealed in his words: "He who despises music, as all fanatics do, will never be my friend." He wished that all children might be taught to sing; "for," he says, "I would fain see all arts, especially music, in the service of Him who has bestowed and created them."[9]

He began to write hymns soon after he had completed his New Testament translation and from this time on he was an active reformer of church music and hymns, enlisting in the same work the large circle of friends whom he gathered about him. Luther had recourse to the Latin hymns, adapting and translating many of those which would lend themselves best to his purposes. Altogether he wrote thirty-seven hymns, most of them dating from the year 1524; more are frequently ascribed to him though on doubtful authority. Luther's hymns which are characterized by simplicity and strength, had a popular churchly tone; his style is plain and often rugged and quaint but he throws into his poems all his own fervent faith and deep devotion. His most famous hymn "Ein' feste Burg ist unser Gott," written in 1529 when the German princes made their formal Protest against the revocation of their liberties, thus gaining the name of Protestants, has passed into English hymnody in no less than sixty-three versions.[10]

Of the many hymnists inspired by Luther's example the more eminent were Justus Jonas, Luther's friend and colleague in the preparation of metrical German versions of the Psalms, Paul Eber, the faithful assistant of Melanchthon, Markgraf Albrecht of Brandenburg, Hans Sachs, the shoemaker, and later Gerhardt.

[8] But cf. L. F. Benson: *The English Hymn*, N. Y. 1915, p. 20 ff.
[9] Cf. *Tischreden:* "Von der Musica" and "Die Musicam sol man nicht verachten."
[10] Cf. Julian: *Dictionary of Hymnology*, pp. 324-5.

The German hymnody of the Reformation period was enriched by the hymns of the Bohemian and Moravian Brethren, who as followers of John Huss, had in 1467 formed themselves into a separate and organized church; their archbishop Lucas in 1501 collected hymns and published the first hymn book in the vernacular to be found in Bohemia or Germany.   The adherents of this cult are commonly called Moravians, because the first founders of the settlement in Saxony immigrated from Moravia.   They assumed this name in England and America and it is very largely through their hymn book[11] that German hymns have found their way into English hymnody.

The Lutheran hymnody which followed closely upon the Moravian contributions concluded its productive period with the *Formula of Concord*[12] in 1577 which gave final shape to the Lutheran creed.   In this period there were over a hundred poets whose verses have expressed the highest Christian praises.   It is an era which, for its productiveness, may be compared with the time of Watts and Doddridge and their immediate successors in England.

The hymns from this time to the close of the Thirty Years' War are of a more subjective[13] experimental type of sacred poetry, that is, writers made their songs more and more expressive of personal feelings.   In point of refinement and grace of style the hymn writers of the period of the Thirty Years' War, whose taste was chiefly formed by the influence of Martin Opitz[14] the founder of the First Silesian School of German poetry, excelled their predecessors.   His finest hymn, "O Licht, geboren aus dem Lichte" is a special favorite in Silesia where he was born, and has passed into English in several translations, notably that of Miss Winkworth, "O Light, who out of Light wast born."[15]

Near the close of the war, when the hope of peace had begun to dawn, Martin Rinckart (1586-1649) composed that noble expression of trust and praise, "Nun danket alle Gott."   It has been translated many times and is included in nearly all American and English hymnals.   The hymn of trust in Providence by Neumarck (1621-1681), "Wer nur den lieben Gott läszt walten," is hardly inferior to that of Gerhardt on the same theme.[16]

The two most famous and most copious hymn writers of this time were however Rist and Heermann; the former wrote between 600 and 700 hymns, such as were intended to supply every possible requirement of public worship or private experience.   In so great a mass of writings it is inevitable that there should be much that is poor, but over 200 may be said to be in

---

[11] Cf. the frequent references to the *Moravian Hymn Book,* p. 38 ff.

[12] Cf. p. 4.

[13] Cf. p. 14.

[14] For his influence on Gerhardt cf. pp. 2, 14, 18.

[15] Cf. *Christian Singers of Germany,* p. 173.

[16] "Befiehl du deine Wege," cf. p. 114 ff.

common use in Germany and at least fifteen have appeared in the hymn books of English-speaking countries. Not so prolific as Heermann and Rist but superior to them in poetical genius was Simon Dach (1605-1659), who was Professor of Poetry at Königsberg and the most important poet of the Königsberg School.[17]

While the Lutheran churches were superior to the Reformed churches of Germany and Switzerland in original hymnody, they were inferior to them in the matter of psalmody. Zwingli and Calvin held firmly to the principle that in public worship the word God should have supreme dominion, a principle which raised the Psalter to new dignity and power. Versified versions of the Psalms became the first hymn books of the Reformed Churches.[18] The first German Reformed hymn book appeared at Zürich, 1540. It contained not only versified psalms but also hymns, with a preface in defense of congregational singing. The most popular collection however was the versified Psalter of Lobwasser of Königsberg. While its poetry is but a poor translation of the French Psalter of Marot and Beza,[19] its pious contents made it a rich source of devotion for a hundred years. It is a parallel to the Scottish Psalter of 1641 by Francis Rous.[20]

Simon Dach was the last poet of any note to write in the Reformation period of German hymnody. After him a new era of poetry, the Confessional (1648-1680), opens and it is at this time that Paul Gerhardt appears. He, however, although living in the midst of this churchly atmosphere, profound in Lutheran orthodoxy, feels the tendencies of a still later period, that of the Devotional era. Like many other great men he saw beyond his time. He combined in his poems all the strong qualities of the century in which he lived, and of the later epoch, the period of the Pietists.

---

[17] Of the 165 hymns that he wrote, five have found places in modern English hymnals. One of the best known popular songs is his love-song written in East Prussian dialect "Anke von Tharaw." This is made familiar to English readers through Longfellow's translation, "Annie of Tharaw."

[18] For their effect on English hymnody cf. p. 28 ff.

[19] Cf. p. 29.

[20] Cf. Julian: *Dictionary of Hymnology,* p. 1023.

CHAPTER III.

FROM the close of the Thirty Years' War until 1680 there occurred in German hymnody a transition from the churchly and confessional to the pietistic and devotional hymns.[1] It is during this transitional period that the religious song of Germany finds its purest and sweetest expression in the hymns of Paul Gerhardt, who is as much the typical poet of the Lutheran, as Herbert is of the English church. In Gerhardt more than in any other author all the requisites for the religious poem are united. He possessed a firm conviction of the objective truth of the Christian doctrine of salvation and also a genuine sentiment for all that is purely human. His deep Christian feeling together with sterling good sense, and a fresh and healthy appreciation of life in the realm of nature and in the intellectual world are the sources for his splendid work. His hymns are among the noblest contributions to sacred poetry, giving him a place second only to Luther and even surpassing Luther's work in poetic fertility. Gervinus says of him:[2]

"He went back to Luther's most genuine type of hymn in such a manner as no one else had done, only so far modified as the requirements of his time demanded. In Luther's time the belief in Free Grace and the work of the Atonement in Redemption and the bursting of the gates of Hell was the inspiration of his joyful confidence; with Gerhardt it is the belief in the Love of God. With Luther the old wrathful God of the Romanists assumed the heavenly aspect of grace and mercy; with Gerhardt the merciful Righteous One is a gentle loving man. Like the old poets of the people he is sincerely and unconstrainedly pious, naive and hearty; the blissfulness of his faith makes him benign and amiable; in his way of writing he is as attractive, simple and pleasing as in his way of thinking."

Scherer[3] gives an even clearer characterization of the two hymn writers:

"Geistlicher Ernst des Vortrags schlieszt Heiterkeit des Gemütes nicht aus, und diese bildet in der That den sittlichen Grundcharakter von Gerhardts Poesie. Wenn bei Luther die Welt voll Sturm und Gewitter ist, so liegt sie bei Gerhardt in beständigem Sonnenglanz; die Wohltaten des

---

[1] Or as the German says: From the "Bekenntnislied" to the "Erbauungslied."
[2] *Geschichte d. d. Nationallitteratur*, ed. 1842, Pt. III, p. 366.
[3] *Geschichte d. d. Literatur*, 1899, pp. 340-341.

Schöpfers erfreuen das Herz; alles ist so schön zum Besten der Menschen eingerichtet; Tod und Hölle haben längst ihre Macht verloren; die Seele frohlockt in der Gewiszheit der Erlösung; Gnade geht vor Recht, Zorn musz der Liebe weichen. Luther steht wie ein Mann dem Bösen, Gerhardt sieht wie ein Jüngling darüber hinweg; und schlieszlich weisz er zu trösten und Zufriedenheit, Geduld zu predigen, das rechte Mittelmasz zu preisen und auch dem Uebel gute Seiten abzugewinnen; selbst die Sünde dient zum Heil. Bei Luther ruft die Gemeinde zu Gott, bei Gerhardt redet der Einzelne. Seine Lyrik ist nicht mehr Chorpoesie; sie beschränkt sich nicht auf das, worin alle betenden Christen einig sind; sie holt aus der Tiefe des individuellen Seelenlebens ihre Schätze; sie macht (um die Schulausdrücke zu gebrauchen) den Uebergang vom objektiven Bekenntnisliede zum subjektiven Erbauungsliede."

Gerhardt sings his hymns with conviction, embodying in them such phases of feeling as might be experienced by any large body of sincere Christians. In all the religious lyrics even in the congregational hymns from the middle of the seventeenth century on we note a more personal and individual tone and with it a tendency to reproduce special forms of Christian experience often of a mystical character. Gerhardt's whole tone and style of thought belong to the confessional school, but the distinct individuality and expression of personal sentiment which are impressed on his poems already point to the devotional school.

Many of our poet's hymns show the influence of Opitz' *Trostgedichte in Widerwärtigkeit des Krieges.* Critics[4] have gone so far as to say that "without Opitz there would be no Gerhardt." There can be no doubt but that the smoothness and elegance of form, the complete mastery of technique and the purity of language are a distinct heritage from him. But without consciously differing from Opitz and his school, Gerhardt has brought into prominence the popular expression of feeling, using the popular form of verse in which there prevails the natural flow of rhythm, so that no striving after correctness of form is evident.

Compared with most authors of his time Gerhardt wrote but little. His contemporary, Rist (1607–1667), and his successor, Schmolk (1672–1737), composed respectively 659 and 1188 hymns, while Gerhardt has the modest number of 132 poems in all.[5] Yet a complete hymnal might be compiled from them, so thoroughly do they embrace all religious and domestic experiences. They appeared at intervals from the year 1649 on, many of them for the first time in the *Praxis pietatis melica,* a collection of hymns and tunes by Johann Crüger, the famous organist and composer of chorals.

---

[4] Cf. J. Smend: *"P. Gerhardt u. das evangel. Kirchenlied"* in *"Der Protestantismus am Ende des 19. Jahrh."* I, pp. 301, ff.

[5] Among them are 18 poems for occasions, 27 founded on Psalms and 24 founded on other parts of Holy Scripture.

Crüger died in the year 1662 and Cristoph Runge took over further editions of the book.   Gerhardt made no further contributions to these publications because henceforth he became more intimately associated with Johann Georg Ebeling, Crüger's successor in his church and organ work.   Ebeling was so much pleased with Gerhardt's hymns, that he at once began to set them to music and eventually he published them dividing them by "dozens"[6] into separate books.   Gerhardt put at Ebeling's disposal the first copy of his hymns hitherto published and also thirty-one separate 'strophes which had for various reasons been omitted in previous editions.   Finally he turned over to him twenty-six more poems which the *Praxis pietatis melica* had not published up to this time.   Among them are a number which in all probability belong to his early period of poetic activity, such as: "O Tod, O Tod, du greulichs Bild," a paraphrase of one of Röber's[7] hymns.   Also among them are several which from content and form must be regarded as products of his mature years, and from which the poet himself derived much comfort and strength.[8]

---

[6] The tenth and last "dozen" of Gerhardt's hymns which Ebeling had set to music for four voices and with an accompaniment of two violins and a bass, appeared in 1667.   The full title, characteristic of Ebeling, reads: *Paul Gerhardt's spiritual devotions, consisting of one hundred and twenty hymns, collected into one volume, at the request of a number of eminent and distinguished gentlemen; first to the honor of the Divine Majesty and then also for the consolation of esteemed and distressed Christendom, and for the increase of the Christianity of all believing souls—in sets by dozens, embellished with melodies for six parts.*" With such eagerness were these hymns sought after that Ebeling had to publish a new edition two years later.   The melodies which proved most popular were those set to "Voller Wunder, voller Kunst," "Schwing dich auf zu deinem Gott" and "Warum sollt' ich mich denn grämen." Each single dozen was again dedicated to a particular class of men with a characteristic preface.   The first dozen he dedicated "to the prelates, counts, lords, knights, and estates of the Electorate of Brandenburg, this side the Oder and beyond the Elbe";   the second dozen, "To the high, noble-born, honored, and virtuous women of Berlin" and so on.

[7] Cf. pp. 1 and 2.

[8] "Die güldne Sonne" *Goed.* 293.
"Der Tag mit seinem Lichte" *Goed.* 296.
"Wie schön ists doch, Herr Jesu Christ" *Goed.* 302.
"Voller Wunder, voller Kunst" *Goed.* 304.
"Gib dich zufrieden und sei stille" *Goed.* 274.
"Ich bin ein Gast auf Erden" *Goed.* 284.
"Herr, du erforschest meinen Sinn" *Goed.* 287.
"Herr Gott, du bist ja für und für" *Goed.* 315.
"Ich danke dir mit Freuden" *Goed.* 333.
"Ich, der ich oft in tiefes Leid" *Goed.* 298.
"Johannes sahe durch Gesicht" *Goed.* 319.
"Mein Seel ist in der Stille" *Goed.* 307.
"Merkt auf, merkt Himmel, Erde" *Goed.* 278.

The most important fact about the Ebeling edition is this, that the personality of Gerhardt, the poet, was for the first time presented to the German people's heart and mind. Hitherto his poems had been grouped together in collections of hymns with those of other and perhaps better known authors. Ebeling's publication placed Gerhardt's works on their own merit. The texts of the hymns in the editions of Crüger and Ebeling and later of Feustking[9] in 1707 have often different readings so that it is difficult to determine which the authentic version may be. It is quite within the limits of possibility that Gerhardt himself undertook revisions, as Feustking's title indicates.

Of these 132 poems a large proportion have become embodied in church music of Germany and many of them may be counted among the most beautiful in German hymnody. How widely they have been adopted into general use is shown by the fact that in modern hymnals in Germany there appear either in expanded or cento form,[10] altogether 78 of his hymns, while in the Schaff-Gilman "Library of Religious Poetry," which may be regarded as a representative collection of universal hymnody, the proportion among German hymn writers is as follows:—Luther 10, Goethe 8, Gerhardt 7,[11] Spitta 6, Scheffler 4, Schmolk 4, etc. Pietism and rationalism transferred the centre of gravity in hymnody to a different point; that is, it changed the type of hymn or required of it other features, and thus it is that during the XVIIIth century, while Gerhardt's hymns lived on with others they are rarely accorded a leading place. It was only the reawakening of a life of faith that needed worship and strong evidence of reverence such as followed the wars of liberation that brought his hymns into the forefront once more and prompted further publications of them.

Rarely has there been, taking all in all, a time when there existed a greater gulf between poets and their effusions than in the XVIIth century. Most poets of that time gave forth what they had learned and what they knew,—not what they really were. Theirs was a play of the intellect and imagination on objects outside them. Hence their works displayed a universal lack of inner truth. In the biographical sketch of Gerhardt we have given a broken account of his life. Different from this is the story of the individual in his poems which are his very personality. His work is not what he learned from others. Instead, he gives us his own life unadorned

---

[9] Johann Heinrich Feustking: *Ausgabe, Zerbst, 1707, text "nach des seligen Autors eigenhändigem revidirten Exemplar mit Fleisz übersehen."*

[10] Cf. Dietz: *"Tabellarische Nachweisung des Liederbestandes,"* Marburg, 1904. Fischer-Tümpel: *"Das deutsche evangelische Kirchenlied des 17. Jahrhs."* (Gütersloh, 1906) includes 116 of Gerhardt's hymns.

[11] There is an exact total of 10 of Gerhardt's poems, different versions being given of "O Haupt voll Blut und Wunden," and "Befiehl du deine Wege."

and true, and for the very reason that he leads a rich inner life is he able to give it.   He wrote preeminently as a living member of Christ's church. The same quiet sincerity, depth of feeling and warmth that are seen in his face, stand out in his poetry.

Luther sang: "Ein' feste Burg ist *unser* Gott," but Gerhardt has: "Ist Gott für *mich,* so trete,"[12] and *"Ich* singe dir mit Herz und Mund.[13]   Thus, as has been said in the early part of this chapter,[14] the hymns no longer acknowledge the truths of the Gospel as in the days of the Reformation, but the poet lives them.   Approximately one-eighth[15] of Gerhardt's hymns begin with "Ich," while not one of Luther's begins this way.   Gerhardt's hymns, then, proclaim his own personal experiences, many of them having their inspiration in the intimate circle of his own family and friends.   Yet observe that in none of them is there any personal experience that is not enlightened by its relation to the external truths of Christian Belief so that it has a universal significance.   Assuming that one takes for granted the incontestable truth of evangelistic Philosophy of Life as does Gerhardt, one may find one's own thoughts and feelings expressed in these poems. Every pious worshipper can follow Gerhardt, every one may find in him peace for the soul, the consecration of happiness and comfort in dark hours. Universal life and not merely the life of one reared in the church is unfolded in his hymns.

Mention has several times been made of Luther[16] in connection with Gerhardt.   Every Protestant hymn writer must undergo comparison with the great father of German hymnody and none can stand the test better than Gerhardt.   Let us take the hymns cited above: "Ein' feste Burg," and "Ist Gott für mich."   In the very choice of material the likeness is striking. In Luther's song of defiance the XLVIth Psalm is born anew.   In Gerhardt it is the triumphant song of Paul that they who are in Christ are free from condemnation.   We see, then, that while the one is concerned with the congregation of God's church, the other treats of life's experiences.   In the form of the verse Luther displays the greater strength and Gerhardt the greater art.

Although Gerhardt's hymns are written in the vernacular of the XVIIth century, at a time when many of the forms characteristic of the writers of the two preceding centuries still survived, nevertheless his hymns are remarkably free from the tendency of this period to use words coined from foreign tongues.   He belongs to no poetic school or literary circle of the

---

[12] *Goed. 229.*
[13] *Goed.* 118.
[14] Cf. p. 14.
[15] There are 16 beginning with "ich."
[16] Cf. pp. 1 and 13.

XVIIth century. He never sought any laurels. He goes on his way writing because his heart is so full, and not from any desire or intention to devote himself to poetry. A fine feeling for rhythm schooled under the principles of Opitz, language taken from the best sacred literature including Luther's Bible and almost entirely free from foreign words,[17] avoidance of bombast and coarseness[18] of which so many contemporary writers were guilty, richness in figures and analogies, tenderness which on occasion yields to sternness, are all attributes of his writing. The mother of Hippel[19] says of him:

"Er war ein Gast auf Erden[20] und überall in seinen 120 Liedern ist Sonnenwende gesäet. Diese Blume dreht sich beständig nach der Sonne[21] und Gerhardt nach der seligen Ewigkeit."

Gerhardt's poems are all permeated with this hope for future happiness in Heaven and with a childlike joy in this hope. He may sing of the beauties of summer, yet with that his thoughts go further and he soon begins to reflect upon the greater beauties of Heaven. In his "Reiselied" (*Goed.* 248) he begins by urging on his horse; suddenly he changes from the beauties of the hill and vale to the joy of eternity. Even in an uncouth poem about health (*Goed.* 244) appear the lines:

> "Gib mir meine Lebenszeit
> Ohne sonderm Leide,
> Und dort in der Ewigkeit
> Die vollkommene Freude!"

We have said that biblical phraseology plays a large part in Gerhardt's hymns. In fact many lines are a direct translation of passages in scripture. In two or three of them a single dogma appears very plainly, but elsewhere pure doctrine is the basis of each poem. God is a friendly and gracious God, not a "bear or lion,"[22] but a Father reconciled by Christ's death,— entirely a New Testament conception. He even addresses the Almighty as a good companion:

> "Sollt aber dein und unser Feind
> An dem, was dein Herz gut gemeint,
> Beginnen sich zu rächen:
> Ist das mein Trost, dasz seinen Zorn
> Du leichtlich könnest brechen."[23]

---

[17] He uses the following: *Clerisei, Fantasei, Victoria, Policeien, Regiment, Summa, Ranzion, Compagnie, Regente, studieren, formieret, vexieren, jubilieren.*
[18] Lines such as "Trotz sei dir, du trotzender Kot!" (*Goed.* 5, 65) were comparatively inoffensive to XVIIth century standards.
[19] Cf. Frau Th. v. Hippel, "*Sämmtliche Werke,*" Berlin, 1827, I, 27 ff.
[20] Cf. "Ich bin ein Gast auf Erden" *Goed.* 284.
[21] Sonnenwende, "heliotrope," from the Greek, literally "turning toward the sun."
[22] Cf. *Goed.* 62, 17—"Er ist ja kein Bär noch Leue."
[23] Cf. *Goed.* 217, 56-60.

The Redeemer is mentioned in barely half of Gerhardt's poems. It has therefore been often said that the poet esteemed the graces of Redemption less than those of Creation. He is fully conscious of the former, hence he can resign himself to the latter and dwell upon them in all their phases. On the basis of the Atonement there springs up in his mind the whole Christian life with all its experiences of salvation, consolation, patience, mastery of sin and suffering. Since he does not sing solely for church worship, but for family devotion and for personal edification, he necessarily must observe and discourse upon the various vicissitudes of life in sickness and health, in strife and peace.

Inasmuch as Gerhardt is a poet of unusually fine feeling for the rhythmical and melodious peculiarities of the German tongue, he appreciates the interdependence of verse rhythm and thought showing always a nicety in choosing the right word to suit the measure. The lines:

> "Nun ruhen aller Wälder,
> Vieh, Menschen, Stadt, und Felder . . ."[24]

are at once suggestive of Nature in repose. The harmonious connection of words of kindred meaning, "Ruh und Rast," "Gnad und Gunst,"[25] and frequent use of assonance, "Not und Tod," "Füll und Hüll," etc. are introduced not merely to catch the ear, but to accentuate the artistic effect, which shows us that Gerhardt is more than a master of the language, that he writes with an inexhaustible naturalness. He intended his style to be popular in the sense of appealing to the people, and it is here that he manifests the intimate relation of his poetry to the Volkslied without forsaking the proper limits of artistic poetry.

In observing certain defects such as the awkwardness and imperfect rhyme in the couplet:

> "Aber nun steh ich
> Bin munter und frölich."[26]

even Gerhardt's most devoted admirers must regret that he did not feel the necessity of giving to his verses the final rounding-off, or did not possess the ability to do so. Yet what many critics have regarded as faults, must, when fairly analyzed, be recognized as contributing much to the effect and as being in accord with the *Sprachpoesie* of the people. For example, the richness in alliteration, "Ich mein Heil und Hülfe hab,"[27] "Ich lechze wie ein Land,"[28] the juxtaposition of words of the same root, "Erbarm dich, o

---

[24] *Goed.* 60, 1 and 2.
[25] For a tabulation of Alliteration, Assonance, etc., cf. Appendix, pp. 149 ff.
[26] *Goed.* 293, 8 and 9.
[27] *Goed.* 93, 6.
[28] *Goed.* 65, 46.

barmherzigs Herz,"[29] "Ich lieb ihr liebes Angesicht,"[30] as well as the frequent repetition of words or use of refrains[31] show the power of his language and offer a striking method of expressing inmost sympathy. What real fervor is indicated in the lines:

> "Dasz ich dich möge für und für
> In, bei und an mir tragen."[32]

Just as Gerhardt was a loyal devotee to his mother-tongue, so also he stood aloof from the tendency of his time to adopt foreign characteristics in verse. Only twice[33] has he employed the Alexandrine so fashionable in the period, and other foreign verse-forms he avoids entirely. On the other hand in so comparatively small a number of poems the variety of his verse structure is unusual. Gerhardt knew Buchner[34] in his Wittenberg student days and owes to him his technical training in versification which his strophes show. He uses in them iambic, trochaic and especially dactyllic-anapaestic metres which Buchner had declared permissible. Hahne[35] enumerates in Gerhardt's poems fifty-one kinds of strophe among which six are quite complicated. Three of these, as appear in the poems, "Frölich soll mein Herze springen," *Goed.* 155; "Gib dich zufrieden," 274; and "Die güldne Sonne," 293, must be regarded as original with Gerhardt. While these three are not artistic and harmonious, they are, nevertheless, in exact accord with the type of melody prevalent in the XVIIth century.

Our poet has shown preference for the older German strophes which belong to popular poetry and had most firmly held their own in the spiritual song because of its relation to the Volkslied and also for the Nibelungen strophe of eight lines. Eighteen[36] times he uses the well known seven-line ballad strophe and twice[37] the six-lined strophe of the Wanderlied "Innsbruck, ich musz dich lassen"[38] which even as early as the Reformation had come into wide use in hymnody. He has also frequently employed the rhymed couplet in the four-lined stanza. The verse-structure in the remainder of his poems may generally be traced back to lays long since

---

[29] *Goed.* 7, 76.

[30] *Goed.* 260, 41.

[31] Cf. the refrains in *Goed.* 106; 139; 235.

[32] *Goed.* 158, 94.

[33] "Du liebe Unschuld du, wie schlecht wirst du geacht!" (*Goed.* 3) and "Herr Lindholtz legt sich hin und schläft in Gottes Namen" (*Goed.* 252).

[34] Cf. p. 2.

[35] Hahne, F., *P. Gerhardt und A. Buchner* in *Euphorion* 15, p. 19-34.

[36] *Goed.* 10; 21; 23; 51; 125; 134; 158; 171; 190; 209; 253; 271; 298; 315; 317; 325; 331; 335.

[37] *Goed.* 60 and 71.

[38] Regarding this melody cf. p. 100.

native to the church, though one strophe "Sollt ich meinem Gott nicht singen"[39] appears for the first time, as far as we know, in Johann Rist's[40] hymns. Realizing, furthermore, that a composition becomes truly a poem only through its harmony Gerhardt clung to the well known melodies, adapting his new text to them that through the music his hymns might the more easily become familiar. Thus he composed "Ein Lämmlein geht und trägt die Schuld" to the melody "An Wasserflüssen Babylon," and "O Welt, sieh hier dein Leben" and "Nun ruhen alle Wälder" to "Innsbruck, ich musz dich lassen,"[41] and in fact his hymns were known at first only through their musical setting. Like Luther, he wished to teach the people song[42] and it is evident that in composing he usually had some definite melody in mind, and what Johann Walther had been to Luther, Crüger[43] was to Gerhardt. To this choir master we owe the first significant publication of our poet's hymns. Many musicians have adapted his hymns to music; Bach made use of them in a number of his cantatas and his Passion music,[44] and five[45] times in his rapturous *Weihnachtsoratorium* do we find Gerhardt's words. Of recent musicians who have been interested in his poetry as a basis for their compositions mention must be made of Albert Becher (d. 1899), H. von Herzogenberg (d. 1900) and especially the Bavarian clergyman, Friedrich Mergner[46] (1818-1891), who has so thoroughly caught the spirit of Gerhardt. As early as 1732-1800 six Catholic hymn books in quite general use throughout Germany had included in all, thirteen of Gerhardt's hymns, and "O Haupt voll Blut und Wunden" can be heard in many Catholic churches to-day, even in the Cologne Cathedral.[47]

Gerhardt was essentially a "Gelegenheitsdichter," a poet of occasions, choosing for his themes the various vicissitudes of life and such events as would present themselves to an earnest pastor devoted to the flock under his care. We may define him more precisely as a poet of consolation, for at least seventeen of his hymns are to be classed as "Songs of the Cross and Consolation,"[48] and fully half his work contains much that is intended as a source of comfort in the many afflictions of the troublous times in which

---

[39] *Goed.* 235.

[40] Rist, 1607-1667.

[41] Cf. p. 100.

[42] Cf. p. 10.

[43] Cf. p. 2.

[44] Cf. p. 43.

[45] From *Goed.* 25; 310; 150; 155; 158.

[46] Cf. *P. Gerhardt's Geistl. Lieder in neuen Weisen von Fr. Mergner. 30 ausgewählte Lieder von Karl Schmidt,* Leipzig, C. Deichert, 1907.

[47] Cf. J. Smend: *P. Gerhardt u. das evangel. Kirchenlied* in *Der Protestantismus am Ende des 19. Jahrh.* I, pp. 301, ff.

[48] Cf. Index by subjects, Appendix, pp. 158 ff.

he lived.   An enumeration of "Trost" words shows the use of "Trost" 51 times, "getrost" 11, "trösten" 10, "trostlos," "tröstlich" 2, besides numerous phrases such as "Erschrecke nicht,"[49] "Sei unverzagt,"[50] "Sei ohne Furcht,"[51] "Gott hat mich nicht verlassen."[52]   In this connection we should consider Gerhardt's use of the word "Trost."   With him it seems often to have a wider meaning than merely solace, or comfort.   At times it approaches even its English cognate *trust,* or at least that comfort or assurance which is born of trust.[53]   In the poem beginning "Schwing dich auf zu deinem Gott" the word seems clearly to be used in this sense in line 7:

> Merkst du nicht des Satans List?
> Er will durch sein Kämpfen
> Deinen *Trost,*[54] den Jesus Christ
> Dir erworben, dämpfen.

At other times the meaning is apparently the *ground* of confidence or reliance, as in the line: "Dein Arm ist mein Trost gewesen."[55]   Since joy is to Gerhardt innately associated with the theme of comfort, we find in his verses a host of phrases embodying cheer and joy:

> Lasz deine Frömmigkeit
> Sein meinen Trost und Freud.[56]

By enumeration we find the use of "Freude" 161 times; of "Freudenlicht" (-quell, -schein, etc.) 33 times; of "freuen" and "erfreuen" 22 times; of "froh," "frö(h)lich," "freudig," "freudenvoll," "selig," etc. 50 times; of other kindred expressions, such as "Lust," "Wonne," "Seligkeit," "Freudigkeit," etc. 8 times.   Stanza VI of the "Adventgesang" (*Goed.* 108) is a fair example of Gerhardt's fondness for singing of joys both temporal and spiritual:

> Aller Trost und aller Freude
> Ruht in dir, Herr Jesu Christ;
> Dein Erfreuen ist die Weide,
> Da man sich recht frölich iszt.
> Leuchte mir, o Freudenlicht,
> Ehe mir mein Herze bricht;
> Lasz mich, Herr, an dir erquicken!
> Jesu, komm, lasz dich erblicken!

---

[49] *Goed.* 271, 8.
[50] *Goed.* 185, 42.
[51] *Goed.* 289, 3.
[52] *Goed.* 296, 31.
[53] Cf. the meaning of the modern German "getrost."
[54] *Goed.* 135, 7; cf. also *Goed.* 135, 132; 30, 127; 150, 74; 217, 59; 317, 40.
[55] *Goed.* 145, 19; cf. also *Goed.* 46, 16; 150, 43.
[56] *Goed.* 65, 22.   For the frequent use of "Trost und Freude" and "Freude und Trost," cf. Appendix, p. 155 and p. 153.

Compare with this the lines from the hymn based on Johann Arndt's "Gebet um Geduld in groszem Creutz" (*Goed. 209*):

> St. XIV.   "O heilger Geist, du Freudenöl,
> Das Gott vom Himmel schicket,
> Erfreue mich, gib meiner Seel
> Was Mark und Bein erquicket!
> Du bist der Geist der Herrlichkeit,
> Weiszt, was für Freud und Seligkeit
> Mein in dem Himmel warte."

A pastor and poet whose spirit amidst the hardships of the war can not only remain undaunted but bring so large a measure of cheer to his flock is indeed destined to have an immortal name.   It was the everpresent hardships of war, however, that made him long not merely for an earthly peace but also for spiritual rest.   As an advocate of peace and contentment he has among his contemporaries no equal.   Having hoped and prayed during the war for a cessation of hostilities and horrors he could at last burst forth at the conclusion of the Peace of Westphalia in his magnificent

> Gott Lob! nun ist erschollen
> Das edle Fried- und Freudenswort.[57]

Furthermore he preaches patience and contentment with life's experiences. Notably does this appear in the poem "Gib dich zufrieden" (*Goed.* 274) where each stanza has these words as the refrain.   Taking as his theme "Rest in the Lord, and wait patiently for him" (*Ps*. XXXVII, 7) he reveals to his fellow-men the joys and comforts that await the true believers even though they must pass through pain, anxiety, and even death.   As their tears are counted and their sighs are heard, so a day of rest is at hand when God shall receive the meek in the abundance of peace, and 'they shall then be exalted to inherit the land.'[58]   But how very deeply Gerhardt felt this yearning for spiritual as well as material peace is best seen from the constant recurrence of the root "Friede."   Of this word and its compounds we note 33 examples, and of "Ruhe," "Stille," Rast" and similar words, 16.

Aside from the hymns of Cross and Consolation discussed above,[59] which among Gerhardt's poems are by far the most numerous, and which gave him the widest opportunity to grasp the inner life of the Christian believer in its different tendencies and phases, the subjective development of his spiritual songs is shown in two directions—in the poetic glorification of

---

[57] *Goed.* 95.
[58] Cf. also the poem "Geduld ist euch vonnöten" (*Goed.* 267), where each of the 14 stanzas begins with the word "Geduld."
[59] Cf. p. 21.

nature and of family life. Gerhardt's knowledge of nature is limited to
the ideas set forth in Johann Arndt's[60] *Viertes Buch vom wahren Christen-
tum*. Following Arndt, Gerhardt believes the material as well as the spiritual phenomena on earth are influenced in a mysterious way by the heavens
and their constellations; hence the prophetic significance of comets which
he mentions in two poems.[61]   In the year 1618 just such a threatening
"torch" had appeared to announce the frightful war. Fourteen years later
another comet was regarded as prophecy of the death of the Swedish King.
Naturally, then, in 1652 Gerhardt is terrified with all others at the appear-
ance in the sky of the third "Flammenrute" (*Goed.* 104).

However, within this limited knowledge nature appears to him as of inde-
pendent grandeur, wholly subservient to God and freely enjoyed by all
Christians. In his life, too, as well as in his songs, Gerhardt is open to all
the world and is at all times sensible to the appreciation of nature. It is
a noteworthy characteristic of him that in one glance he includes with
sense of fitness and artistic certainty both large and small, the most sublime
and the most commonplace. In this wise he sings:

> Die Erd ist fruchtbar, bringt herfür
> Korn, Oel, Most, Brot, Wein und Bier,
> Was Gott gefällt.
>   (*Goed.* 139, 49 ff.)

To Gerhardt the world lies in continual sunshine.[62]   He scorns trouble,
distress seems merely to accentuate happiness; from the horrors of the
Thirty Years' War he turns to thank God for the return of peace,[63] and
to inspire his people with gratitude for the infinite mercy of the Most High.
He celebrates evening and morning and takes us in summer through the
flowering gardens of God, portrays rain and sunshine, earth's sorrows and
joys.

The other direction of the subjectivity of Gerhardt's writing is that of
the family life. In a time so bereft of virtues as the XVIIth century the
firmly grounded idea of the home must be given first place. His own family
life, cheered by domestic felicity, and the many contributions he made to
occasional poetry bear testimony to this. For married life he sings the

---

[60] Joh. Arndt, a Protestant theologian, 1555-1621. The "Vier Bücher" appeared in
1605. Cf. the references on pp. 63 ff. to his *Paradiszgärtlein aller christl. Tugenden,*
1612.

[61] *Goed.* 104 and 142.

[62] Even no. 15 which begins with a seemingly very pessimistic complaint about the
disastrous weather and consequently meagre harvest closes with a prayer full of hope
for the future.

[63] *Goed.* 95.

praise of quiet domesticity,[64] picturing the Christian housewife in the midst of her surroundings, bringing joy and cheer to her husband, faithful in her tasks, ministering to the poor and teaching her children the Word of God. He closes the poem with the eulogy:

> Die Werke, die sie hie verrichtt,
> Sind wie ein schönes helles Licht;
> Sie dringen bis zu Himmelspfort
> Und werden leuchten hier und dort.

Before Gerhardt, Mathesius[65] had sung the praises of domestic happiness in "Wem Gott ein ehrlich Weib beschert," but the sincere note of Gerhardt's "Wie schön ist's doch, Herr Jesu Christ" (*Goed.* 302) placed German home-life in a poetic light it had not known before.

For the dying he allays the fear of death; man is but a stranger on earth[66] and has spent many a day in distress and care; his home is yonder where hosts of angels praise the Mighty Ruler. The sympathetic pastor takes his place with the parents beside the bier of their deceased child.[67] He speaks as a father who has lost his son, and he imagines the child in heaven joining the chorus of the angels. But Gerhardt has written very few hymns of death or of penitence. When he does speak of sin and its curse of death with its terrors, he still contrives at once to take from them the sting. The poem beginning "O Tod, O Tod, du greulichs Bild,"[68] bears the title *"Freudige* Empfahung des Todes," and concludes with the lines:

> Was solls denn nun, O Jesu, sein,
> Dasz mich der Tod so schrecket?
> Hat doch Elisa Todtenbein,
> Was todt war, auferwecket:
> Viel mehr wirst du, den Trost hab ich,
> Zum Leben kräftig rüsten mich;
> Drum schlaf ich ein mit *Freuden.*

In hymnody both before and since Gerhardt there has often been a vivid portrayal of the tortures of hell to terrify the soul. Gerhardt scrupulously avoids this and is therefore able to reduce everything to the simplicity of beauty. Every pain and every punishment in which his poems abound at once lose their bitterness because on them is reflected the sunlight of God's love. Gerhardt towers above his time in that amid all his despondent fellow-men he is always fearless and shows a cheerful heart reliant on God;

---

[64] *Goed.* 242.
[65] Johann M., a Lutheran theologian, 1504-1565. His *Leben Luthers* (1566) is his most famous work.
[66] "Ich bin ein Gast auf Erden" (*Goed.* 284).
[67] "Weint; und weint gleichwol nicht zu sehr" (*Goed.* 335).
[68] *Goed.* 317.

just because the severe afflictions of his own life cannot break his spirit, he has in his power the cure for others.

The candid reader must admit that there is evident in some passages of Gerhardt's poetry a certain dogmatic constraint, ("Gebundenheit").   The devil[69] is to him a terrible reality, the Christchild in the manger is the creator[70] of the world, and the problem of the Trinity is dismissed without consideration.   The Atonement, too, of the Savior is easily understood on the theory of punishment, while the resurrection[71] of the flesh is an undeniable truth.   But in other respects Gerhardt is far less dogmatic than Luther.

Critics have sought in vain for traces of poetic development in Gerhardt's work.   Such findings as have been claimed can be regarded only as more or less probable conjecture, a fact which shows that his personality was immediately poetically endowed, giving itself out whenever it composed poetry.   If his individuality shows no development as such, his poetry can bear no marks of development.

It has often been said that "Gerhardt had and sought no laurels"; nor was he ever "hailed as the Homer or Vergil of his time."   As he knew neither himself nor the greatness of his gift, so his contemporaries failed to appreciate him.   He never regarded himself as a poet by calling as did Opitz, Johann Franck and Rist, but only a poet by avocation.   To quote Goethe, he sang "as the bird sings that lives in the branches."   In the same proportion that Gerhardt's poetry brought strength and comfort in the grievous period of the Thirty Years' War and later eras of confusion, it is destined through the present world disaster to bring its message of hope.

---

[69] Cf. "Will Satan mich verschlingen" (*Goed.* 60, 46) ; "Dazu kommt des Teufels Lügen" (*Goed.* 108, 17) ; also 62, 55 ; 122, 31 ; 135, 41 ; 171, 40 ; 173, 40 ; 185, 33 ; 232, 18 ; 256, 34 ; 312, 6 ; 328, 14.

[70] Cf. "Es wird im Fleisch hier fürgestellt,
    Der alles schuf und noch erhält ;" (*Goed.* 310, 37-38).

[71] Cf. *Goed.* 51.

PART TWO.

. . .

CHAPTER I.

HISTORY OF ENGLISH HYMNODY AND THE GERMAN INFLUENCE UPON
ENGLISH HYMN WRITING FROM THE EARLY XVITH
THROUGH THE XIXTH CENTURY.[1]

ANY direct traces of literary intercourse between Germany and England
before the XVIth century are hard to find; however, with the invention
of printing, the establishment of the universities, the Renaissance and the
Reformation the literary relations were increased and became important.

In the wide region of satire which was at that time serious and often
steeped in theological ideas Germany's works left enduring traces. Brant's
"Narrenschiff" translated in the first years of the century helped essentially
in accelerating the development of this type of literature in England:
reprinted there after an interval of sixty years it was still an inexhaustible
model of satire. Another source of dramatic effect destined to have great
success on the English stage was found in some hero endowed with super-
natural powers, such as Faustus. Thus by introducing a new class of
situations into English drama the unusually gifted Germany of the sixteenth
century was of great moment for its neighbor, England. Not a little of the
quality of the Minnelied, too, reappears in much of the verse of the English
lyric writers of this century, when the rose, the nightingale and daisy serve
as interpretations of the play of love. In the Mystery Plays there existed
doubtless germs of the Meistersänger school: the occasional strophic passages in the Towneley plays resembled to a great extent the normal Meistergesang. This germ, however, did not develop markedly because in England
the cultivation of poetry never became a serious occupation. These literary
influences from Germany in satire, in Minnelied and in Meistergesang had
direct effect upon English intellectual life, and continued uninterrupted
through the centuries. The record, on the other hand, of German influence
in History, Lyrics and Hymns was more broken and disconnected.

---

[1] Inasmuch as Gerhardt's influence was not fully felt in England till the middle of
the XIXth century, this chapter deals with the development of the English hymn up
to that period.

In order to get the story of the development of the hymn we must go back a little. Church music in the mediaeval times belonged to the choir, not to the congregation. The choral hymns in England, as in Germany, were in Latin and many of them were exceedingly beautiful. Although the early English Church received from the continent the most of the Latin hymns used in its service, nevertheless there were a few English authors of Latin hymns. Among this number were Bede, commonly called Venerable Bede (673-735?) who wrote "Adeste, Christi, vocibus," and Anselm of Canterbury, a great architect and theologian, and Thomas à Becket. While psalms and hymns have been used by the Christian Church since its beginning, the particular form of psalms and hymns now in use originated with the Reformation. A wonderful development of this religious lyric poetry sprang up in England and Germany at the beginning of the XVIth century. The reformers in both countries were chiefly concerned in simplifying religious worship, and in giving to the laity a more active participation in it; the choir and anthem, the old liturgic hymn and antiphonal chant gave way to a great extent to hymns in the vernacular, set to the simplest music and sung by the whole congregation. This change was first made by Luther and eagerly copied in England.

When Miles Coverdale in his ungifted way translated Luther's hymns into English his unpoetical and lumbering versions were ill received and were soon proscribed by the Crown. Sternhold and Hopkins who were translators of the psalms became more noticed, but their versions too seem to have been deficient in taste and feeling of lyric poetry. The criticism of the poet Campbell seems to be justified when he says of the authors that "with the best intentions and the worst taste they degraded the spirit of Hebrew Psalmody by flat and homely phraseology; and mistaking vulgarity for simplicity turned into bathos what they found sublime." Although these bleak translations were read in England for a time, they soon disappeared leaving only small traces which were picked up by Wesley more than two centuries later.

So with the royal proscription of Coverdale's work,[2] the dying out of Sternhold and Hopkins' and other similar attempts at translation, the

---

[2] It must be remembered, however, that although Coverdale's writings had little influence upon the people of his own time, they have been appreciated by later generations and are among the most sincere monuments to Luther in the English language. Cf. A. Mitchell: *The Wedderburns*, Edinb., 1868.

An example will show the nature and degree of Coverdale's imitation. Here is the first stanza of his version of "Ein' feste Burg":

> "Oure God is a defence and towre
> A good armour and good weapen,
> He hath ben ever oure helpe and sucoure

imaginative poetry of German Protestantism which had been caught up in England with such momentary enthusiasm was as rapidly forgotten. Church music was again sung by the choir.   The first effort, therefore, in the early XVth century to introduce Lutheran hymnody into the English world contributed little.

This disappearance in England of the work of the Reformers in church music was due not only to the lack of great translators but also to many other causes.   Early in the Renaissance England came to think of the Reformation as her own movement, and therefore casting aside all suggestions from other countries wished to study history and hymns of English sources only.   The few men at this time who recognized Germany as the mother country of the Reformation and a seat of literary accomplishments had no wide influence in England.   All German residents in England belonged exclusively to the commercial class and brought no literary influence with them; also a reason for the literary alienation at this time was the fact that Germany did not enter the religious wars in which Englishmen were so deeply interested.   To men like Jonson and Fletcher Germany was famous only as a land of magicians and conjurers such as Paracelsus and Dr. Faustus.   In short, for nearly two centuries England knew little of Germany except what booksellers found it to their profit to advertise on their sign directories as the "wonderful strange Newes from Germany," and the satires of Brant, Dedekind, and Fischart.[3]

Another most vital cause of the retardation of the development of hymnody in Great Britain so soon after the Reformation was the example and influence of Geneva.   Calvin was organizing his ecclesiastical system at Geneva, and introduced into it Marot's Psalter[4] which was then very fashionable.   This example produced in England the translation commonly known as the *Old Version of the Psalms* begun in the reign of Henry VIII (1509–1547).   In this collection are eleven metrical versions of the "Te Deum" and "Da pacem, Domine," two original hymns of praise, two

---

In all the troubles that we have ben in.
Therefore wyl we never drede
For any wonderous dede
By water or by londe
In hilles or the sea-sonde.
Our God hath them al i his hond."

[3] For a good account of contemporary German drama and satire in England, cf. Herford: *The Literary Relations of England and Germany in the XVIth. Century.* Ch. IV-VII.

[4] Clement Marot, valet de chambre to Francis I of France, collaborated with Theodore Beza on a metrical translation of the Old Testament Psalms.   The work appeared about 1540.

penitential and a hymn of faith.   The tunes which accompanied the words were German.[5]   Therefore, although the religious influence of the Reformation was always strong in England from the beginning of the movement, the influence of Luther from a literary standpoint early in the Renaissance ceased to exist in England and was replaced by Calvin's stern rule.   These narrower canons admitting nothing but paraphrases of scripture and even of scripture little outside the Psalms became the firm fashion of English hymnody for the next century and a half.

In spite of the fact that Luther had little influence on English literature in the early Reformation his hymns came to their own in England in the middle of the XVIIIth century.   In the meantime, although the English people used the stern canons of Calvin, they began to feel the want of a more lyric hymn.   While German Protestantism had developed at once a rich hymnody there was actually no English hymnody until the XVIIIth century.   Isaac Watts, a representative of the English Independents, may be justly considered the real founder of modern English hymnody.   He was the first to understand the nature of the want, and by the publication of his *Hymns* in 1707–1709 and *Psalms* (hymns founded on psalms) he led the way in providing for this want.   His immediate followers were Simon Browne and Doddridge; and later in the century Grigg, Miss Steele, Beddome and Swain succeeded them.   Of these writers Watts and Doddridge are certainly preeminent, the hymns of the former are of unusual fervor and strong simplicity, and those of Doddridge while perhaps more artificial in general than those of his predecessor Watts are nevertheless distinguished by their graceful style.

About 1738 came the "Methodist" movement which afterward became divided into three sects, the Arminian under John Wesley, those who adhered to the Moravians,[6] and the Calvinists of whom Whitfield was the leader.   Each of these factions had its own hymn writers, some of whom did, and others did not, secede from the Church of England.   These are the years when a renewed strong current of influence from Germany is felt.   The translation movement first sprang up in the middle of this century when Count Zinzendorf and A. G. Spangenberg came to England[7] and established a branch of the Moravian Church there.   The *Gesangbuch,* the first of the hymn books for the congregation at Herrnhut, had been published in 1735 by Count Zinzendorf.   The Moravians in England began to translate many of the hymns contained in the German *Moravian Hymn Book.*[8]

---

[5] Cf. Barney: *History of Music.*
[6] The Moravians were a vigorous religious cult established in Herrnhut, Saxony.
[7] In 1737 and 1741, respectively.
[8] Cf. p. 11.

These translations, however, were for the most part poor, mere doggerel, but in later editions they were somewhat improved, especially in the one revised in the XIXth century by James Montgomery, the well known hymn writer, who was for a long time a member of the English Moravian Church. Among these many English hymn writers at this time whether writing entirely from English sources, or influenced by German ideas and philosophy or merely translators of the German hymn, the Wesley brothers are deserving of the first place.

After determining upon missionary lives John and Charles Wesley embarked on October 14, 1735, for the new colony of Georgia. Among their fellow passengers were twenty-six Moravian colonists, who in all the changes of weather, especially during storms, made a great deal of hymn singing. John Wesley was much impressed with the fervor and piety of these hymns and with their spiritual possibilities. One of the German sources which had great influence upon Wesleyan hymnody was Freyling-hausen's *Geist-reiches Gesang-Buch* (Halle 1704 and 1714). John Wesley introduced hymn singing into the "companies" formed in Georgia and his first hymn book appeared as a *Collection of Psalms and Hymns. Charles-Town 1737*, without his name. Of the seventy lyrics in the book, one half are from Watts, fifteen of the remainder are hymns of the Wesleys, five of which were translated from the German by John Wesley. In his third collection printed in England in 1750 the immediate impression the hymns produce is that of foreignness because of the many lengthy stanzas and the unusual metres. The reason for this is the fact that the authorities insisted that the melodies sung at Herrnhut be kept, irrespective of the language in which they might be sung. Although Charles Wesley knew no German, and therefore derived his impressions of the Moravian hymnody indirectly, nevertheless he caught much of its tone and manner and its atmosphere of confiding love. In all he wrote about 6500 hymns, through a large portion of which may be traced this Moravian influence.

Of great value to English hymnody are the contributions of the Calvinistic Methodists, and few writers of hymns have had higher gifts than A. M. Toplady, the author of "Rock of Ages." His hymns have the same warmth, richness and spirituality as German hymns, and are meditations after the German manner, owing direct obligation to German originals. During the first quarter of the nineteenth century came the practice of hymnodists of altering without scruple the compositions of other men, notably Latin and German hymn writers, to suit their own doctrines and tastes, with the result all too often of spoiling the originals thus altered, though English hymnody was undoubtedly enriched by this process of adaptation. Two publications in 1827, Bishop Heber's *Hymns* and Keble's *Christian Year* introduced a new epoch into English hymnody, destroying the barrier which had previously existed between the different theological schools of the Church of England.   This movement received a great additional impulse from the publication in 1833 of Bunsen's *Gesangbuch*.   From this time hymns and hymn writers multiplied not only in the Church of England, but in Scotland and America also.   With such influences as we have mentioned the more recent collections have evidenced an improved standard of taste, and there has been a larger and more liberal admission of good hymns from the German.   In this XIXth century when the study of the German language and literature became so much more common than before it is natural that an impulse be given also to translation of German hymns.

Beside the improvement in the standard of taste, additional interest in hymnody had been aroused by the prominence given to congregational singing in English churches.   "To love hymns in eighteenth century Scotland was to be accused of heresy: in England, it was to be convicted of that worse thing, 'enthusiasm.'"   Since the days of Luther Germany had given her hymns general esteem, but in England it was the middle of the nineteenth century before hymns won anything like popular favor.   The congregational hymn in England is the direct although exceedingly slow outgrowth of the German Reformation but it must be borne in mind that the foundations of congregational singing were laid even before Luther. When the Hussites in Bohemia created this hymnody in the vernacular their hymns were designed for worshippers rather than for the choir.[9] While German Protestantism developed at once a rich hymnody there was actually no English hymnody until the XVIIIth century.

German hymns and chorals had a place in the *Church Psalter and Hymn Book* of William Mercer of Sheffield (1854).   One who took much interest in its preparation was James Montgomery of whom mention has already been made.[10]   This was the most successful of all the books of the decade for the reason that it aided in placing the hymnody back in the people's hands and making it congregational.   Thus we see that the success of congregational singing of the better type required a return to the Reformation practice of including the tunes, as well as words, in the people's hymn books.

If general congregational singing after the manner that prevailed in Germany for so long has been an incentive to the development of English hymnody, the interest in German hymnody has at the same time been quickened by the good work done in Frances E. Cox's *Sacred Hymns from the German* (1841) and Henry J. Buckoll's *Hymns translated from the*

---

[9] The earliest extant hymn book is that in the Bohemian Museum at Prague, and bears the date Jan. 13, 1501, but this hymn book is, singularly, never mentioned among the works of the Brethren (Moravians).

[10] Cf. p. 31.   For Gerhardt's influence on Montgomery cf. p. 139.

German (1842).   This also found expression in the *Psalms and Hymns, partly original, partly selected* (Cambridge 1851) of Arthur T. Russell, in which the German hymns played a very large part, the Latin a very small one; even the arrangement of the hymns is based on an old Lutheran hymn book.   In 1854 appeared Richard Massie's *Martin Luther's Spiritual Songs,* and the first four parts (1854–1862) of *Hymns from the Land of Luther* by Jane Borthwick and her sister Mrs. Findlater.   In 1855 and 1858 Catherine Winkworth published the first and second series of her *Lyra Germanica,* following them in 1863 with the *Chorale Book for England,* and *Christian Singers of Germany* (1869).   The work of this group of translators which has secured so firm a place in English hymnody for a number of German hymns and more particularly those of Paul Gerhardt will be discussed in the following chapter.

ABBREVIATIONS AND EXPLANATIONS.

Bachmann = Bachmann: Gerhardts Geistliche Lieder, 1866.

C.B. = Chorale Book for England, by Catherine Winkworth, 1863.

C.P.&H.Bk. = Mercer's Church Psalter and Hymn Book, 1854 etc.

Crü.Praxis = Crüger's Praxis pietatis melica, Berlin and Frankfurt a/M. 1648 etc.

Crü.—Runge = Runge's edition of the above.

Ebeling = P. Gerhardi Geistliche Andachten, 1667 etc. (The numbers following the date refer to the "dozen" in which the poem appeared. Cf. p. 15 and note 6.)

G.B. = Gesangbuch.

G.L.S. = Geistlicher Liederschatz, 1832.

Goed. = Goedeke: Gedichte von Paulus Gerhardt, 1877. (In this thesis the poems are numbered according to the page on which they begin in this Goedeke text.)

H.L.L. = Hymns from the Land of Luther, by Mrs. Findlater and Miss Jane Borthwick, 1854 etc.

H.Bk. = Hymn Book.

Kelly = J. Kelly: Paul Gerhardt's Spiritual Songs, 1867.

Lib.R.P. = Library of Religious Poetry, 1881.

Lyra Ger. = Lyra Germanica, by Miss Winkworth, 1855 etc.

Songs of G. and G. = Songs of Grace and Glory, by Charles B. Snepp, 1872.

st. = stanza.

Unv.L.S. = Unverfälschter Liedersegen, Berlin, 1851.

Wackernagel = Wackernagel: Gerhardts Geistliche Lieder, 1843.

When merely the translator's name is given, the complete title of the work is usually to be found in the respective biographical note in the Appendix, pp. 144 ff.

The citation of hymn books is by no means exhaustive. Selections from Gerhardt's hymns are to be found in nearly all modern hymnals. The aim has been to give mainly those which first included versions of his hymns.

As a rule, the German stanzas are indicated by the Roman numerals I, II, III, etc., the English stanzas by the Arabic 1, 2, 3, etc.

CHAPTER II.

ENGLISH VERSIONS OF GERHARDT'S HYMNS.

WHILE the first influence of Gerhardt on English hymnody dates from the earlier part of the XVIIIth century it was not until the middle of the following century[1] that his influence was most fully felt. For it was then that the whole subject of church music and congregational singing in England received renewed and special attention. The English hymn writers and compilers of hymn books naturally appropriated all embodiment of Christian experience and devotion that Germany, a country so nearly akin to their own, could offer. The translators of all German hymns were subjected to certain limitations the observance of which affected the character of the rendering. The accompanying versions of Gerhardt's poems are illustrations of this statement.

A parallel arrangement of these various versions reveals the following interesting facts. First, that literalness has been rarely attained for the reason that a certain measure of freedom has to be used in any metrical rendering. Some, as for example, Dr. J. Kelly, have striven to maintain fidelity to the sense of the original and thereby have often sacrificed euphony to fidelity. Secondly, there has been made necessary the frequent use of the double rhymes which are as common in the German language, on account of its peculiar structure, as monosyllabic rhymes are in English. The limited number of double rhymes in English has presented a serious obstacle in the way of rendering German hymns with their native force and simplicity without which qualities the hymns cannot become truly naturalized. In so many cases have the German hymns and tunes been considered as one and inseparable, that the translators have sought to preserve the original metres for the sake of the tunes which would not of course admit of any deviation without harm to their characteristic beauty.

In the following pages we shall discuss those of Gerhardt's hymns (84 in number) which have been translated into English, and cite in most cases the hymn books which have been among the first to recognize the excellence of the English versions.[2]

---

[1] Cf. p. 27 and note.

[2] The hymns selected for discussion with their respective English versions are arranged according to the sequence in the Goedeke text (*Gedichte von Paulus Gerhardt*, Leipzig 1877). The ten most widely translated hymns (nos. 25, 49, 59, 60, 68,

Du liebe Unschuld du, wie schlecht wirst du geachtt!—(*Goed.* 3.)

Appeared in the *Crii. Praxis,* 1656, p. 650.

English Version:

1.   By *J. Kelly,* under the heading, "Under the vexations of the wicked prosperous world," the first stanza as follows:

> Ah! lovely innocence, how evil art thou deemed,
> How lightly oft thy work by all the world's esteem'd!
> Thou servest God, thy Lord, and to His word thou cleavest.
> For this, from men thou nought but scorn and hate receivest.

This translation is somewhat labored as is especially evident in line 4 above for the German:

> "Darüber höhnt man dich und drückt dich aller Orten."

Goedeke in his note to this hymn points out that from the use of the Alexandrine verse, the freedom from biblical phraseology and from the generality of the expressions it is probable that this is one of Gerhardt's earliest poems composed at a time when he patterned his writings after the model of Opitz.[3]

Wie ist so grosz und schwer die Last.—(*Goed.* 7.)

Appeared in *Crii.—Runge,* 1653, no. 299.

This fervent appeal for protection during the Thirty Years' War has been translated into English only by *J. Kelly* 1867, p. 246.   In line 36 he renders (from the Wackernagel text which he used):

> "Behold! *my heart,* on every hand."

As *mein Herr* is very evidently the proper reading from the sense of the context and the character of the other stanzas, it is unfortunate that his otherwise excellent rendering should be made to suffer by this one weak stanza.

"Protection of God in hitherto dangerous times of war."

> Stanza 1.   How heavy is the burden made
> That Thou upon our backs hast laid,
> O God! the Lord of Hosts,
> O God, whose anger rises high
> 'Gainst workers of iniquity.

122, 150, 185, 229, 239) and hymns showing adaptations are treated in a separate part of this chapter, pp. 82 ff.   In some instances specimen stanzas selected from the English versions have been added for comparison or reference.

[3] On Gerhardt's use of the Alexandrine cf. p. 20 f, and on the influence of Opitz cf. p. 18.

O Herrscher in dem Himmelszelt.—(*Goed.* 15.)

Appeared in *Crü.—Runge*, 1653, no. 315.

This poem and "Nun ist der Regen hin" (cf. *Goed.* 17, below) were both written during the Thirty Years' War and inspired by the same occasion. Gerhardt in two instances uses the same set of rhymes:

Goed. 15		*Goed.* 17	
1.	1 zelt	1.	31 feld
	2 feld		32 zelt
	51 bekehrt		5 gekehrt
	52 erhört		6 erhöret

The long metre lends itself well to English translation, and Kelly in his English version has observed with precision the pleading and melancholy tone of the original.

> Stanza 1. O God! who dost Heav'n's sceptre wield,
> What is it that now makes our field,
> And everything that it doth bear,
> Such sad and ruined aspect wear?[4]
> *J. Kelly*, 1867, p. 294.

His last stanza forms by its fervor an even stronger conclusion than Gerhardt's. The alteration from "bis in unsern Tod" to "as long as we may live" is a decided improvement, and more consistent with the thought of the context:

Verleih uns bis in unsern Tod	And, Lord, as long as we may live
Alltäglich unser liebes Brot	Our daily bread in bounty give
Und dermaleins nach diser Zeit	And when the end of time we see
Das süsze Brot der Ewigkeit!	The bread give of eternity.

Nun ist der Regen hin.—(*Goed.* 17.)

First published in *Crü.—Runge*, 1653, no. 315.

This simple nature poem expressing to the Almighty thanks for gracious sunshine after a storm has appeared but once in English verse, the version of *J. Kelly*, 1867, p. 298. The many poetic allusions and references to nature he has imitated very acceptably, at times even surpassing the thought of the original. In the first stanza the rhymes "gekehret" and "erhöret" have been especially aptly rendered by the accented *ed* in "turnéd" and "spurnéd."

> Stanza 1. Now gone is all the rain,
> Rejoice my heart again,

---

[4] On the pessimistic tone in this stanza cf. p. 24.

Sing after times of sadness
To God thy Lord with gladness!
Our God His heart hath turned
Our pray'r He hath not spurned. . . .

How successfully Kelly has caught the spirit of Gerhardt's nature description is evident in stanza 9:

Die Bäume werden schön	The trees so very fair
In ihrer Fülle stehen,	Fruit-laden will stand there;
Die Berge werden flieszen,	From hill-sides like a river
Und Wein und Oele gieszen,	Will wine and oil flow ever
Das Bienlein wird wol tragen	In warm and quiet weather
Bei guten warmen Tagen.	Will bees their honey gather.

Nun laszt uns gehn und treten.—(*Goed.* 19.)

[*New Year.*]

Evidently written during the Thirty Years' War. It first appeared in *Crü.—Runge,* 1653, no. 106, in 15 stanzas of 4 lines; thence in *Wackernagel:* no. 12; *Bachmann:* no. 24; Berlin *G. L. S.:* 1863, no. 200.

English Versions:

1. **In prayer your voices raise ye.**
In full, by *J. Kelly,* 1867, p. 45. From this 8 stanzas are included in the Ohio *Lutheran Hymnal,* 1880.

2. **Now let each humble creature.**
In the *Suppl. to Ger. Psal.,* 1765, p. 4, and *Select Hymns from Ger. Psal.,* Tranquebar, 1754, p. 7. In the *Moravian Hymn Bk.,* 1789, no. 507 (1849, no. 1106) greatly altered and beginning, "Year after year commenceth."

3. **O come with prayer and singing.**
R. Massie in the *British Herald,* Jan., 1865, p. 8.

4. **Christians all, with one accord.**
E. Massie, 1867, p. 168.

5. **With notes of joy and songs of praise.**
Dr. R. Maguire, 1883, p. 24.

Noch dennoch must du drum nicht ganz.—(*Goed.* 23.)

Appeared in the *Crü. Praxis,* 1656, no. 814.

This hymn of consolation seems to refer to some particular disaster that had befallen the community during the Thirty Years' War. The "drum" in line 1 may possibly refer to some address or announcement made to the congregation.

The poem has been well translated in full by *J. Kelly*, 1867, p. 230.   He makes no attempt to render the doubtful meaning above referred to in the word "drum."   On the other hand his interpretations of several rather obscure lines (cf. lines 29 and 43 below) are undoubtedly correct.

> Stanza 1.   Thou must not altogether be
> O'ercome by sad vexation,
> God soon will cause to shine on thee
> The light of consolation.
> In patience wait, and be thou still
> And let the Lord do what He will,
> He never can do evil.

Lines 29, 30[5] are rendered:

> God therefore all our *joys* doth *blight*.
> Lets trials overtake us,

and lines 43, 44:[6]

> Afflicted *band!* oh, fall ye now
> With contrite hearts before Him,

In this last citation Kelly is right in assuming it is not literally the "army" but rather the congregation or community that Gerhardt is here addressing.

Wie soll ich dich empfangen.—(*Goed.* 25.)
(Cf. p. 82.)

Nun du lebest, unsre Krone.—(*Goed.* 28.)

This poem was appended to an address delivered in Berlin on the 23d of March, 1648, at the funeral of Peter Fritzen, the President of the Consistory.

English Version:

> 1.   On thy bier how calm thou'rt sleeping
> Yet thou livest, oh our crown!
> Watch eternal art thou keeping,

---

[5] Gerhardt, lines 29, 30:

> Drum fährt uns Gott durch unsern Sinn
> Und läszt uns Weh geschehen;

[6] lines 43, 44:

> Drum falle, du betrübtes Heer,
> In Demut für Ihm nieder;

> Standing near thy Savior's throne.
> Endless joy thy portion now!
> Why should tears so freely flow?
> What should thus in sorrow sink us?
> Up! aright let us bethink us!

A complete translation by *J. Kelly*, 1867, p. 338.

Sei mir tausendmal gegrüszet.—(*Goed.* 40.)

Taken from the "Salve mundi salutare," ascribed to St. Bernard of Clair-vaux.[7] The text of this beautiful poem is in St. Bernard's *Opera Omnia*, Paris, 1609, cols. 1655-56. Here it is entitled "A rhythmical prayer to any-one of the members of Christ suffering and hanging on the Cross," and is divided into 7 parts viz:

    I. **Salve mundi salutare** (*to the Feet*).
    II. **Salve Jesu, Rex sanctorum** (*to the Knees*).
    III. **Salve Jesu, pastor bone** (*to the Hands*).
    IV. **Salve Jesu, summe bonus** (*to the Side*).
    V. **Salve salus mea, Deus** (*to the Breast*).
    VI. **Summi Regis cor aveto** (*to the Heart*).
    VII. **Salve caput cruentatum** (*to the Face*).

The whole poem has been frequently translated into German. The best known translations are those by Paul Gerhardt, which are free versions of all the seven parts from the Latin text of 1609. Of Gerhardt's versions, nos. I, V, VI, and VII have passed into English, as follows:

I. Sei mir tausendmal gegrüszet.—(*Goed.* 40.)

This appeared in the 5th ed., Berlin, 1653, and the Frankfort ed., 1656, of *Crü. Praxis*, no. 150; thence in *Wackernagel:* no. 16; *Bachmann:* no. 48; *Unv. L. S.:* 1851, no. 116.

English Versions:

  1. **Thousand times by me be greeted.**
     In pt. I of the *Moravian H. Bk.* 1754. Repeated in later editions.

  2. **Ever by my love be owned** (st. I, III, IV).
     A. T. Russell in his *Psalms and Hymns*, 1851.

---

[7] Bernard of Clairvaux, saint, abbot, and doctor, was born in Burgundy in 1091, entered the monastery of Citeaux in 1113. In 1146 he spent much time in traversing France and Germany to rouse the people to participate in the ill-fated second crusade. He died in 1153. The hymns by which he is best known are (1) "Jesu dulcis memoria," a long poem on the "Name of Jesus," and (2) "Salve mundi salutare," an address to the various members of Christ on the cross. Hymns, translated from, or founded on, St. Bernard's will be found in almost every modern hymnal.

V.   Gegrüszet seist du, Gott, mein Heil.—(*Goed.* 46.)

Appeared in the Frankf. ed., 1656, of *Crü. Praxis;* thence in *Wackernagel:* no. 20; *Bachmann:* no. 52.

English Versions:

1. **All hail to Thee, my Savior and my God.**

    Mrs. Stanley Carr in her translation of *Wildenhahn's Paul Gerhardt,* ed. 1856, p. 116.

2. **All hail! my Savior and my God.**

    R. Massie in the *British Herald,* Feb., 1865, p. 18.

VI.   O Herz des Königs aller Welt.—(*Goed.* 47.)

Appeared in the Frankf. ed., 1656, of *Crü. Praxis,* no. 155; thence in *Wackernagel:* no. 21; *Bachmann:* no. 53; Berlin, *G. L. S.:* 1863, no. 258.

English Version:

1. **O Heart of Him who dwells on high.**

    R. Massie in the *British Herald,* May, 1866, p. 260.

VII.   O Haupt voll Blut und Wunden.—(*Goed.* 49.)
(Cf. p. 86 ff.)

Wach auf, mein Herz, und singe.—(*Goed.* 59.)
(Cf. p. 95 ff.)

Nun ruhen alle Wälder.—(*Goed.* 60.)
(Cf. p. 98 ff.)

Weg, mein Herz, mit den Gedanken.—(*Goed.* 62.)
[*Lent.*]

Founded on *St. Luke* XV. Appeared in *Crü. Praxis,* 1648, no. 36 in 12 stanzas.

English Versions:

1. **Let not such a thought e'er pain thee.**

    J. *Kelly,* 1867, p. 83.

2. **Hence, my heart, with such a thought.**

    Miss Winkworth, 1869, p. 210.

Herr, höre, was mein Mund.—(*Goed.* 65.)

Appeared in *Crü. Praxis,* 1648, no. 37.

This prayer for favor in judgment is based on *Psalm* CXLIII.   It is pervaded with deep humility and devoutness.

English Versions:

1. Lord, lend a gracious ear
    To my desire sincere
    From heart all free from guile
    And glad me with Thy smile,
    Accept my petition.
    > *J. Kelly,* 1867, p. 92.

His rendering of the similes and metaphors of this hymn is especially good.   Cf. stanza VI :

Betrachte, wer ich bin,	Consider what we be—
Im Hui fahr ich dahin,	A moment, what are we?
Zerbrechlich wie ein Glas,	As brittle as frail glass
Vergänglich wie ein Gras	As fading as the grass,
Ein Wind kann mich fällen.	By a breath we're swept off.

and in stanza X :

Ich lechze wie ein Land,	I'm like a thirsty land,

also stanza XI :

Gleich wie auf der Heid	Like hart upon the heath . . .
Ein Hirsch . . .	

Warum machet solche Schmerzen.—(*Goed.* 67.)
[*New Year.*]

Based on *St. Luke* II, 21.   It appeared in *Crü. Praxis,* 1648, no. 97 in 4 stanzas.   Bunsen, in his *Versuch* 1833, no. 120, gives stanzas III, IV, altered to "Freut euch, Sünder, allerwegen."

English Versions:

1. **Mortals, who have God offended.**
    Miss Cox, 1841, p. 21, from *Bunsen.*

2. **Why should they such pain e'er give Thee.**
    J. Kelly, 1867, p. 43.

Ein Lämmlein geht und trägt die Schuld.—(*Goed.* 68.)
(Cf. p. 104 ff.)

O Welt, sieh hier dein Leben.—(*Goed.* 71.)[8]
[*Passiontide.*]

Cf. *Koch* IV, 161, 711, 787.   First published in *Crü. Praxis,* 1648, no. 119, in 16 stanzas of 8 lines, reprinted in *Wackernagel:* no. 15; *Bachmann:* no. 8; *Unv. L. S.:*

---

[8] For adaptations of this hymn cf. p. 137.

1851, no. 113. Stanzas III-V were favorites with J. S. Bach and used by him in his St. Matthew and St. John Passion Music.[9]

English Versions:

1. **Extended on a cursed tree.**

A free translation in long metre by J. Wesley, of stanzas I, III, IV, VI, VIII-XI, XVI, in *Hymns and Sacred Poems,* 1740 (P. Works, 1868-72, vol. I, p. 232), and thence in the *Wesleyan H. Bk.,* 1780, and since in other hymn books of the Methodists. The translation of stanzas IX-XI, XVI, beginning "My Savior, how shall I proclaim" were included in the American *Sabbath Hymn Book,* 1858, and the Baptist *Service of Song,* Boston, 1871.

2. **See, World, upon the bloody tree.**

A translation by P. H. Molther of stanzas I-X in the *Moravian H. Bk.,* 1742, 1754. In the 1789 and 1886 eds. it is altered to "See, World, upon the shameful tree." The hymn appears in several English hymn books in different abridged forms.

3. **O, World! behold upon the tree.**

A good translation omitting stanza VII, by Miss Winkworth, in the 2d Series, 1858, of her *Lyra Ger.,* and thence in Schaff's *Christ in Song* ed. 1869, p. 174, and slightly altered and beginning:

> "Lord, be Thy Cross before our sight."
> In *Kennedy,* 1863.

4. **Here, World, see thy Redeemer.**

> In the *Suppl. to Ger. Psalmody,* ed. 1765, p. 16.

5. **O World! attention lend it.**

J. Gambold, as no. 442 in pt. I of the *Moravian H. Bk.,* 1754. Altered to "O World, see thy Creator." (1886, no. 94.)

6. **O World! see thy life languish.**

J. D. Burns, in the *Family Treasury,* 1859, pt. I, p. 54, also in his *Memoir and Remains,* 1869, p. 246.

7. **See World! thy Life assailed.**

> J. Kelly, 1867, p. 54.

8. **Here, World, thy great Salvation see.**

> Dr. J. Guthrie, 1869, p. 87.

9. **O World! see here suspended.**

> In Reid's *Praise Book,* 1872, no. 1009.

10. **Behold, O World, thy Life, thy Lord.**

> Dr. R. Maguire, 1883, p. 143.

Selected Stanzas:

J. Gambold in Part I of the 1734 edition of the *Moravian Hymn Book.*

> 1. O World! attention lend it,
>   Thy Life's on Cross suspended

---

[9] Cf. p. 21.

Thy Healer sinks in death:
The sov'reign Prince of Glory
(Tis no fictitious story)
With Shame and torment yields his Breath.

P. H. Molther in Part I of the 1754 edition of the *Moravian Hymn Book*.

1.   See, world, upon the bloody tree
Thy Life there sinks in Death,
Cover'd with Stripes and wounds for thee
Thy Savior yields his breath.

2.   Behold his Body swims in blood;
Out of his tender Heart,
Deep sighs and Groans he sends to God
In his excessive smart.

Note in the above stanzas the inconsistencies in capitalization.

Miss Winkworth, in her *Lyra Germanica*, 1865.

1.   Oh world! behold upon the tree
Thy Life is hanging now for thee,
Thy Savior yields His dying breath;
The mighty Prince of glory now
For thee doth unresisting bow
To cruel stripes, to scorn and death.

Auf, Auf, mein Herz mit Freuden.—(*Goed.* 74.)

[Easter.]

It appeared in *Crü. Praxis,* 1648, no. 141, in 9 stanzas.

English Versions:

1. **Up! up! my heart with gladness, See.**
J. Kelly, 1867, p. 71.

2. **Up, Up, my heart, with gladness, Receive.**
H. L. Frothingham, in his *Metrical Pieces,* 1870, p. 228.

O du allersüszste Freude!—(*Goed.* 76.)

[Whitsuntide.]

First published in the 3d ed., 1648, of *Crü. Praxis,* no. 155 in 10 stanzas of 8 lines; thence in *Wackernagel:* no. 30; *Bachmann:* no. 10. Cf. *Koch* IV, 232.

This is a fine hymn of supplication to the Holy Spirit for His gifts and graces. It is widely popular in Germany, and is included in the Berlin *G. L. S.*: 1863, no. 366. Through the version of J. C. Jacobi it has also been very largely used in various forms, in Great Britain and America.

English Versions:

1. O Thou sweetest source of gladness.

A full and good translation by J. C. Jacobi, in his *Psal. Ger.*, 1725, pt. II, p. 6. Jacobi's stanzas I-IV, IX, X, were considerably altered, as "Holy Ghost, dispel our sadness," by A. M. Toplady, in the *Gospel Magazine,* June, 1776. In Sedgwick's ed. of Toplady's *Hymns and Sacred Poems,* 1860, p. 169, these stanzas appear:

1. Holy Ghost, dispel our sadness;
2. From that height which knows no measure.
3. Come, Thou best of all donations.
4. Known to Thee are all recesses.
5. Manifest Thy love for ever.
6. Be our Friend on each occasion.

The alteration in Sedgwick is, therefore, as follows:

Gerhardt:	I	II	III	IV	V	VI	VII	(VIII	IX)	X
Toplady:	1	3	2		4		5			6

The hymn appears in many centos, though it usually begins with the first stanza of the text above, "Holy Ghost, dispel our sadness." There are many centos in the original metre, but other metre has been employed also, as:

(1) 8.7.8.7.4.7 metre. Cf. a greatly altered version of stanzas I, III, in Bickersteth's *Christian Psalmody,* 1883.

(2) 8.7.8.7. metre. 10 centos. Cf. *Cong. H. Book,* 1836, 2 stanzas, and Pennsylvania *Lutheran Ch. Book,* 1868, in 3 stanzas of 8 lines.

Other centos are:

(1) **Holy Spirit, Source of gladness,** in the American Unitarian *Bk. of Hymns* 1848, and other collections.

(2) **Come, Thou Source of sweetest gladness,** in Stopford Brooke's *Christian Hymns,* 1881. Both these centos are altered forms of the Jacobi-Toplady text.

2. Sweetest joy the soul can know.

A good translation, omitting stanzas VIII and IX, by Miss Winkworth, in her *Lyra Ger.,* 2d Series, 1858, p. 55, and again, altered in metre, as "Sweetest Fount of holy gladness," in her *C. B. for England,* 1863, no. 73. In this, stanzas II and IV, as in *Lyra Ger.,* are omitted. From this text is derived no. 408 of the American *Hymns of the Spirit,* 1864. Cf. also no. 108 in Stryker's *Christian Chorals,* N. Y., 1885, which is taken from the *Chorale Book* text.

Selected Stanzas:

J. C. Jacobi, 1722, altered by A. M. Toplady, 1776, in the Schaff-Gilman *Library of Religious Poetry,* 1881.

1. Holy Ghost, dispel our sadness,
Pierce the clouds of sinful night;
Come, thou source of sweetest gladness,

Breathe thy life and spread thy light!
Loving Spirit, God of peace!
Great distributer of grace!
Rest upon this congregation,
Hear, oh, hear our supplication!

Miss Winkworth, in her *Chorale Book for England,* 1863.

1. Sweetest Fount of holy gladness,
    Fairest light was ever shed
    Who alike in joy and sadness
    Leavest none unvisited;
    Spirit of the Highest God,
    Lord, from whom is life bestow'd,
    Who upholdest ev'rything,
    Hear me, hear me, while I sing.

Nun danket all und bringet Ehr.—(*Goed.* 78.)
Appeared in *Ebeling,* 1648, no. 181.

It is based on the Apocryphal book *Sirach* L. 24, and inspired also of
course by the famous hymn of Martin Rinckart[10] "Nun danket alle Gott,"
which may be called the German Te Deum.   As a great part of Rinckart's
life, was, like Gerhardt's, spent amid the horrors of the Thirty Years' War
it is natural that Gerhardt should have been influenced by this voluminous
writer.   Rinckart's hymn was translated by Miss Winkworth in her *Chorale
Book,* but for some reason she has passed over Gerhardt's verses.   As
Rinckart was a good musician and his melody[11] was well calculated to please
the popular ear it is not strange that his hymn has maintained itself ahead
of Gerhardt's.

The only English version published is that of *J. Kelly,* 1867, p. 238.

Stanza 1.   In grateful songs your voices raise,
             All people here below,
             To Him whom angels ever praise
             In heav'n His glory show.

The translation has much more flowery language than the original and is
far less direct, cf. "In grateful songs" as compared with "Nun danket all,"
and in the second stanza a virtual repetition of this "with gladsome songs
now fill the air" for the very forceful reflexive construction "Ermuntert

---

[10] Cf. p. 11.
[11] The melody as it appeared in Crüger's *Praxis,* etc., is marked with Crüger's initials,
but it was quite likely adapted from a motet by Rinckart.

euch." Throughout the poem the English version brings out more emphatically than the German the idea of *life in eternity*. Cf. stanza 6:

> And may his blessing ever rest.

and the last two lines of stanza 8:

> Our portion when from earth we part,
> To all eternity.

In the closing stanza the translation by losing the fervor of Gerhardt's verses is almost anticlimactic. The German is a fervent prayer that *God* may close our eyes and appear to us in eternity, while the English, in too evident an effort to effect a rhyme with *rest*, would seem to assign to the Deity a place almost secondary in importance to "our eyes." Cf. stanza 9.[12]

> When sinks the heart, when strength decays,
> By Him our eyes be press'd
> Then may we see His open face,
> In everlasting rest.

Zweierlei bitt ich von dir.—(*Goed*. 80.)

Appeared in *Crü. Praxis*, 1648, no. 240. Based on *Proverbs*, XXX, 7-9.

English Version:

> 1. Twofold, Father, is my pray'r,
>   Twofold the desire I there
>   Lay before Thee, who dost give
>   What's good for us to receive;
>   Grant the pray'r that Thou dost know,
>   Ere my soul to Thee must go
>   From the body's bands below.
>   *J. Kelly*, 1867, p. 107.

The rhyme of the German has offered great difficulties in the last three lines of each stanza. The translator's success in meeting this obstacle has been indifferent. Cf.:

stanza 2	stanza 3	stanza 4	stanza 5	stanza 6
poverty	mood	swell	artifice	graciously
may	good	well	practices	me
lay	bestowed	extol	is	be

---

[12] Er drücke, wann das Herze bricht
Uns unsre Augen zu
Und zeig uns drauf sein Angesicht
Dort in der ewign Ruh.

O Gott, mein Schöpfer, edler Fürst.—(*Goed.* 81.)

Based on the Apocryphal book *Sirach,* XXIII 1-6. It appeared in *Crü. Praxis,* 1648, no. 248.

English Versions:

    1. Creator, Father, Prince of might!
        Who life to me art giving,
        Unless Thou guid'st my life aright
        In vain here am I living.
        For while I'm living I am dead,
        To sin devoted ever;
        Whose life in mire of sin is led,
        The true life he hath never
        Beheld one moment even.

                J. Kelly, 1867, p. 109.

    2. God, my Creator, and my Lord,
        Thou Father of my spirit,
        To me thy constant grace afford,
        Or life—I well may fear it:—
        Nay, e'en while living were I dead,
        And in my sins must perish;
        Whose with Christ, the living bread,
        Shall fail his soul to nourish,
        Must sink to death eternal.

        Dr. H. Mills in his *Horae Germanicae,* 1856.

Ich hab in Gottes Herz und Sinn.—(*Goed.* 83.)

[*Resignation.*]

It appeared in *Crü. Praxis,* 1648, no. 249, in 12 stanzas.

English Versions:

    1. **I into God's own heart and mind.**
        J. Kelly, 1867, p. 219.

    2. **To God's all-gracious heart and mind.**
        Miss Winkworth, 1869, p. 213.

Nicht so traurig, nicht so sehr.—(*Goed.* 89.)

[*Christian Contentment.*]

Founded on *Psalm* CXVI, 7; *Psalm* XLII, 6-12; *1 Tim.* VI, 6. Appeared in the 3d ed., 1648, of *Crü. Praxis,* no. 251, in 15 stanzas of 6 lines; thence in *Wackernagel:* no. 53; *Bachmann:* no. 16; Berlin *G. L. S.:* 1863, no. 851.

English Versions:

    1. **Ah! grieve not so, nor so lament.**

A free rendering by Mrs. Findlater and Miss Borthwick of stanzas I, II, VII-X, XIII, XV, in the first Series, 1854, of the *H. L. L.*, p. 48 (1884, p. 50).

2. **Why this sad and mournful guise.**
   Miss Dunn, 1857, p. 85.

3. **Not so darkly, not so deep.**
   Miss Warner, 1858 (1861, p. 58).

4. **O my soul, why dost thou grieve.**
   J. Kelly, 1867, p. 155.

Selected Stanza:

Mrs. Findlater (and Miss Borthwick) in their *Hymns from the Land of Luther,* 1884.

> 1. Ah! grieve not so, nor so lament,
>   My soul! nor troubled sigh,
>   Because some joys to others sent
>   Thy Father may deny;
>   Take all as love that seems severe—
>   There is no want if God is near.

Nach dir, O Herr, verlanget mich.—(*Goed.* 91.)

Based on *Psalm* XXV. Appeared in *Crü. Praxis,* 1648, no. 276.

English Version:

> 1. For thee, Lord, pants my longing heart,
>   My hope and confidence Thou art;
>   My hope can never shaken be,
>   Nor e'er be put to shame by Thee.

A full translation by *J. Kelly,* 1867, p. 88. This is one of the best pieces of interpretation as regards harmony and rhythm and the spirit of the original, that he has given us. Kelly is at his best in rendering the "long metre" hymns (cf. *Goed.* 260, 287, etc.). Stanza 9 is especially noteworthy:

Nun, Herr, ich bin dir wolbekannt,	Ah! Lord full well Thou knowest me,
Mein Geist, der schwebt in deiner Hand;	My spirit lives and moves in Thee;
Du siehst, wie meine Seele thränt	Thou seest how my bleeding heart
Und sich nach deiner Hülfe sehnt.	Longs for the help Thou canst impart.

Ich erhebe, Herr, zu dir.—(*Goed.* 93.)

Based on *Psalm* CXXI. It appeared in *Crü. Praxis,* 1648, no. 279.

English Version:

> 1. Lord! to Thee alone I raise
>   Evermore mine eager eyes,

Upturn'd is my constant gaze
To the hills that pierce the skies:
To the hills whence flow to me
Help and saving health from Thee!

Stanza 1 of the complete translation by *J. Kelly,* 1867, p. 135.

Gott Lob! nun ist erschollen.—(*Goed.* 95.)

[*Thanksgiving for the Proclamation of the Peace of Westphalia in 1648 after the Thirty Years' War.*]

It appeared in *Crü. Praxis,* 1653, no. 401, 1656, no. 409, in 6 stanzas of 12 lines; *Wackernagel:* no. 64; *Bachmann:* no. 84; *Unv. L. S.:* 1851, no. 589.

English Versions:

1.   Thank God it hath resounded,
The blessed voice of joy and Peace!
And murder's reign is bounded,
And spear and sword at last may cease.
Bright hope is breaking o'er us
Arise, my land once more,
And sing in full-toned chorus
Thy happy songs of yore; . . .

Miss Winkworth in her *Lyra Ger.,* 1858, p. 156, and her *Chorale Book,* 1863. Stanzas I, V, VI, form no. 49, in M. W. Stryker's *Christian Chorals,* 1885.

2. **Praise God! for forth hath sounded.**
J. Kelly, 1867, p. 251.

Du bist zwar mein und bleibest mein.—(*Goed.* 100.)

[*For the Bereaved.*]

This is a beautiful hymn for consolation of parents on the loss of a son. The occasion of the poem was the death of Constantin Andreas, younger son of Johannes Berkov, pastor of St. Mary's Church, Berlin. It was first printed as one of the *Dulcia amicorum solatia* at the end of the funeral sermon by Georg Lilius, Berlin, 1650. Included in *Ebeling,* 1667, 6, no. 72, in 12 stanzas.

English Versions:

1. **Thou'rt mine, yes, still thou art mine own.**
Miss Winkworth, in her *Lyra Ger.,* 1858, p. 123.

2. **Yes, thou art mine, still mine, my son.**
J. D. Burns, in the *Family Treasury,* p. 8, and his *Remains,* 1869, p. 249.

3. **Mine art thou still, and mine shalt be.**
J. Kelly, 1867, p. 333.

4. **Thou art mine own, art still mine own.**

Dr. J. Guthrie, 1869, p. 100.

Selected Stanza:

  1. Thou'rt mine, yes, still thou art mine own!
   Who tells me thou art lost?
   But yet thou art not mine alone,
   I own that He who cross'd
   My hopes, hath greatest right in thee;
   Yea, though He ask and take from me
   Thee, O my son, my heart's delight,
   My wish, my thought, by day and night.
         Miss Winkworth, 1858.

Lobet den Herren, alle die Ihn fürchten!—(*Goed.* 106.)
[*Morning.*]

Included in the *Crü.—Runge,* 1653, no. 7, in 10 stanzas of 5 lines; thence in *Wackernagel:* no. 100; *Bachmann:* no. 21; Berlin *G. L. S.:* 1863, no. 1063.

English Versions:

1. **Praise God! revere Him! all ye men that fear Him!**

This is from the version in Bunsen's *Allg. G. B.,* 1846, no. 167; stanza 1 being from Gerhardt and stanzas 2, 3, from "Lobet den Herren, denn er ist sehr freundlich" (which Wackernagel quotes from a Nürnberg broadsheet about 1560). It appeared in the *Dalston Hospital H. Bk.,* 1848, no. 55, signed "A. G."

2. **Our Lord be praising, All His glory raising.**

H. J. Buckoll, 1842, p. 27.

3. **Praise ye Jehovah, all ye men who fear Him.**

J. Kelly, 1867, p. 279.

Warum willst du drauszen stehen.—(*Goed.* 108.)
[*Advent.*]

Suggested by *Gen.* XXIV, 31. It appeared in *Crü.—Runge,* 1653, no. 78, in 9 stanzas of 8 lines; viz. stanzas I-VII, XI, XII, of the full form; stanzas VIII-X being added in *Ebeling,* 1667, 5, no. 50. The full text, in 12 stanzas, appeared also in *Wackernagel:* no. 2; *Bachmann:* no. 23; *Unv. L. S.:* 1851, no. 20.

English Versions:

1. **Wherefore dost Thou longer tarry.**

Miss Winkworth, omitting stanzas VIII-X, in her *Lyra Ger.,* 2d Series, 1858, p. 6. In her *C. B. for England,* 1863, no. 153, the translation of stanzas III, V, XI, are omitted.

2. **Wherefore dost Thou, blest of God.**

R. Massie, in *Lyra Domestica,* 1864, p. 90.

3. **Why, without, then, art Thou staying.**

   J. Kelly, 1867, p. 5.

Selected Stanza:

> 1. Wherefore dost Thou longer tarry
>   Blessed of the Lord afar?
>   Would it were Thy will to enter
>   To my heart, O Thou my Star,
>   Thou my Jesus, Fount of pow'r,
>   Helper in the needful hour!
>   Sharpest wounds my heart is feeling,
>   Touch them, Savior, with Thy healing!
>
>   *Miss Winkworth,* 1858.

Zeuch ein zu deinen Thoren.—(*Goed.* 111.)[13]

[*Whitsuntide.*]

Cf. *Koch* IV, 231. Appeared in *Crü.—Runge,* 1653, no. 157, in 12 stanzas, viz: stanzas I-VIII, XII, XIII, XIV, XVI, of the full poem. Stanza XV was added in *Ebeling,* 1666-67, no. LXXX, and stanzas IX-XI in *J. H. Feustking's* ed., 1707. The full form in 16 stanzas is in *Wackernagel:* no. 32; and *Bachmann:* no. 25; and the *Unv. L. S.:* 1851, no. 184. The hymn was undoubtedly written during the Thirty Years' War.

English Versions:

1. **Retake thy own Possession.**

This is a free translation omitting stanzas X-XII, in pt. II, 1725, of J. C. Jacobi's *Psalmodia Germanica,* p. 9. In his ed. of 1732, it is greatly altered, and begins "In me resume thy dwelling." From this form the translations of stanzas I, VI, XVI, were included unaltered in the Scottish *Evang. Union H. Bk.,* 1856.

2. **Come to Thy temple here on earth.**

A good translation omitting stanza IV, by Miss Winkworth in her *Lyra Ger.,* 1st Series, 1855, p. 113. From this the translations of stanzas I, II, VIII, XII, were repeated in the Pennsylvania *Luth. H. Bk.,* 1865.

3. **O enter, Lord, Thy temple.**

A good translation by Miss Winkworth in her *Chorale Book,* of stanza I, II, V-VIII, XIV, XVI, based on her *Lyra Ger.* version. Included in full and unaltered as no. 482, 483 in Dr. Thomas' *Augustine H. Bk.,* 1866. No. 483 begins "All love is thine, O Spirit" (stanza VII). In the Pennsylvania *Luth. Ch. Bk.,* 1868, no. 250, is stanzas I-III, VI, VIII, and in the *Ohio Luth. Hyl.,* 1880, no. 106, is stanzas I, II, V, XIV, XVI.

4. **Retake thy own possession, Thou glorious Guest of Hearts.**

In *Select H. from Ger. Psal.,* Tranquebar, 1754, p. 43, and the *Suppl. to Ger. Psalt.,* ed. 1765, p. 26.

---

[13] For adaptations of this hymn cf. p. 136.

5. **Come, O Thou Holy Dove.**
   Miss Dunn, 1857, p. 104.

6. **Come, enter Thine own portal.**
   Miss Cox, 1864, p. 117.

Stanzas 1 of Miss Winkworth's versions are given below:

Come to Thy temple here on earth,	O enter, Lord, Thy temple,
Be Thou my spirit's guest,	Be Thou my spirit's guest!
Who givest us of mortal birth	Who at my birth didst give me
A second birth more blest;	A second birth more blest.
Spirit beloved, Thou mighty Lord,	Thou in the Godhead, Lord,
Who with the Father and the Son	Though here to dwell Thou deignest,
Reignest upon an equal throne,	Forever equal reignest,
Art equally adored!	Art equally adored.
Lyra Ger., 1855.	*Chorale Book,* 1863.

Du Meine Seele, singe.—(*Gocd.* 115.)
[*Psalm* CXLVI.]

Appeared in *Crü.—Runge,* 1653, no. 183, in 10 stanzas.

English Version:

1. **O Come, my soul with singing.**

Miss Burlingham, in the *British Herald,* Jan., 1866, p. 207, and as no. 423 in Reid's *Praise Bk.,* 1872.

Ich singe dir mit Herz und Mund.—(*Gocd.* 118.)
[*Thanksgiving.*]

Cf. *Koch* IV, p. 95. First published in *Crü.—Runge,* 1653, no. 186, in 18 stanzas of 4 lines; thence in *Wackernagel:* no. 85; *Bachmann:* no. 27; *Crü. Praxis:* 1656; Berlin *G. L. S.:* 1863.

English Versions:

1. **O Lord! I sing with mouth and heart.**

Translated in full by *J. Kelly,* 1867, p. 225. A cento in 6 stanzas is found in the *Ohio Lutheran Hymnal,* 1880, no. 364.

2. **He never yet has made mistakes.**

Stanzas XVII, XVIII, as no. 475, in part I of the *Moravian H. Bk.,* 1754.

3. **I sing to Thee with Heart and Tongue.**

Appeared in the *Suppl. to Ger. Psalmody,* ed. 1765, p. 65. Included in the *Moravian H. Bk.,* 1789, no. 802 (1886, no. 647), altered, and beginning: "I'll praise Thee with my heart and tongue."

4. **I'll sing to Thee with mouth and heart.**

Miss Cox, 1864, p. 154.

5. **I'll sing to Thee with heart and mouth.**
   Miss Manington, 1863, p. 108.

6. **My heart's warm gush breaks forth in mirth.**
   E. Massie, 1867.

Der Herr, der aller Enden.—(*Goed.* 120.)

Founded on *Psalm* XXIII. Appeared in the *Crü.—Runge,* 1653, no. 224.

English Version:

> Stanza 1.   The Lord, the earth who ruleth,
> And with His hand controlleth,
> Whose goodness never endeth,
> He watcheth me and tendeth. . . .

A good and full translation by *J. Kelly,* 1867, p. 266, with a rather unusual combining of literality and metre, especially in stanza 9:

Du salbst mein Haupt mit Oele	My head with oil anointest
Und füllest meine Seele,	My empty soul appointest
Die leer und dürstig sasze,	Of every good and pleasure
Mit vollgeschenktem Masze.	A full o'erflowing measure.

Warum sollt ich mich denn grämen.—(*Goed.* 122.)

(Cf. p. 108 ff.)

Wol dem Menschen, der nicht wandelt.—(*Goed.* 124.)

Appeared in *Crü.—Runge,* 1653, no. 241.

It would be inconceivable that Gerhardt should omit the first Psalm from his themes, and his hymn adapts so well the biblical text that we should expect more than the one English version of *J. Kelly,* 1867, p. 130. In his rendering the translator has done well to infuse much of the poetic language of the English Bible.

> Stanza 1.   Bless'd is he who never taketh
> Counsel of ungodly men!
> Bless'd, the right who ne'er forsaketh,
> Nor in sinners' paths is seen,
> Who the scorners' friendship spurns,
> From their seats away who turns,
> Who delight in God's word taketh,
> This his meditation maketh.
>
> Stanza 2.   Bless'd is he who pleasure taketh
> (Lines 1 & 2.) In God's laws' most perfect way.

Stanza 3.   He will truly ever flourish
(Lines 1 & 2.) Who God's word delights to do.

Stanza 4.   But he who in sin's ways goeth
(Lines 1 & 2) Is like chaff the wind before.

Wol dem, der den Herren scheuet.—(*Goed.* 130.)

Appeared in *Crü.—Runge,* 1653, no. 243.

The CXIIth Psalm of David celebrating the prosperity of the godly is the basis for Gerhardt's beautiful hymn which has found great popularity in German hymn-books. The translation by *J. Kelly,* 1867, p. 132, is the only English version published. While Gerhardt follows quite closely the poetic language of the Bible, the translator departs often from what might be expected as the normal English equivalent of Gerhardt's diction. In the following stanzas the translation brings out excellently Gerhardt's simile and metaphor.

Stanza 1.   Bless'd is he the Lord who loveth,
                     At His word doth tremble aye!
                     Bless'd whose heart him freely moveth
                     God's commandments to obey.
                     Who the Highest loves and fears,
                     Findeth increase with the years.
                     Of all that to him is given
                     By the bounteous hand of Heaven.

Stanza 5.   When the black clouds o'er them lighten,
                     And the pealing thunders shock
                     They shall sit and nought shall frighten,
                     Like the dove hid in the rock;[14]
                     They'll remain eternally,
                     And their memory shall be
                     Upon every side extending,
                     As their branches trees are sending.[15]

Cf. also lines 1 and 2 of stanza 2:

His dear children shall stand ever[16]
Like to roses in their blow; . . .

Schwing dich auf zu deinem Gott.—(*Goed.* 135.)

Appeared in *Crü.—Runge,* 1653, no. 288, under the title "Trost in schwerer Anfechtung."

---

[14] Cf. line 36: "Wie ein Vöglein in der Kluft."
[15] Line 40: "Wie die edlen Zweig ausbreiten."
[16] Seine Kinder werden stehen
Wie die Rosen in der Blüt.

The only English version of this fervent hymn of consolation in despondency and temptation is that of *J. Kelly,* 1867, p. 195. Nearly every line has the force and directness of the original especially in the verses addressed to the Soul, charging it to defy the wiles of Satan and to seek strength and consolation in Nature's bounties. Gerhardt's poem is one of close introspection and self analysis, and the translator interprets with feeling its spirit of "Trost."

IN DESPONDENCY AND TEMPTATION.

Stanza 1.   Look up to thy God again,
Soul, sunk in affliction!
Shall He be reproach'd by men
Through thy sore dejection?
Satan's wiles dost thou not see?
By severe temptation,
Gladly would he keep from thee
Jesu's consolation.

Was Gott gefällt, mein frommes Kind.—(*Goed.* 139.)

[Resignation to "what pleases God."]

First appeared in *Crü.—Runge,* 1653, no. 290, in 20 stanzas of 5 lines; thence in *Wackernagel:* no. 60; *Bachmann:* no. 37; *Unv. L. S.:* 1851, no. 723.

English Versions:

1. **What God decrees, child of his love.**

A good rendering of stanzas I, II, V, VI, VIII, XII, XV, XVIII, XX, by Mrs. Findlater in the 3d Series, 1858, of the *H. L. L.,* p. 49 (1884, p. 170). Included in full in Bishop Ryle's *Collection,* 1860, no. 171, and abridged in *Christian Hymns,* Adelaide, 1872, and beginning "What God decrees, take patiently," in *Kennedy,* 1863, no. 1344.

2. **What pleaseth God with joy receive.**

    Miss Dunn, 1857, p. 94.

3. **What pleases God, O pious soul.**

    Miss Winkworth, 1858, p. 193.

4. **What pleaseth God, my faithful child.**

    J. Kelly, 1867, p. 189.

Selected Stanzas:

Miss Winkworth, in her *Lyra Germanica,* 1865.

1. What pleases God, O pious soul,
Accept with joy; though thunders roll
And tempests lower on every side,
Thou knowest nought can thee betide
    But pleases God.

Mrs. Findlater in her *Hymns from the Land of Luther,* 1884.

1. What God decrees, child of his love,
Take patiently, though it may prove
The storm that wrecks thy treasure here;—
Be comforted! thou needst not fear
    What pleases God.

2. The best will is our Father's will,
   And we may rest there calm and still,
   Oh make it hour by hour thine own,
   And wish for nought but that alone,
       Which pleases God.

3. His thought is aye the wisest thought;
   How oft man's wisdom comes to nought;
   Mistake or weakness in it lurks,
   It brings forth ill, and seldom works
       What pleases God.

2. The wisest will is God's own will:
   Rest on this anchor, and be still;
   For peace around thy path shall flow,
   When only wishing here below
       What pleases God.

Die Zeit ist nunmehr nah.—(*Goed.* 142.)
[*Day of Judgment—Second Advent.*]

Based on *Acts* III, 20. It first appeared in the *Crü.—Runge*, 1653, no. 367, in 18 stanzas of 6 lines; thence in *Wackernagel:* 1843, no. 119 (1874, no. 124); *Bachmann:* no. 40; Berlin *G. L. S.:* ed. 1863, no. 1517.

English Versions:

1. **O Christ! how good and fair.**
A translation of stanzas III, IV, VI, VII, X-XIII, XVII, by Mrs. Charles in her *Voice of Christian Life in Song*, 1858, p. 242.

2. **May I when time is o'er.**
A translation of stanzas VII, VIII, in the *Moravian H. Bk.*, 1789, (in later eds.) "I shall when time is o'er."

3. **The time is very near.**
       J. Kelly, 1867, p. 341.

Wir singen dir, Emanuel.—(*Goed.* 150.)
(Cf. p. 110 ff.)

O Jesu Christ! dein Kripplein ist.—(*Goed.* 153.)
[*Christmas.*]

At the Manger in Bethlehem. It appeared in *Crü. Praxis*, 1653, 1656, no. 101, in 15 stanzas.

English Versions:

1. **Be not dismay'd—in time of need.**
       (Stanza XI) in the *Moravian H. Bk.*, 1789, no. 236.

2. **O blessed Jesus! This.**
       Miss Winkworth, in her *Lyra Ger.*, 1858, p. 18.

3. **O Jesus Christ! Thy cradle is.**
       Miss Manington, 1864, p. 41.

4. **Thy manger is my paradise.**
    J. *Kelly,* 1867, p. 26.

Selected Stanza:

Miss Winkworth in her *Lyra Germanica,* 1858, p. 18.

GOD WITH US.

Stanza 1.   O Blessed Jesus! This
Thy lowly manger is
The Paradise where oft my soul would feed:
Here is the place, my Lord,
Where lies the Eternal Word
Clothed with our flesh, made like to us indeed.

Frölich soll mein Herze springen.—(*Goed.* 155.)
[*Christmas.*]
(Cf. *Koch* IV, p. 130.)

Appeared in *Crü. Praxis,* 1653 and 1656, no. 104, in 15 stanzas of 8 lines; reprinted in *Wackernagel:* no. 5; and *Bachmann:* no. 44; *Unv. L. S.:* 1851, no. 35.

Lauxmann, in *Koch,* VIII, 26, thus analyses it:

"First a trumpet blast: Christ is born, God's Champion has appeared as a Bridegroom from his chamber (I, II). In the following 4 stanzas the poet seeks to set forth the mighty value of the Incarnation: is it not love when God gives us the Son of His Love (III), the Kingdom of Joy (IV) and His Fellowship (V)? Yes, it is indeed the Lamb of God who bears the sin of the world (VI). Now he places himself as herald by the cradle of the Divine Child (VII). He bids, as in *Matt.* XI, 28, all men (VIII), all they that labor (IX), all the heavy laden (X), and all the poor (XI), to draw near. Then in conclusion he approaches in supplication like the shepherds and the Wise Men (XII-XV). He adores the child as the source of life (XII), his Lamb of God (XIII), his Glory (XIV), and promises to be ever true to Him (XV). It is a glorious series of Christmas thoughts, laid as a garland on the manger at Bethlehem."

Crüger gave the hymn an original melody in 1656 (as in L. Erk's *Choralbuch,* 1863, no. 86), but the melody generally used (in *Church Hymns* called "Bonn") is that by J. G. Ebeling in the *Geistliche Andachten,* 1666, to "Warum sollt ich mich denn grämen."[17] The hymn is very beautiful, but somewhat long, hence generally abridged.

English Versions:

1. **Let the voice of glad thanksgiving.**
    A good translation of stanzas I-III, VI-IX, by A. T. Russell, as no. 15, in the *Dalston Hospital Hymn Bk.,* 1848, and repeated, in part, as no. 56, in his own *Psalms and Hymns,* 1851.

---

[17] Cf. p. 108.

2. **All my heart this night rejoices.**

A beautiful, but rather free translation omitting stanzas III-V, XIII, XIV, by Miss Winkworth in the 2d series of her *Lyra Ger.*, 1858, p. 13. In America it appeared in the Dutch Reformed *Hymns of the Church*, 1869, the *Hymns and Songs of Praise*, N. Y., 1874, etc. Parts have appeared also in the *New Zealand Hymnal*, 1872, the *Evangelistic Hymnal*, N. Y., 1880, and *Laudes Domini*, N. Y., 1884, etc. It is very generally included in cento form in nearly all current American hymnals.

3. **All my heart with joy is springing.**

A free translation by Dr. Kennedy in his *Hymnologia Christiana*, 1863, no. 100, omitting stanzas III-V, IX, XIII, XIV.

4. **Lightly bound my bosom, ringing.**

A translation in full, by Dr. M. Loy, in the *Ohio Luth. Hymnal*, 1880.

5. **Now in His manger He so humbly lies.**

A translation of stanza V in the *Moravian H. Bk.*, 1754, no. 435.

6. **Up, my heart! rejoice with singing.**

As a broadsheet for Christmas, 1770.

7. **Rise, my soul, shake off all sadness.**

P. H. Molther, in the *Moravian H. Bk.*, 1789 and 1886.

8. **Now with joy my heart is bounding.**

J. Kelly, 1867, p. 18.

9. **Up, with gladness heavenward springing.**

E. Massie, 1867, p. 24.

10. **Joyful be my spirit singing.**

M. L. Frothingham, 1870, p. 260.

11. **Joyful shall my heart, upspringing.**

M. W. Stryker, 1883, p. 30.

Selected Stanzas:

A. T. Russell, in his *Psalms and Hymns*, 1851.

> 1. Let the voice of glad thanksgiving
> Upward rise, to the skies—
> Praises from all living.
> Hark! the angel-choirs from heaven
> Hither fly! hark! they cry,
> Christ to earth is given!

Miss Winkworth, 1858, in her *Lyra Germanica*.

> 1. All my heart this night rejoices,
> As I hear, far and near,
> Sweetest angel voices:
> "Christ is born," their choirs are singing,
> Till the air everywhere
> Now with joy is ringing.

Ich steh an deiner Krippen hier.—(*Goed.* 158.)
[*Christmas.*][18]

Included in *Crü. Praxis:* 1653, no. 105, 1656, no. 105, in 15 stanzas of 7 lines; *Wackernagel:* no. 9; *Bachmann:* no. 45; Berlin *G. L. S.:* 1863, no. 167.

This is a beautiful hymn in which the poet puts himself in the place of the shepherds and the wise men visiting Bethlehem; and in praise and adoration tenders his devotion, his love and his all to the Infant Savior in the manger.

English Versions:

1. Stanzas I, IV, VII, XV, have been translated by Rev. A. T. Russell in his *Ps. and Hys.*, 1851, no. 57. His translation of stanza I is as follows:

My faith Thy lowly bed beholds,
My Life and my Salvation;
Thee in my heart my faith enfolds,
And brings Thee her oblation.
My heart and soul, will, spirit, mind,
Oh, take them all, to Thee resign'd:
Make all to Thee well-pleasing.

2. **I stand beside Thy manger-bed.**
Miss Manington, 1864, p. 38.

3. **Now at the manger here I stand.**
J. Kelly, 1867, p. 32.

Hör an! mein Herz, die sieben Wort.—(*Goed.* 161.)
[*Passiontide.* (The seven words from the Cross.)]

Founded on the hymn of J. Böschenstein: "Da Jesus an dem Kreuze stund" (which was called a translation from the Latin of Peter Bolandus, "Stabat ad lignum crucis"). It appeared in *Crü. Praxis,* 1653, no. 137, 1656, no. 137, in 15 stanzas.

English Versions:

1. **Come now, my soul, thy thoughts engage.**
Dr. H. Mills, 1845, 1856, p. 309.

---

[18] This is Gerhardt's third Christmas hymn (cf. also *Goed.* 150, 153, 155, 310, 312). It is very probable that in composing it the poet had in mind the words of St. Jerome of Strido, abbot of a monastic brotherhood in Bethlehem 386-420: "As often as I gaze on this place (the manger at Bethlehem), so often does my heart converse with the Infant Jesus which lay there in the manger . . . I say . . . "I must give Thee something, Dear Child! I will give Thee all my wealth," and the child answered—"Give it to the poor, I will accept it as if it were given me."—cf. *Koch* IV, p. 137.

2. **Seven times the Savior spake—my heart.**
    R. Massie, in the *British Herald,* Sept., 1865, p. 133.

3. **My heart! the seven words hear now.**
    J. *Kelly,* 1867, p. 63.

Selected Stanza:

    Dr. H. Mills in his *Horae Germanicae,* 1856.

      1. Come now, my soul, thy thoughts engage
        On what by Christ was spoken,
        When on the cross man's deadly rage
        With griefs his heart had broken.
        His words may prove A gift of love,
        The best his love could offer;
        Keep them in store, And learn their pow'r,
        When call'd thyself to suffer.

Sei frölich alles weit und breit.—(*Goed.* 171.)

Appeared in *Crü. Praxis,* 1656, no. 171.[19]

English Version:

      1. Be joyful all, both far and near,
        Who lost were and dejected:
        To-day the Lord of glory here,
        Whom God Himself elected
        As our Redeemer, who His blood
        Upon the cross shed for our good,
        Hath from the grave arisen.
                J. *Kelly,* 1867, p. 75.

    This is stanza 1 of a complete translation of the seven stanzas of Gerhardt's Easter hymn, keeping well the spirit and fervor of the original, at the same time observing the literality in an unusually difficult metre.   Cf. stanza 7:

Nu Gott sei Dank, der uns den Sieg	Now praised be God, who vict'ry hath
Durch Jesum hat gegeben	To us through Jesus given,
Und uns den Frieden für den Krieg	Who peace for war, and life for death,
Und für den Tod das Leben	With entrance into Heaven,
Erworben, der die Sünd und Tod,	Hath purchas'd, who death, sin, and woe,
Welt, Teufel, Höll und was in Not	World, devil, what our overthrow
Uns stürzet, überwunden.	Would seek, for aye hath vanquish'd.

---

[19] Goedeke states in his note to this hymn (p. 171): "In Crüger's Praxis ist Christ(ian) Bartholdi unterzeichnet, aber von Ebeling als Gerhardt's aufgenommen, und auch wol von ihm selbst mitgetheilt. . . ."

Gott Vater, sende deinen Geist.—(*Goed.* 173.)

Appeared in *Crü. Praxis,* 1656, no. 198.

English Version:

Stanza 1.   O Father! send Thy spirit down,
Whom we are bidden by Thy Son
To seek, from Thy high heaven; . . .

A complete translation by *J. Kelly,* 1867, p. 78, a version of very varying excellence. For example, stanza 15 seems hopelessly weak when compared with the vigorous and simple German:

O selig, wer in dieser Welt	Oh! happy are the souls and bless'd
Läszt diesem Gaste Haus und Zelt	Who while on earth permit this Guest
In seiner Seel aufschlagen!	To make in them His dwelling;
Wer Ihn aufnimmt in dieser Zeit	Who now receive him joyfully,
Den wird er dort zur ewgen Freud	He'll take up to God's house on high,
In Gottes Hütte tragen.	Their souls with rapture filling.

On the other hand in stanza 5 the translator has coped very successfully with the many difficulties of rhyme and metre:

Und das ist auch ein Gnadenwerk	This is a work of grace indeed,
Und deines heilgen Geistes Stärk;	The Holy Spirit's strength we need,
In uns ist kein Vermögen.	Our pow'r is unavailing;
Wie bald würd unser Glaub und Treu,	Our faith and our sincerity
Herr, wo du uns nicht stündest bei	Would soon, O Lord! in ashes lie
Sich in die Aschen legen!	Were not Thy help unfailing.

Was alle Weisheit in der Welt.—(*Goed.* 176.)

[*Trinity Sunday.*]

Appeared in *Crü. Praxis:* 1653, no. 206, 1656, no. 212, in 8 stanzas of 9 lines; thence in *Wackernagel:* no. 1; *Bachmann:* no. 59; Berlin *G. L. S.:* 1863, no. 50.

English Versions:

1. **Scarce Tongue can speak, ne'er human ken.**
   A translation in full, by *J. Kelly,* 1867, p. 1.

2. **The mystery hidden from the eyes.**
   R. Massie, in his *Lyra Domestica,* 1864, p. 87.

Wie lang, O Herr, wie lange soll.—(*Goed.* 178.)

Appeared in *Crü. Praxis,* 1656, no. 365.

Translated by *J. Kelly,* 1867, p. 235, in seven stanzas of seven lines each. The rhyme and metre have been altered after the first four lines in each stanza, with the result that the version is one of this translator's least successful contributions.

> Stanza 1. How long, Lord, in forgetfullness
> And darkness wilt Thou leave me?
> How long will sorrow on me press
> And deep heart-anguish grieve me?
> Wilt Thou Thy face, Lord, utterly
> Turn from me? wilt ne'er look on me
> In grace and in compassion?

Befiehl du deine Wege.—(*Goed.* 185.)

(Cf. p. 114 ff.)

O Jesu Christ, mein schönstes Licht.—(*Goed.* 200.)

[*Love of Christ.*]

Cf. *Koch* IV, 402, VIII, 294. Included in the 5th ed., Berlin, 1653, and the Frankfurt ed., 1656, of *Crü. Praxis*, in 16 stanzas of 9 lines; thence in *Wackernagel:* no. 45; *Bachmann:* no. 73; *Unv. L. S.:* 1851, no. 771. This is one of the finest hymns on the Love of Christ. It is founded on Prayer V of Class II in Johann Arndt's *Paradiszgärtlein*, 1612.[20]

English Versions:

(A.)   Wesley.

1. **Jesus, Thy boundless love to me.**

A full and very fine translation by J. Wesley in *Hymns and Sacred Poems*, 1739 (P. Works, 1868-72, vol. I, p. 138). In the *Wesleyan Hymn Book*, 1780, it was reduced to 9 stanzas.

Centos of the Wesley version are:

(1.)   **O Love, how cheering is Thy ray.**   (Stanza III.)
    Bk. of Hymns, Boston, U. S. A., 1848.

(2.)   **My Savior, Thou Thy love to me.**   (Stanza V.)
    Moravian H. Bk., 1789.

(3.)   **More hard than marble is my heart.**   (Stanza VI.)
    American *Sabbath H. Bk.*, 1858.

(4.)   **O draw me, Savior, after Thee.**   (Stanza IX.)
    Snepp's *Songs of G. and G.*   Pennsylvania *Luth. Ch. Bk.*, 1868.

---

[20] This hymn led Philipp Friedrich Hiller to think of turning all of these prayers in the *Paradiszgärtlein* into hymns. The result was his work entitled "Arndt's Paradiszgärtlein . . . in teutsche Lieder," Nürnberg (no date given). The book is in four parts and contains 301 hymns, 297 being founded on Arndt and 4 original.

(5.) O draw me, Father, after Thee. (Stanza IX altered.)

> *Bk. of Hymns,* Boston, U. S. A., 1848. Amer. *Unitarian H. Bk.,* 1869.

(6.) Still nigh me, O my Savior stand.

This stanza is taken from a hymn "Peace, doubting heart, my God's I am," by C. Wesley. To this is added in Snepp's *Songs of G. and G.,* stanzas XII, XIV, XVI, and in J. L. Porter's *Collection,* 1876, stanzas XII, XV, XVI, of this translation of J. Wesley.

(7.) Thou Friend of Sinners! Who hast bought.

This is stanzas V, IV, XVI, rewritten by E. Osler and published in the *Mitre H. Bk.,* 1836.

(B.) Other English versions:

1. O Christ, my sweetest Life and Light.

In the *Suppl. to German Psal.,* ed. 1765, p. 29, and the *Moravian H. Bk.,* 1754 (and with slight change in the ed. of 1789, and 1849), viz: In the 1746 ed. in part II there appear as a separate hymn stanzas V-VII, beginning "Thou cam'st in love to my relief." In the 1789, and 1849 ed., it begins "O Christ, my only Life and Light."

2. O Jesus Christ! my fairest Light.

> *J. Kelly,* 1867, p. 122.

3. O Christ, my Light, my gracious Savior.

> In the *Moravian H. Bk.,* 1886.

Selected Stanzas:

In the *Moravian Hymn Book,* 1754 (author's name not given).

> 1. O Christ my sweetest Life and Light!
> Whose loving Condescension
> Embraces me by day and night
> Beyond my comprehension:
> Lord! grant me to return thy Love
> With due and true devotion,
>   That my notion
> Of Mercy may improve
> With ev'ry thought and motion.

J. Wesley, 1739, in the 1754 ed., Part I, of the *Moravian Hymn Book.*

> 1. Jesu, thy boundless Love to me
> No thought can reach, no tongue declare:
> O knit my thankful heart to Thee
> And reign without a rival there.
> Thine wholly, thine alone I am:
> Be thou alone my constant Flame.

J. Wesley, 1739, in *Snepp's Songs of Grace and Glory,* 1872. It is stanza 2 of a hymn beginning "Still nigh me, O my Savior stand" in *Snepp,* and Gerhardt's stanza XII: "Was ists, o Schönster, dasz ich nicht / In deiner Liebe habe?" etc.

Stanza 1.   What in Thy love possess I not?
My star by night, my sun by day;
My spring of life, when parched with drought,
My wine to cheer, my bread to stay,
My strength, my shield, my safe abode,
My robe before the throne of God!

Ich danke dir demütiglich.—(*Goed.* 205.)

Appeared in the *Crü. Praxis,* 1656, no. 318.   From Johann Arndt's *Paradiszgärtlein*
(Goslar, 1621, 4), 3, 17, p. 294, "Gebet um zeitliche und ewige Wolfahrt."

English Version:

Stanza 1.   O God, my Father! thanks to Thee
I bring with deep humility,
That Thou Thine anger endest,
And that Thy Son
Our Joy and Crown
Into the world Thou sendest. . . .

A complete translation by *J. Kelly,* 1867, p. 117.   In stanza 14 the translator has, in honor to Queen Victoria, altered the original which reads:

Insonderheit nimm wol in Acht
Den Fürsten . . . etc.

to

Make Her Thy care especially,
Whom Thou as monarch hast raised high
This land and nation over; . . . etc.

Ach! treuer Gott, barmherzigs Herz.—(*Goed.* 209.)
[*Cross and Consolation.*]

Founded on a prayer "for patience under great trial," no. XXV in Class III of
J. Arndt's[21] *Paradiszgärtlein,* 1612.   It appeared in *Crü. Praxis,* Frankfurt, 1656, no.
391, in 16 stanzas of 7 lines, and was included in many subsequent hymn books, as
recently as the *Unv. L. S.:* 1851, no. 693; also in *Wackernagel:* no. 57; and in *Bachmann:* no. 80.

English Versions:

1.   **O God most true, most merciful!**

A good adaptation in 4 stanzas by Rev. A. T. Russell in his *Psalms and Hymns,* as
follows:

Gerhardt stanza	I	(II III)	IV	V	(VI VII VIII IX)	X	XI
Russell stanza	1		2	3		4	

This version appears in an altered form in *Kennedy,* 1863, no. 665.   "O God of mercy
full and free."

---

[21] Cf. pp. 24 and 63.

2. **O faithful God! O pitying heart.**

A good translation in 11 stanzas by Miss Winkworth in the 2d Series, 1858, of her *Lyra Ger.,* and thence in the Gilman-Schaff *Lib. of R. P.,* 1883, p. 837.   The correspondence of stanzas is as follows:

Gerhardt stanzas   I II (III) IV V VI VII VIII (IX) X (XI) XII (XIII) XIV XV XVI
Winkworth stanzas   1 2   3 4 5 6 7   8   9   10   11

The translation of stanzas X, XII, XIV, XVI, beginning "O Thou, who diedst to give us life," appear as no. 327, in *Church Praise,* 1883.

3. **Ah! faithful God, compassionate heart.**
    J. Kelly, 1867, p. 169.

Barmherziger Vater, höchster Gott.—(*Goed.* 212.)

Based on Joh. Arndt's *Creutzgebet.* It appeared in *Crü. Praxis,* 1656, no. 382.

English Version:

> Stanza 1.   Father of mercies! God most high,
> Deign graciously to hear me,
> Thou say'st, "Knock at my door and cry,
> In time of need draw near to me.
> As urgently
> Thou long'st, to thee,
> That with thy mouth,
> In very truth,
> Thou joyfully may'st praise me." etc.
> *J. Kelly,* 1867, p. 175.

Ich weisz, mein Gott, dasz all mein Thun.—(*Goed.* 217.)
[*Supplication.*]

A prayer for success in all Christian works and purpose; founded on *Jeremiah* X, 23, and *Acts* V, 38, 39.   Cf. *Koch* IV, 98.   Included in *Crü. Praxis,* 1653, no. 321, 1656, no. 332, in 18 stanzas of 5 lines; thence in *Wackernagel:* no. 40; *Bachmann:* no. 71; Berlin, *G. L. S.:* 1863.

In the *Ebeling* edition the hymn has the title: "Um Glück und Segen zu allem christlichen Thun und Vorhaben."   It has on many occasions been given as a farewell injunction by parents to their children on leaving home.

English Versions:

1. **I know, my God, and I rejoice.**
    (Stanzas I-III, VIII, XI, IX) by Miss Winkworth in her *Chorale Book,* 1863, no. 121.

2. **My God! my works and all I do.**
    J. Kelly, 1867, p. 102.

Selected Stanzas:

Miss Winkworth in her *Chorale Book,* 1863.

> 1. I know, my God, and I rejoice
>   That on Thy righteous will and choice
>   All human works and schemes must rest:
>   Success and blessing are of Thee,
>   What Thou shalt send is surely best.

> 2. It stands not in the power of man
>   To bring to pass the wisest plan
>   So surely that it cannot fail;
>   Thy counsel, Highest, must ensure
>   That our poor wisdom shall avail.

Du bist ein Mensch, das weiszt du wol.—(*Goed.* 220.)

Appeared in *Crü. Praxis,* 1656, no. 330.

A hymn of self-abnegation, even self-denunciation, emphasizing the frailty and insignificance of mortals, and closing with an admonition of resignation to God's wise dispensations. Though Gerhardt frequently employs this form of rhyme[22] only rarely does he combine it with this metre. Both have been strictly observed by *J. Kelly,* 1867, p. 148:

> Stanza 1.   Thou art but man, to thee 'tis known,
>   Why dost thou then endeavor
>   To do what God should do alone,
>   Or can accomplish ever?
>   A thousand griefs thou goest through,
>   In spite of all thy wit can do;
>   Upon thine end thou pond'rest
>   What it will be thou wond'rest.

Ich habs verdient.   Was will ich doch.—(*Goed.* 224.)

Appeared in the *Crü. Praxis,* 1656, 817, no. 374.

English Version:

> Stanza 1.   I have deserv'd it, cease t'oppose
>   The Lord's will, shall I never?
>   Thou bitter cup, thou heavy cross,
>   Come hither to me ever!
>   From pain all free
>   May never be
>   He 'gainst the Lord who fighteth,

---

[22] I.e. ab ab cc dd.   Cf. nos. 62, 76, 100, 108, 124, 127, 130, 145, 149, 256, 263, 307, 321.

As I each day,
Who trod the way
Wherein the world delighteth. . . .
J. Kelly, 1867, p. 165.

This is one of the least adaptable poems of Gerhardt and it is evident that the translator has struggled with the many difficulties of metre and frequent rhyme.

Ich hab oft bei mir selbst gedacht.—(*Goed.* 226.)

Appeared in *Crü. Praxis,* 1656, no. 331.

English Version:

Stanza 1.   Full often as I meditate
Upon the world's disordered state,
I ask myself if earthly life
Be good, and worthy of the strife,
Has he not acted for the best
Who laid himself betimes to rest?
J. Kelly, 1867, p. 143.

A free, but very acceptable rendering in which the easy colloquial style of the original has been well retained.   Cf. lines 7 and 8:

"Denn, Lieber, denk und sage mir: "Reflect, my friend, say, if you know
Was für ein Stand ist wol allhier."   What station is there here below . . ."

Ist Gott für mich, so trete.—(*Goed.* 229.)

(Cf. p. 126 ff.)

Auf den Nebel folgt die Sonne.—(*Goed.* 232.)

[*Thanksgiving after great sorrow and affliction.*]

It appeared in *Crü. Praxis,* 1653, no. 236, and 1656, no. 249, in 15 stanzas of 7 lines; thence in *Wackernagel:* no. 87; *Bachmann:* no. 64; *Unv. L. S.:* no. 402. Cf. *Koch* IV, 545.

English Versions:

1.   **Cometh sunshine after rain.**

Miss Winkworth in her *Lyra Ger.,* 1st Series, 1855, p. 100 (omitting stanzas IV-VII, X, XI).   In her 1856 ed. the translation of stanzas X and XI is added.   In the *Christian H. Bk.,* Cincinnati, 1865, no. 799 begins with her stanza no. XIII "Now as long as here I roam."

2.   **After clouds we see the sun.**

J. Kelly, 1867, p. 261.

Selected Stanzas:

Miss Winkworth in her *Lyra Ger.,* 1855.

1. Cometh sunshine after rain,
   After mourning joy again,
   After heavy bitter grief
   Dawneth surely sweet relief;
   And my soul, who from her height
   Sank to realms of woe and night,
   Wingeth now to heav'n her flight.

2. He, whom this world dares not face,
   Hath refreshed me with his grace,
   And his mighty hand unbound
   Chains of hell, about me wound;
   Quicker, stronger, leaps my blood,
   Since his mercy, like a flood,
   Poured o'er all my heart for good.

Soll ich meinem Gott nicht singen.—(*Goed.* 235.)

[*Thanksgiving.*]   Cf. *Koch,* IV, 91 ff.

One of Gerhardt's finest hymns, setting forth God's love in His creation, redemption and sanctification of the world, His care in trouble. It closes with a prayer which R. Massie renders:

Grant me grace, O God, I pray Thee,
That I may with all my might
Love and trust Thee and obey Thee,
All the day and all the night;
And when this brief life is o'er
Love and praise Thee evermore.

The hymn was included in the 5th ed., Berlin, 1653, and in the Frankfurt ed., 1656, of *Crü. Praxis,* no. 230; thence in *Wackernagel:* no. 81; *Bachmann:* no. 60; *Unv. L. S.:* 1851, no. 722.

English Versions:

1. **Shall I not his praise be singing.**
Dr. Mills in his *Horae Germanicae,* 1845, p. 141, and 1856, p. 195.
This is a mediocre version, as it misses the characteristic points of the German. His stanzas II, IV-VII beginning "As the eagle fondly hovers," were included in the Amer. Luth. Gen. Synod's *Collection,* 1850-52, no. 35.

2. **Shall I not sing praise to Thee.**
A full and good translation by Miss Winkworth in her *Lyra Ger.,* 1st Series, 1855; p. 200; also, omitting stanzas III-VI, VIII in her *C. B. for England,* 1863, no. 10. Included in full in *Cantate Domino,* Boston, U. S. A., 1859.

3.   I will sing my Maker's praises.

A good translation omitting stanzas VI, VIII, contributed by R. Massie to the 1857 ed. of Mercer's *C. P. & H. Bk.*, no. 185, reprinted in his own *Lyra Domestica*, 1864.

4.   Can I fail my God to praise.

A translation of stanzas I, III, IV, by F. C. C., as no. 218, in Dr. Pagenstecher's *Collection*, 1864.

5.   Should I not, in meek adoring.

A translation of stanzas I-III by M. W. Stryker in his *Hymns & Verses*, 1883, p. 38, and *Christian Chorals*, 1885, no. 36.

6.   Can I cease, my God, from singing.

In *Lyra Davidica*, 1708, p. 22.

7.   Shan't I sing to my Creator.

J. C. Jacobi, 1732, p. 153.   Repeated in the *Moravian Hymn Books*, 1754-1886, in some editions beginning, "I will sing to my Creator."

8.   Shall I not my God be praising.

J. Kelly, 1867, p. 240.

Selected Stanzas:

Dr. Mills in his *Horae Germanicae*, 1856.

> 1.   Shall I not His praise be singing
> Who in glory reigns above:—
> Him my thanks and honors bringing,
> For the blessings of his love?
> Those, who with sincere endeavor
> Keep the way that He has shown,
> He will as his children own,
> Yielding them a father's favor.
> All things else their time will last
> But His love, when Time is past.

Miss Winkworth, in her *Chorale Book for England*, 1863.

> 1.   Shall I not sing praise to Thee,
> Shall I not give thanks, O Lord?
> Since for us in all I see
> How thou keepest watch and ward;
> How the truest tend'rest love
> Ever fills Thy heart, my God,
> Helping, cheering, on their road
> All who in Thy service move.

M. W. Stryker, 1882, in his *Christian Chorals*, 1885.

> 1.   Should I not, in meek adoring,
> Thank my gracious God above
> Whom I see on all things pouring
> Forth the sunshine of His love?

For 'tis naught but Love's own loving
In his constant heart, doth care
Endlessly to love and bear
Those their love, in service proving.
All things last their portioned day—
God's love to eternity.

Geh aus, mein Herz, und suche Freud.—(*Goed.* 239.)
(Cf. p. 131 ff.)

Also hat Gott die Welt geliebt.—(*Goed.* 256.)
[*Good Friday.*]

Founded on *John* III, 16. It appeared in *Crü. Praxis,* 1661, no. 372, in 17 stanzas.

English Version:

1. **Be of good cheer in all your wants.**

P. H. Molther, of stanza 16, as no. 181 in the *Moravian H. Bk.,* 1789 (1886, no. 217).

Herr, aller Weisheit Quell und Grund.—(*Goed.* 260.)
Appeared in *Crü. Praxis,* 1661, 576, no. 373.

English Version:

O God! from Thee doth wisdom flow,
All I can do Thou well dost know;
If Thine own grace doth not sustain,
Then all my labor is in vain. . . .

A complete and very good translation by *J. Kelly.* The long metre of 8 syllables seems to lend itself more readily to adaptation into English. In the fourth stanza, first line, Kelly has resorted to a device common to translators, that of making up the extra accent where the corresponding English cognate has lost the ending, by selecting instead of a monosyllabic adverb an adverb of two syllables. Here, of course, "very" for "sehr" makes literality and meter perfect.

Mein Leben ist sehr kurz und schwach
My life is very short and weak.

As exact and appropriate a translation as is possible word for word is found in stanza 11:

Ich lieb ihr[23] liebes Angesicht,	I love her lovely face so bright.
Sie ist meins Herzens Freud und Licht;	She is my joy and heart's delight
Sie ist die schönste, die mich hält	The fairest is that holdeth me
Und meinen Augen wolgefällt.	Mine eyes she pleaseth wondrously.

---

[23] i.e. Weisheit.

Jesu, allerliebster Bruder.—(*Goed.* 263.)

Based on Johann Arndt's *Paradiszgärtlein,* I, 33, 92. It appeared in *Crü. Praxis,* 1661, no. 374.

English Version:

> 1. Jesus! Thou, my dearest Brother,
> Who dost well to me intend,
> Thou mine Anchor, Mast, and Rudder
> And my truest Bosom-Friend.
> To Thee, ere was earth or heaven,
> Had the race of man been given;
> Thou, e'en me, poor guest of earth,
> Chosen hadst before my birth. . . .

A complete translation by *J. Kelly,* 1867, p. 112. The translator has well rendered a hymn of rather unusual difficulty of interpretation in a foreign tongue.

An unavoidable weakening by translation appears in the last stanza:

Nun, Herr lasz dirs wolgefallen,
Bleib mein Freund bis in mein Grab!
Bleib mein Freund und unter allen
Mein getreuster stärkster Stab!

Gracious Savior! let it please Thee,
Be my Friend in every hour
Be my Friend, till death release me
Be my faithful Staff of pow'r!

Geduld ist euch vonnöten.—(*Goed.* 267.)

Based on *Hebrews* X, 35-37. It appeared in *Crü. Praxis,* 1661, no. 375.

English Version:

> 1. 'Tis patience must support you
> When sorrow, grief, or smart,
> Or whate'er else may hurt you
> Doth rend your aching heart.
> Belov'd and chosen seed!
> If not a death will kill you,
> Yet once again I tell you
> 'Tis patience that you need. . . .

By *J. Kelly,* 1867, p. 184. A complete translation of the 14 stanzas, and in general very true to the original. It is noteworthy that the first line of each stanza contains the word "patience" as does the poem of Gerhardt the word "Geduld." Kelly's rendering of the last four lines illustrates as well as any the faithfulness of his version.

Kommt dann der letzte Zug,
So gib durch deine Hände
Auch ein geduldigs Ende!
So hab ich alles gnug.

And in my dying hour,
Thy mercy still extending,
Oh! grant a patient ending
Then need I nothing more.

Nun sei getrost und unbetrübt.—(*Goed.* 271.)

Subjoined to a funeral address by Johann Meiszner.

This is one of Gerhardt's many "Trostgesänge," and though less well known than most of his hymns is deserving of wider recognition than it has hitherto received. As far as is at present known there has been published but one English version, that of *J. Kelly*, 1867, p. 329, the first stanza of which is as follows:

"JOYFUL RESIGNATION TO A HAPPY DEPARTURE FROM
THIS WEARY WORLD."

Stanza 1.   Be glad, my heart! now fear no more,
Let nothing ever grieve thee;
Christ lives, who lov'd thee long before
Thy being He did give thee,
And ere He made thy wondrous frame;
His love remaineth still the same,
It ne'er can change to hatred.

It is unfortunate that the translator has been satisfied with "glad" for the forceful "getrost" which connotes "confidence" and "trust" (to which it is indeed cognate)[24] and even "comfort in that confidence" to the point of being "courageous." More pardonable is his balking at the characteristic alliterative "Geist und Gemüte" which must mean not only the "feelings," but also "soul" and "intellect" as well. If "heart" be accepted in this broadest sense it is undoubtedly the best English equivalent. The psychology of language would presumably never allow in poetry a literal word-for-word rendering of "Geblüte, Fleisch, Haut," and the English reader is denied the poetic force of "ward"[25] also beautifully illustrated so frequently in the German Bible. Again it must be accounted a defect that the passive "ward zugericht" (1. 5) is changed to an active construction. The German passive is never used without sufficient reason, and Gerhardt chooses here to imply the divine mystery of birth. Here the English is too specific. On the other hand where the German is direct, "Dein Jesus" (1. 3), "Geblüte, Fleisch, Haut," (1. 4, 5), "Der" (1. 6), the English descends to the general.

Stanza 7 preserves more of the "Stimmung" of the original:

Thou Jesus! O thou sweetest Friend,
My light and life art ever!
Thou holdest me, dost me defend,
The foe can move Thee never.

---

[24] Cf. p. 22.
[25] Und Fleisch und Haut *ward* zugericht; line 5.

In Thee I am, Thou art in me,
As we are here, we'll ever be,
Nought here or there can part us.

It is difficult to see, however, why "allerliebster Freund" (line 43) could not have its logical equivalent "dearest Friend";[26] and similarly in line 48, "Und wie wir stehen," might equally be "And as we are," instead of "As we are here," which seems rather forced.

Gib dich zufrieden, und sei stille.—(*Goed.* 274.)

[*Cross and Consolation.*]

Founded on *Psalm* XXXVII, 7. It appeared in *Ebeling*, 1666, I, no. 11, in 15 stanzas.

English Versions:

1. **Be thou content: be still before.**
Miss Winkworth, 1855, p. 156, and in Bishop Ryle's *Collection,* 1860, no. 269.

2. **Be thou contented! aye relying.**
    J. Kelly, 1867, p. 202.

3. **Tranquilly lead thee, peace possessing.**
    N. L. Frothingham, 1870, p. 246.

Selected Stanza:

Miss Winkworth in her *Lyra Germanica,* 1855, p. 156.

Stanza 1.   Be thou content; be still before
His face, at whose right hand doth reign
Fulness of joy forever more,
Without whom all thy toil is vain.
He is thy living spring, thy sun, whose rays
Make glad with life and light thy dreary days.
Be thou content.

Ich bin ein Gast auf Erden.—(*Goed.* 284.)

[*Eternal Life.*]

Based on *Psalm* XXXIX, 12, "I am a stranger with thee, and a sojourner, as all my fathers were." Cf. also *Psalm* CXIX, "I am a stranger in the earth." It was first published in *Ebeling,* Berlin, 1666; reprinted in *Wackernagel:* 1843, no. 112; and *Bachmann:* no. 98; and included as no. 824, in the *Unv. L. S.:* 1851.

English Versions:[27]

1. **A pilgrim and a stranger,**
   I journey here below.

---

[26] Line 43: "Thou Jesus! O Thou sweetest Friend."
[27] For adaptations of this hymn cf. p. 140 ff.

A good translation in 7 stanzas by Miss Jane Borthwick, in *H. L. L.*, 3d Series, 1858, p. 13, 1884, p. 139, as follows:

Gerhardt:	I	II	III	IV	(V)	VI	VII	VIII	IX	(X)	XI	XII	XIII	XIV
Borthwick:	1	2		3			4		5			6		7

2. **A pilgrim here I wander,**
   On earth have no abode.

A translation in 10 stanzas by Miss Winkworth in her *Lyra Ger.*, 2d Series, 1858, p. 173, and in her *Chorale Book*, 1863, no. 148, altered by stanzas as follows:

Gerhardt:	I	II	III	(IV	V	VI	VII)	VIII	IX	X	XI	XII	XIII	XIV
Winkworth:	1	2	3					4	5	6	7	8	9	10

In *Holy Song*, 1869, it begins: "As pilgrims here we wander."

3. **A rest here have I never,**
   A guest on earth am I.
      J. Kelly, 1867, p. 316.

4. **On earth I'm but a pilgrim.**
      G. Wade in the *U. P. Juvenile Missionary Magazine*, 1859, p. 252.

Selected Stanzas:

Miss Winkworth in her *Chorale Book*, 1863.	Miss Borthwick in her *Hymns from the Land of Luther*, 1858, 1884.
Stanza 1.	Stanza 1.
A pilgrim here I wander,	A Pilgrim and a stranger,
On earth have no abode,	I journey here below;
My fatherland is yonder,	Far distant is my country,
My home is with my God,	The home to which I go.
For here I journey to and fro,	Here I must toil and travel,
There in eternal rest	Oft weary and opprest;
Will God his gracious gift bestow	But there my God shall lead me
On all the toil-oppress'd.	To everlasting rest.

Herr, du erforschest meinen Sinn.—(*Goed.* 287.)
Appeared in *Ebeling*, 1666, 2, no. 23.

English Version:
1. **Lord, Thou my heart dost search and try.**
      J. Kelly, 1867, p. 138.

In his last stanza Kelly has nearly equalled the original in happily choosing for many of the words the exact English cognate:

Erforsch, Herr, all mein Herz und Mut	Lord, search and know my heart and mood,
Sieh, ob mein Weg sei recht und gut,	See if my way be right and good,
Und führe mich bald himmelan	The everlasting joyful road
Den ewgen Weg, die Freudenbahn.	Lead me that brings me home to God.

Was traurest du, mein Angesicht.—(*Goed. 289.*)

Appeared in *Ebeling, 1666, 2, 24.*

Of Gerhardt's hymns treating of Death, the Last Day, and Eternal Life, this is one of the least well known, and has not been retained in many German hymn books, mainly because of the mixed metaphor and the many unpoetic lines. It is translated in full by *J. Kelly,* 1867, no. 322, in stanzas of 7 lines, the long fifth line with the double rhyme being written as two short lines,

> Stanza 1. My face, why should'st thou troubled be
> When thou of death art hearing?
> Know it, it cannot injure thee,
> Contemplate it, ne'er fearing.
> When thou dost know
> Death, all its woe
> Will soon be disappearing.

In stanza 19 Kelly has made the first personal pronoun predominant with the result that greater smoothness is obtained. He has, however, been obliged to omit what in the German are the best touches, namely the thoughts contained in "mein Hirt," "leiten" and "immergrün":

O süsze Lust, o edle Ruh,
O fromme Seelen Freude,
Komm, schleusz mir meine Augen zu,
Dasz ich mit Fried abscheide
Hin, da mein Hirt mich leiten wird
Zur immergrünen Weide.

O sweetest joy, O blessed rest!
To all true-hearted given,
Come, let mine eyes by Thee be pressed,
In peace take me to heaven.
May I roam there
'Mong pastures fair
Where day ne'er knoweth even.

Die güldne Sonne.—(*Goed. 293.*)

[*Morning.*]

First appeared in *Ebeling, 1666, 3,* no. 25, entitled "Morgensegen"; thence in *Wackernagel:* no. 98; *Bachmann:* no. 101; *Crü. Praxis:* 1672; *Unv. L. S.:* 1851, no. 449. (The melody is by Ebeling. It is called in the *Irish Ch. Hymnal* "Franconia.")

Lauxmann in *Koch,* VIII, 185, calls this "A splendid hymn of our poet, golden as the sun going forth in his beauty, full of force and blessed peace in the Lord, full of sparkling thoughts of God."

English Versions:

1. **The golden sunbeams with their joyous gleams.**

A translation by Miss Winkworth in her *Lyra Ger.,* 1855. Her translations of verses as follows:

Gerhardt:	I	II	III	IV	(V	VI	VII)	VIII	IX	(X	XI)	XII
Winkworth:	1	2	3	4				5	6			7

Her version appears in *Kennedy*, 1863, no. 814, with the omission of the translation of Gerhardt's stanzas II, VIII, IX.

2. Evening and Morning.

A good translation beginning with stanza IV ("Abend und Morgen") by R. Massie in the 1857 ed. of Mercer's *Church Psalter and Hymn Book*. The version has these stanzas:

Gerhardt:	IV	VIII	IX	X	XI	XII
R. Massie:	1	2	3	4	5	6

This version in whole or in part appears in various hymn books. In *Kennedy*, 1863, no. 636, it begins with the translation of stanza IX ("Gott, meine Krone") "Father, O hear me." Massie subsequently added a translation of stanzas I, II, III, and included it in his *Lyra Domestica*, 1864, p. 106, and this full form appears in Reid's *Praise Bk.*, 1872, no. 379.

3. The sun's golden beams.

    Miss Dunn, 1857, p. 21.

4. Sunbeams all golden.

    Miss Cox, 1864, p. 13.

5. What is our mortal race.

    (Beginning with stanza VII) by *E. Massie*, 1866, p. 87.

6. See the sun's glorious light.

    E. Massie, 1867, p. 8.

7. The golden morning.

    J. Kelly, 1867, p. 270.

Selected Stanza:

Miss Winkworth in her *Lyra Germanica*, 1865, p. 216.

> Stanza 1. The golden sunbeams with their joyous gleams,
> Are kindling o'er earth, her life and mirth,
> Shedding forth lovely and heart-cheering light;
> Through the dark hours' chill I lay silent and still,
> But risen at length to gladness and strength,
> I gaze on the heavens all glowing and bright.

Der Tag mit seinem Lichte.—(*Goed.* 296.)

Appeared in *Ebeling*, 1666, 3, 26.

Compare with this:

(a) The hymn of J. A. Freylinghausen (1704)

    "Der Tag ist hin, mein Geist und Sinn."

(This has been translated by Miss Winkworth, R. Massie, Miss Borthwick and others, and has much similarity of thought to Gerhardt's hymns.)

also (b) "Der Tag vergeht, die müde Sonne sinket" in Knapp's *Evang. Liederschatz*, 1837.

English Version:

    1. The daylight disappeareth,
        It fleeth and night neareth,
        Its gloom is spreading o'er us.
        With slumber to o'erpower us
        And all the wearied earth. . . etc.

Stanza 1 of a complete translation by *J. Kelly*, 1867, p. 282.

Ich, der ich oft in tiefes Leid.—(*Goed.* 298.)

Based on *Psalm* CXLV. First published in *Ebeling*, 1666, 3, no. 27, in 18 stanzas of 7 lines; thence in *Wackernagel:* no. 95; *Bachmann:* no. 103; Berlin *G. L S.:* 1863, no. 1004.

English Versions:

    1. **I who so oft in deep distress.**

Miss Winkworth in her *Lyra Ger.,* 2d Series, 1858, p. 149. The translation omits Gerhardt's stanzas II, III, IV. An alteration and adaptation of stanzas VI, VIII, IX, XI, beginning "O God! how many thankful songs," appeared as no. 168 in *Holy Song,* 1869.

    2. **Who is so full of tenderness.**

A translation of stanza VIII as stanza 4 in the *Moravian Hymn Book,* 1886, no. 537.

Selected Stanza:

Miss Winkworth, in her *Lyra Germanica,* 1865.

    1. I who so oft in deep distress
        And bitter grief must dwell,
        Will now my God with gladness bless,
        And all His mercies tell;
        Oh hear me then, my God and King,
        While of Thy Holy Name I sing,
        Who doest all things well.

Wie schön ists doch, Herr Jesu Christ.—(*Goed.* 302.)
[*Marriage.*]

Founded on *Psalm* CXXVIII. First published in *Ebeling*, 1666, 4, no. 38, in 8 stanzas of 12 lines; thence in *Wackernagel:* 1843, no. 108, 1874, no. 109; *Bachmann:* no. 105; *Unv. L. S.:* 1851, no. 680.

English Version:

    1. **Oh Jesus Christ! how bright and fair.**

In full by *J. Kelly*, 1867, p. 307; repeated altered, and omitting stanzas III-V, in the Ohio *Lutheran Hymnal,* 1880, no. 339.

Voller Wunder, voller Kunst.—(*Goed.* 304.)

[*Holy Matrimony.*]

First published in *Ebeling*, 1666, 4, no. 40, in 17 stanzas.   The hymn is often used in Germany at marriages.

English Versions:

1. **Full of wonder, full of skill.**
   Dr. H. Mills, 1845, 1856, p. 215.

2. **Full of wonder, full of skill.**
Mrs. Stanley Carr, in her translation of *Wildenhahn's Paul Gerhardt*, ed. 1856, p. 52.

3. **Full of wonder, full of art.**
   J. Kelly, 1867, p. 302.

4. **Full of wonder, full of art.**
   Miss Winkworth in her *Lyra Ger.*, 1869, p. 215.

Selected Stanza:

Dr. H. Mills in his *Horae Germanicae*, 1856.

> 1. Full of wonder, full of skill,
>   Full of wisdom, full of might,
>   Full of mercy and good will,
>   Full of comfort and delight,—
>   Full of wonder—once again—
>   Is of love the marriage chain.

Schaut! Schaut! was ist für Wunder dar?—(*Goed.* 310.)

[*Christmas.*]

First published in *Ebeling*, 1667, 5, 55, in 18 stanzas of 4 lines; thence in *Wackernagel:* no. 4; *Bachmann:* no. 109.

English Version:

1. **Behold! Behold! what wonders here.**
In full by *J. Kelly*, 1867, p. 14.   From this 12 stanzas were included in the Ohio *Lutheran Hyl.*, 1880, as no. 25, no. 26: no. 26 beginning with the translation of stanza XIII, "It is a time of joy today."

Kommt, und laszt uns Christum ehren.—(*Goed.* 312.)

[*Christmas.*]

Founded on *St. Luke*, II, 15.   First published in *Ebeling*, 1667, 5, no. 56, in 8 stanzas of 4 lines; thence in *Wackernagel:* no. 6; *Bachmann:* no. 110; *Unv. L. S.:* 1851, no. 43.

English Versions:

1. **Come, unite in praise and singing.**

(Omitting stanzas VI, VII.) Contributed by Rev. A. T. Russell to Maurice's *Choral H. Bk.,* 1861, no. 707.

2. **Bring to Christ your best oblation.**

A full and good translation by R. Massie in his *Lyra Domestica,* 1864, p. 96; repeated in Snepp's *Songs of Grace and Glory,* and Reid's *Praise Bk.,* 1872.

3. **Come and let us Christ revere now.**

    Miss Manington, 1864, p. 25.

4. **Come, and Christ the Lord be praising.**

    J. Kelly, 1867, p. 24.

Herr Gott, du bist ja für und für.—(*Goed.* 315.)

Based on *Psalm* XC. It appeared in *Ebeling,* 1667, 6, no. 68.

English Version:

> 1. Lord God! Thou art forevermore
> Thy people's habitation,
> And Thou existence hadst before
> Was laid the earth's foundation!
> Ere yet the hills began to be
> Thou livedst in eternity,
> Of all things the beginning.

Stanza 1 of a complete translation by *J. Kelly,* 1867, p. 312.

In this version the translator has lost much of the poetry and spirit not only of Gerhardt but of the ninetieth Psalm on which Gerhardt's poem is based. Witness the second and fourth lines above, where Kelly offers the feeble Latin derivatives for the virile "Die Zuflucht deiner Heerde" and "Grund."

Johannes sahe durch Gesicht.—(*Goed.* 319.)

Based on Chap. VII, 9. ff. of *Revelations.* It appeared in *Ebeling,* 1667, 7, 84.

English Version:

> 1. By John was seen a wondrous sight,
> A noble light,
> A picture very glorious:
> A multitude stood 'fore him there
> All bright and fair,
> On heav'nly plain victorious;
> Their heart and mood
> Were full of good,
> That mortal man

> With gold ne'er can
> Procure, so high 'tis o'er us. . . .

Stanza 1 of a complete translation by *J. Kelly,* 1867, p. 347.

Wie ist es müglich, höchstes Licht.—(*Goed.* 324.)
Appeared in *Ebeling,* 8, 96.

The English version by *J. Kelly,* 1867, p. 259, is throughout more moderate in tone and does not reflect the utter self-abnegation of Gerhardt.[28]

> Stanza 1.   How can it be, my highest Light!
> That as before Thy face so bright
> All things must pale and vanish,
> That my poor feeble flesh and blood
> Can summon a courageous mood
> To meet Thee, and fear banish?

Ich weisz, dasz mein Erlöser lebt.—(*Goed.* 331.)
[*Easter.*]

Founded on *Job.* XIX, 25-27.   First published in *Ebeling,* 1667, 10, no. 119, in 9 stanzas of 7 lines; thence in *Wackernagel:* 1843, no. 118 (1847, no. 123); *Bachmann:* no. 119; Berlin *G. L. S.:* 1863, no. 301.

English Versions:[29]

1. **I know that my Redeemer lives.   In this my faith is fast.**

A full and spirited translation by J. Oxenford, in *Lays of the Sanctuary,* 1859, p. 122. His translation of stanzas I, III, VII-IX were included, altered as no. 779 in *Kennedy,* 1863.

2. **I know that my Redeemer lives, This hope,**
   Miss Manington, 1863, p. 78.

From the foregoing statements it is evident that even of Gerhardt's less well-known hymns there has been a comparatively large representation in English and American hymnals.   The ten hymns which follow are so widely known through the excellent versions of Miss Winkworth and others, that making the treatment more detailed, I shall discuss the individual merits of the different versions and compare their relative values as interpretations of the originals.

---

[28] This is almost the only poem in which Gerhardt has not employed his characteristic alliteration or assonance, or introduced "Friede" or "Freude" words.   On these characteristics cf. p. *22* ff.

[29] For adaptations from this hymn cf. p. 135 ff.

Wie soll ich dich empfangen.—(*Goed.* 25.)
[*Advent.*]

First published in *Crü.—Runge,* 1653, no. 77, in 10 stanzas of 8 lines; thence in *Wackernagel:* no. 3; *Bachmann:* no. 22; *Unv. L. S.:* 1851, no. 21.   Cf. *Koch* IV, 119 ff.

The hymn is founded on *St. Matthew* XXI, 1-9, the Gospel for the first Sunday in Advent.   It is one of Gerhardt's finest productions, and is probably the best German Advent hymn.   It is inferable from stanzas VI-IX that the poem was written during the Thirty Years' War.   The entire first stanza has been set to music by Bach in the *Weihnachtsoratorium,* Part I.

English Versions:

1.   **How shall I meet my Savior.**

A translation in full, by J. C. Jacobi, in his *Psalmodia Germanica,* 1722, p. 3 (1732, slightly altered).   Included in the *Moravian Hymn Book,* 1754, and also in later editions with alterations.   Varying centos of this version are found in Montgomery's *Christian Psalmist,* 1825; Dr. Pagenstecher's *Collections,* 1864; and Bishop Ryle's *Collection,* 1860.   Other forms are:

(a) "We go to meet Thee, Savior" (stanza I altered), in Reid's *Praise Book,* 1872, mainly from the *Moravian H. Bk.,* 1801;

(b.) "Love caused Thine Incarnation" (stanza V altered), in Walker's *Collection,* 1855, and Snepp's *Songs of G. and G.,* 1872, from the *Moravian H. Bk.,* 1801.

2.   **Oh, how shall I receive Thee.**

A good translation of stanzas I, II, VII, VIII, X, by A. T. Russell in his *Ps. and Hys.,* 1851, no. 36.   Repeated in *Kennedy,* 1863, and the *People's H.,* 1867; and abridged in J. L. Porter's *Collection,* 1876; *H. and Songs of Praise,* N. Y., 1874; *Laudes Domini,* N. Y., 1884, etc.

3.   **Oh! how shall I receive Thee.**

In the 1857 ed. of Mercer's *C. P. and H. Bk.*   Stanzas 1, 2, are based on A. T. Russell's version and stanzas 3, 4, 5 (Gerhardt's IV, V, VI), are based on Jacobi, as altered in the *Moravian H. Bk.,* 1801.   Altered forms have appeared in other hymnals.

4.   **Ah! Lord, how shall I meet thee.**

A translation of stanzas I, II, V, VI, VIII, X, by Miss Winkworth, in her *C. B. for England,* 1863, no. 71.

5.   **Say with what salutations.**

In full by *J. Kelly,* 1867, p. 10; repeated, abridged, in the Ohio *Luth. Hyl.,* 1880.

6.   **Lord, how shall I be meeting.**

J. W. Alexander, in Schaff's *Kirchenfreund,* 1850, p. 176, and his *Christ in Song,* 1869, p. 20, and his own *Breaking Crucible,* 1861, p. 11.

7.   **How shall I meet Thee? How my heart.**

  Miss Winkworth, 1855, p. 7.

8.   **How shall I come to meet Thee.**

  Miss Manington, 1863, p. 65.

9. **Lord, how shall I receive Thee.**
   R. Massie, 1864, p. 93.

The first hymn in the *Psalmodia Germanica*[30] of Jacobi (1722) is a translation of Luther's "Nun kommt der Heiden Heiland" ("Now the Savior comes indeed").   The second place in the book is given to Gerhardt's "Wie soll ich dich empfangen" which is translated as "How shall I meet my Savior."   In a rather quaint preface Jacobi writes:

"The present S p e c i m e n hopes for a charitable Allowance from those, that may happen to use it.   A Version of this Kind lies under various Disadvantages, known only to those, who in any degree are acquainted with any Poetical Translations of this Kind.   A great Deal is lost of the Life and Spirit of an Hymn, when it appears in another Language."

In this effort as well as in the case of "Befiehl du deine Wege" Jacobi has left out so much, and incorporated so many ideas of his own which are at variance with Gerhardt's theme that it is difficult to recognize its kinship with the original.   The effect Gerhardt produces in the first line by the use of the direct form of address is entirely lost by Jacobi; also the translator creates an unpleasant impression by abruptly changing from the third person in the opening line to the second person in the next line.

Bishop Ryle has altered the last quatrain to this form:

> I wait for Thy salvation;
> Grant me Thy Spirit's light,
> Thus will my preparation
> Be pleasing in Thy sight.

Again, the diction of stanza two is particularly strange, at least to modern readers.

> I'll raise with all my Powers
> More Notes than *Unison*,

would be quite bewildering if we did not have at hand the German which is so forceful in its very simplicity:

> Mein Herze soll dir grünen
> In stetem Lob und Preis.

It is plain that Jacobi had not much appreciation of the spirit of Gerhardt, for the distinctive touches of alliteration, repetition for emphasis, the prevailing note of joy and peace accompanying the Savior's advent are certainly not adequately reproduced.   In fact the impression he leaves is almost one of gloom!

Contrast with this the translation by A. T. Russell, a cento of which (stanzas 1, 2, 7, 8, 10) is given in most American hymnals.   Far more cheer-

---

[30] Cf. p. 96 and note.

ful and more appropriate for the Advent season than anything in Jacobi are such lines as:

> My heart to praise awaking,
> Her anthem shall prepare, (stanza 2)

and

> That in the light eternal our
> Joyous home may be. (stanza 5)

It is apt renderings like these that have won for Gerhardt a place in English hymnody.

Kelly's rendering (1867) is characteristically accurate, but, excepting such lines as:

> My heart shall blossom ever
> O'erflow with praises new (stanza 2)

and

> O come Thou Sun and lead us
> To everlasting light, (stanza 10)

it is uninspired and lacking in fervor.

Of the 20 hymns of Gerhardt which Miss Winkworth translated there are three for which she has made two renderings: "O Haupt voll Blut und Wunden," "Nun ruhen alle Wälder," and for this Advent hymn. The earlier version (1855) of the Advent hymn omits only the third stanza ("Was hast du unterlassen"). The later one (1863) is written in the original metre for church use to be sung to the traditional melody "Wie soll ich dich empfangen" by Johann Crüger[31] (1653) and contains but six stanzas. As Miss Winkworth was so thoroughly at home in the German she was able to reproduce a surprising number of details. Even the alliteration and repetition for emphasis of which Gerhardt is so fond find in her poem at least a partially corresponding place:

> In heavy bonds I languished long (1855, stanza 3, 1)
> This weary world and all her woe (1855, stanza 4, 5)
> And labor longer thus (1855, stanza 6, 2)

The original has been characterized as the best German Advent hymn and Miss Winkworth has transfused it in her earlier version undiminished into her own language so that it reads like an original poem. Her final quatrain is worthy of Gerhardt:

> O Sun of Righteousness! arise,
> And guide us on our way
> To yon fair mansion in the skies
> Of joyous cloudless day.

---

[31] Cf. p. 2 f.

Selected Stanzas:

J. C. Jacobi, 1722, in *Psalmodia Germanica.*

To the Tune: "COMMIT THY WAYS AND GOINGS."[32]

I.

How shall I meet my Savior?
How shall I welcome Thee?
What manner of Behavior
Is now requir'd of me?
Lord, thine Illumination
Set Heart and Hands aright,
That this my Preparation
Be pleasing in thy Sight.

A. T. Russell, 1851, in his *Psalms and Hymns.*[33]

  1. O how shall I receive Thee, How meet Thee on Thy way;
      Blest hope of every nation, My soul's delight and stay?
      (Jesu)(Jesu)   (*Thy)
      O Jesus, Jesus, give me Now by thine own pure light,
      To know whate'er is pleasing And welcome in Thy sight.

        (*Sion)   (*and)
  2. Thy Zion palms is strewing, With branches fresh and fair;
      (*My heart to praise)
      My soul in praise awaking, Her anthem shall prepare.
      Perpetual thanks and praises Forth from my heart shall spring.
      (*I)   (*will)
      And to Thy Name the service Of all my powers I bring.

 (*3.) (Omitted.)

(*4.) 3. Ye who with guilty terror Are trembling, fear no more:
      With love and grace the Savior Shall you to hope restore.
                (*shall)
      He comes, who contrite sinners Will with the children place,
      The children of His Father, The heirs of life and grace.

 (*5.) Omitted.

Miss Winkworth, 1855, in her *Lyra Germanica.*

    Stanza 1.   How shall I meet Thee? How my heart
                Receive her Lord aright?
                Desire of all the earth Thou art!
                My hope, my sole delight!
                Kindle the lamp, Thou Lord, alone,
                Half-dying in my breast,

---

[32] Cf. p. 116.
[33] An asterisk placed before the word indicates the form in the original. This altered cento of three stanzas is the one usually given in American hymn books.

And make Thy gracious pleasure known
How I may greet Thee best.

Miss Winkworth, 1863, in her *Chorale Book*.

Stanza 1.　Ah! Lord, how shall I meet Thee,
How welcome Thee aright?
All nations long to greet Thee
My hope, my sole delight!
Brighten the lamp that burneth
But dimly in my breast,
And teach my soul, that yearneth
To honour such high guest.

O Haupt voll Blut und Wunden.—(*Goed.* 49.)

[*Passiontide.*]

A beautiful but very free translation of the "Salve Caput Cruentatum," which is part VII of the "Rhythmica Oratio," 1153, ascribed to St. Bernard of Clairvaux.[34]　The Latin original follows:

DE PASSIONE DOMINI: AD FACIEM.

1.　Salve, caput cruentatum,
Totum spinis coronatum,
Conquassatum, vulneratum,
Arundine sic verberatum
Facie sputis illita
Salve, cuius dulcis vultus,
Immutatus et incultus
Immutavit suum florem
Totus versus in pallorem
　　Quem coeli tremit curia.

2.　Omnis vigor atque viror
Hinc recessit, non admiror,
Mors apparet in aspectu,
Totus pendens in defectu,
Attritus aegra macie.
Sic affectus, sic despectus
Propter me sic interfectus,
Peccatori tam indigno
Cum amoris intersigno
　　Appare clara facie.

3.　In hac tua passione
Me agnosce, pastor bone,
Cuius sumpsi mel ex ore,

---

[34] Cf. p. 40 and note.

Haustum lactis ex dulcore
Prae omnibus deliciis,
Non me reum asperneris,
Nec indignum dedigneris
Morte tibi iam vicina
Tuum caput hic acclina,
  In meis pausa brachiis.

4. Tuae sanctae passioni
Me gauderem interponi,
In hac cruce tecum mori
Praesta crucis amatori,
  Sub cruce tua moriar.
Morti tuae iam amarae
Grates ago, Jesu care,
Qui es clemens, pie Deus,
Fac quod petit tuus reus,
Ut absque te non finiar.

5. Dum me mori est necesse,
Noli mihi tunc deesse;
In tremenda mortis hora
Veni, Jesu, absque mora,
  Tuere me et libera.
Quum me jubes emigrare,
Jesu care, tunc appare;
O amator amplectende,
Temet ipsum tunc ostende
In cruce salutifera.

Gerhardt's version appeared in the 1656 ed. of *Crü. Praxis,* no. 156, in 10 stanzas of 8 lines; thence in *Wackernagel:* no. 22; *Bachmann:* no. 54; *Unv. L. S.:* 1851, no. 109. Cf. *Koch,* IV, 163; VIII, 47.

In *Koch* VIII, 47, Lauxmann thus characterizes it:

"Bernard's original is powerful and searching, but Gerhardt's hymn is still more powerful and profound, as redrawn from the deeper spring of evangelical Lutheran, Scriptural, knowledge, and fervency of faith."

Stanza X Lauxmann traces not only to Bernard but to stanza II of "Valet will ich dir geben" of Herberger, and to Luther's words on the death of his daughter Magdalen "Who thus dies, dies well."

The melody to which the hymn is sung, usually called "Passion Chorale," first appeared in Hans Leo Hassler's "Lustgarten," Nürnberg, 1601, set to a love song, beginning "Mein G'müth ist mir verwirret."

The hymn has often been signally blessed. The story is told that a Roman Catholic from Bohemia on hearing this hymn sung in a Protestant church was so overpowered that he shed tears of joy, for he saw clearer than ever his own sin and the Savior's grace; he understood better than ever the secret of justification by faith alone, and he became from that time a true evangelical Christian. Frederick William I., King of Prussia from 1713 to 1740, the father of Frederick the Great, ordered in his will that at his funeral this hymn should be played by the band.[35]

The English versions are many, and of some of the versions there are several centos:

1. O Head so full of bruises.

In full, by J. Gambold, in *Some other Hymns and Poems*, London, 1752, p. 12. Repeated in the *Moravian H. Book*, 1754, pt. 1, no. 222 (1789 greatly altered). In the 1789 ed. a new translation of stanza IX was substituted for Gambold's version, his translation of stanza IX "When I shall gain permission" being given as a separate hymn.

Centos of the above version are:

a. "O Head, so pierced and wounded" in Dr. Pagenstecher's *Collection*, 1864.

b. "O Christ! what consolation" in the *Amer. Bapt. H. Bk.*, 1871.

c. "I yield Thee thanks unfeigned" (based on Gambold's version of stanza IX) in E. Bickersteth's *Christian Psalmody*, 1833.

d. "I give Thee thanks unfeigned" in Bishop Ryle's *Collection*, 1860.

2. O Sacred Head! now wounded.

A very beautiful translation by Dr. J. W. Alexander. His translations of stanzas I, II, IV, VII-X, were first published in the *Christian Lyre*, N. Y., 1830, no. 136. These stanzas were revised, and translations of stanzas III, VI, were added by Dr. Alexander for Schaff's *Deutscher Kirchenfreund*, 1849, p. 91. The full text is in Dr. Alexander's *Breaking Crucible*, N. Y., 1861, p. 7; in Schaff's *Christ in Song*, 1869; and the *Cantate Domino*, Boston, U. S. A., 1859. In his note Dr. Schaff says:

"This classical hymn has shown an imperishable vitality in passing from the Latin into the German, and from the German into the English, and proclaiming in three tongues, and in the name of three Confessions—the Catholic, the Lutheran, and the Reformed—with equal effect, the dying love of our Savior and our boundless indebtedness to Him."

Dr. Alexander's version has passed into very many English and American hymnals, and in very varying centos, some of which follow:

a. "O sacred Head, now wounded," *People's H.*, 1867; *Hymnary*, 1872; Hatfield's *Church H. Bk.*, 1872; *Hymns and Songs of Praise*, N. Y., 1874, etc.

b. "O Sacred Head! once wounded" (stanza I altered), *Bapt. Ps. and Hys.*, 1858, etc.

c. "O Sacred Head, sore wounded" (stanza I altered), in the Stoke *Hymn Book*, 1878.

d. "O Sacred Head, so wounded" (stanza I altered), in J. L. Porter's *Collection*, 1876.

---

[35] For other incidents connected with this hymn cf. Th. Kübler: *Historical notes to the Lyra Germanica*, London, 1865.

e. "O blessed Christ, once wounded" (stanza I altered), in Dr. Thomas's *Augustine H. Book,* 1866.

f. "O Lamb of God, once wounded" (stanza I altered), in *Scottish Presb. Hyl.,* 1876.

g. "O Lamb of God, sore wounded" (stanza I altered), in the *Ibrox Hymnal,* 1871.

3. **Ah! Head, so pierced and wounded.**
A good translation by R. Massie, omitting stanza VI, in his *Lyra Domestica,* 1864, p. 114. This version was abridged in Mercer's *Oxford edition,* 1864, and in *Kennedy,* 1863. A cento of this beginning with stanza VIII, line 5, "Oh! that Thy cross may ever," appears in J. H. Wilson's *Series of Praise,* 1865.

4. **Ah wounded Head, that bearest.**
Miss Winkworth, omitting stanza VI, in her *C. B. for England,* 1863, no. 51.

5. **Oh! bleeding head, and wounded.**
   J. Kelly, 1867, p. 59.

6. **Ah wounded Head! must Thou.**
   Miss Winkworth in her *Lyra Ger.,* 1855, p. 80.

7. **Thou pierced and wounded brow.**
   Miss Dunn, 1857, p. 39.

8. **O Head. blood-stained and wounded.**
In the Schaff-Gilman *Lib. of Religious Poetry,* translated by Samuel M. Jackson, 1873, 1880. This version is among those that adhere most closely to the original, at the same time showing traces of the Latin of Bernard.

9. **O sacred Head, surrounded**
   By crown of piercing thorn!
A translation in 3 stanzas by Sir H. W. Baker of stanzas I, III, VII, and X, in the Schaff-Gilman *Lib. of Religious Poetry.*

10. **Oh, wounded head and bleeding.**
A good translation omitting stanzas II, III, V, IX, by Miss Margarete Münsterberg in her *Harvest of German Verse,* 1916.

The earliest known English translation of Gerhardt's Passiontide hymn is that of J. Gambold, published in 1752.[36] It is written in his characteristic vein. Gambold has made no effort to do more than reproduce in doggerel the main ideas of the original without even attempting to gloss over the indelicate expressions which Gerhardt introduced from the Latin of Bernard. The "facie sputis illita" which in Gerhardt is modified to "Wie bist du so bespeit" (line 12) is given by Gambold with extreme literalness. His style becomes often ridiculous if indeed not wholly flippant when he attempts to imitate Gerhardt's familiarity[37] in addressing the Savior.

[36] Cf. p. 92.
[37] Cf. p. 18.

Witness the first quatrain of stanza 7:

> It gives me solid pleasure
> My heart does not recoil
> When I dive in some measure
> Into thy Pangs and Toil.[38]

It is easy to understand why this hymn should be printed in full in the crude *Moravian Hymn Book* of 1754 and even in later editions, but it is also obvious that more recent hymnals should have made drastic alterations and judicious omissions.   Of the centos adapted from Gambold's unpolished verses, that in Reid's *Praise Book* (1872) will show how changes were made to suit the more refined taste of the century following the early Moravian period.   The quatrain cited above appears in *Reid* as follows:

> And oh! what consolation
> Doth in our hearts take place,
> When we Thy toil and passion
> Can joyfully retrace.

An English writer who faithfully transplanted Germany's best hymns and made them bloom with fresh beauty in their new gardens was Catherine Winkworth.   Her two renderings of this hymn are well adapted to awaken responsive feelings in Christian readers.   It would be difficult to judge between the two versions as to which the more successfully retains the force of the German.   In both versions she has omitted stanza VI beginning "Ich will hie bei dir stehen."   The earlier one (1855) does not preserve the metre of the original, while the later one (1863) was written for her *Chorale Book* with the accompanying melody.   In general it may be said that the earlier version with the expanded third and seventh lines follows more closely the fervent thought of Gerhardt, an effect made possible in the longer stanza, as the English can rarely be expressed as concisely as the German.   A comparison of the first quatrains of the two versions of the final stanza illustrates this:

1855.	1863. (Version for church singing.)
Come to me ere I die, My comfort and my shield; Then gazing on Thy cross can I Calmly my spirit yield.	Appear then, my Defender, My Comfort, ere I die This life I can surrender If I but see Thee nigh.

Of the twenty or more forms in which this hymn is familiar to English and American readers that of Dr. Alexander has found most general

---

[38] Cf. lines 49-52: Es dient zu meiner Freuden
> Und kömmt mir herzlich wol,
> Wann ich in deinem Leiden,
> Mein Heil, mich finden soll.

acceptance for church use. The reason is not far to seek. The music to which the hymn is usually sung is the original melody for the hymn "Herzlich tut mich verlangen"[39] and was, as has been stated, written for a secular song, though thoroughly suitable for the expression of the awfulness of Christ's passion. Alexander's version is without question the one which best suits the cadence of this melody. In the version, for example, of Jackson, the stress would fall upon "tortured"[40] in line 2 and, as the music repeats for the third and fourth lines, also on "a" in line 4. This, then, would not be selected as a satisfactory version for church singing. Aside from this feature, however, the flow of Gerhardt's language is more successfully imitated and the deep fervor of the German more effectively brought forth in Alexander's hymn than in any of the other translations unless we except the earlier one of Miss Winkworth.

While Gerhardt's hymn is more searching and profound than its Latin prototype, and an English translator would not ordinarily refer to the original of Bernard, still there seem to be in the phraseology of the Jackson and Winkworth translations evidences that these authors were at least familiar with it. Such lines as "Death triumphs in his pallour"[41] and "The pallor of the dead"[42] are quite suggestive of the Latin: "Totus versus in pallorem";[43] and "Redeemer spurn me not"[44] of the Latin "Non me reum asperneris."[45]

A short paraphrase by Sir H. W. Baker contains several ideas taken from the Latin which Gerhardt has omitted. Stanza 1, lines 7, 8:

> Yet angel hosts adore thee
> And tremble as they gaze

are evidently suggested by:

> Totus versus in pallorem
> Quem coeli tremit curia. (lines 9, 10)

and

> O Love to sinners free!
> Jesu all grace supplying,
> Oh turn thy face to me. (stanza 2)

follows the idea in

> Peccatori tam indigno
> Cum amoris intersigno
> Appare clara facie. (lines 18-20)

---

[39] By Cristoph Knoll, 1563-1650. Cf. p. 87.
[40] Cf. p. 94.
[41] Stanza 3, line 7, Winkworth, 1863.
[42] Stanza 3, line 4, Jackson, 1873.
[43] Line 9, Bernard, p. 86.
[44] Stanza 4, line 8, Winkworth, 1863.
[45] Line 26, Bernard, p. 87.

The same is true in the first quatrain of Baker's stanza 3, with the idea of the word "indigno" above brought into these later lines:

> In this thy bitter passion,
> Good Shepherd, think of me,
> With thy most sweet compassion,
> Unworthy though I be.[46]

In 1860 Bishop Ryle selected and arranged *Three hundred and sixty-six Hymns and Spiritual Songs—a song for every day in the year*. His 166th poem is a cento of this Passiontide hymn and is assuredly deserving of mention, although he omits the first four stanzas entirely, and for no apparent reason changes the order of the others, arranging them as follows:

Ryle:	1	2	3	4	5	6
Gerhardt:	VIII	VI	VII	V	IX	X.

His first quatrain of Gerhardt's stanza VII is almost identical with that given in Reid's *Praise Book* as an alteration of the old Gambold version.

> What heavenly consolation
> Doth in my heart take place,
> When I Thy toil and passion
> Can in some measure trace.

Selected Stanzas:

J. Gambold, 1752, in *Some other Hymns and Poems.*

> 1.   O Head so full of bruises,
>   So full of pain and scorn,
>   'Midst other sore Abuses
>   Mock'd with a crown of Thorn!
>   O head, e'er now surrounded
>   With brightest Majesty,
>   Now pitiably wounded!
>   Accept a kiss from me.
>
> 2.   Thou Countenance transcendent,
>   At other times rever'd
>   By Worlds on thee dependent
>   With Spittle now besmeared!
>   etc.

J. W. Alexander, 1849, in the Schaff-Gilman *Lib. of Religious Poetry.*

> 1.   O Sacred Head, now wounded,
>   With grief and shame bow'd down,
>   Now scornfully surrounded,

---

[46] In hac tua passione
Me agnosce, pastor bone.   Lines 21, 22.

With thorns, Thy only crown.
O Sacred Head, what glory
What bliss till now was Thine
Yet, though despised and gory,
I joy to call Thee mine.

2.   What Thou, my Lord, hast suffered,
(Gerh. IV.)   Was all for sinner's gain:
Mine, mine was the transgression
But Thine the deadly pain.
Lo, here I fall, my Savior:
'Tis I deserve Thy place;
Look on me with Thy favour,
Vouchsafe to me Thy grace.

3.   The joy can ne'er be spoken,
(Gerh. VII.)   Above all joys beside,
When in Thy body broken
I thus with safety hide.
Lord of my life desiring
Thy glory now to see,
Beside Thy cross expiring
I'd breathe my soul to Thee.

4.   What language shall I borrow
(Gerh. VIII.)   To thank Thee, dearest Friend,
For this, Thy dying sorrow,
Thy pity without end?
O make me Thine for ever;
And should I fainting be,
Lord let me never, never
Outlive my love for Thee.

5.   Be near me when I'm dying,
(Gerh. X.)   O show Thy Cross to me:
And to my succour flying,
Come, Lord, and set me free.
These eyes new faith receiving,
From Jesus shall not move;
For he, who dies believing,
Dies safely through Thy love.

Miss Winkworth, 1855, in her *Lyra Germanica,* 1st Series.

1.   Ah wounded Head! must Thou
Endure such shame and scorn!
The blood is trickling from Thy brow
Pierced by the crown of thorn.
Thou who wast crown'd on high
With light and majesty,
In deep dishonor here must die,
Yet here I welcome Thee!

Miss Winkworth, 1863, in her *Chorale Book.*

    1. Ah wounded Head that bearest
         Such bitter shame and scorn,
         That now so meekly wearest
         The mocking crown of thorn!
         Erst reigning in the highest
         In light and majesty,
         Dishonored here Thou diest,
         Yet here I worship Thee.

A cento by J. C. Ryle, 1860, in his *Spiritual Songs.*

    1. I give Thee thanks unfeigned,
(Gerh.   O Jesus, Friend in need,
stanza VIII.) For what Thy soul sustained
         When Thou for me didst bleed.
         Grant to lean unshaken
         Upon Thy faithfulness,
         Until I hence am taken
         To see Thee face to face.

Cento from J. Gambold's version, in Reid's *Praise Book,* 1866.

    1. O Head! so full of bruises,
         So full of pain and scorn;
         Midst other sore abuses,
         Mock'd with a crown of thorn!
         O Head! ere now surrounded
         With brightest majesty,
         In death once bow'd and wounded,
         Accursed on a tree!

    2. Thou countenance transcendent,
         Thou life-creating Sun
         To worlds on Thee dependent,
         Yet bruised and spit upon! . . . etc.

J. Kelly, 1867, in his *Paul Gerhardt's Spiritual Songs.*

    1. Oh! bleeding head and wounded,
         And full of pain and scorn,
         In mockery surrounded
         With cruel crown of thorn!
         O Head! before adornèd
         With grace and majesty,
         Insulted now and scornèd,
         All hail I bid to Thee!

S. M. Jackson, 1873, 1880, in Schaff-Gilman *Lib. of Religious Poetry.*

    1. O Head, blood stained and wounded,
         Tortured by pain and scorn!

O Head in jest surrounded
By a rude crown of thorn!
O Head, once rich adorned
With highest laud and lays,
But now so deeply scorned,
To thee I lift my praise!

Sir H. W. Baker in Schaff-Gilman *Lib. of Religious Poetry.*

1.   O Sacred Head, surrounded
     By crown of piercing thorn!
     O bleeding Head so wounded,
     Reviled and put to scorn!
     Death's pallid hue comes o'er Thee,
     The glow of life decays,
     Yet angel-hosts adore thee
     And tremble as they gaze.

Miss Margarete Münsterberg, in her *Harvest of German Verse,* 1916.

1.   Oh, wounded head and bleeding,
     By pain and scorn bowed down!
     Oh head, the gibes unheeding,
     Bound with a thorny crown!
     Oh head, once decorated
     With honors gloriously,
     Now tortured so and hated,
     I greet and worship Thee!

Wach auf, mein Herz! und singe.—(*Goed.* 59.)

[*Morning.*]

Appeared in *Crü. Praxis,* 1648, no. 1, in 10 stanzas of four lines; thence in *Wacker-nagel:* no. 99; *Bachmann:* no. 1. It was repeated in *Crü.—Runge,* 1653, no. 1, and also in the Berlin *G. L. S.:* ed. 1863, no. 1132. This is one of the finest and most popular of German morning hymns, and soon passed into universal use, stanza VIII being best known. Cf. *Koch,* IV, 595 ff.

English Versions:

1. **My Soul, awake and tender.**
   In full, by J. C. Jacobi, in his *Psalmodia Germanica,* 1720, p. 33 (1722, p. 104), repeated in pt. I of the *Moravian H. Bk.,* 1754. In the *Moravian H. Bk.,* 1789 and 1886, it begins "My soul awake and render," stanzas 1, 2, 4, 5, being from I; V (lines 3, 4); VI (lines 1, 2); X; VIII.

2. **Thy Thanks, my Soul, be raising.**
   H. J. Buckoll, 1842, p. 28.

3. **Wake, my heart, and sing His praises.**
   E. Massie, 1867.

4. **Awake, my heart, be singing.**
    J. *Kelly, 1867, p. 276.*

5. **Wake up, my heart, elater.**
    N. L. Frothingham, 1870.

The third[47] hymn of Gerhardt which Jacobi included in his *Psalmodia Germanica*[48] is "Wach auf, mein Herz, und singe." As this song of trust is one of Gerhardt's oldest pieces and may be said to set the key for all the later hymns, it is appropriate that Jacobi should find for it a place in his very limited selection.

The eighteenth century English versions of German hymns invariably abound in extravagant figures. Just why in this instance the translator has chosen to add to the text, where no mention is made of a "lion," the idea of such an animal in the verse:

> Nay, when that Lyon's Fury,

is difficult to explain. Possibly to his own mind that creature was more terrifying than Satan himself. Still less pardonable is the distortion in stanza IV:

Du sprachst: Mein Kind, nun liege	Thou saidst: my Child, be easy,
Trotz dem, der dich betriege!	My presence shall release Thee
Schlaf wol, lasz dir nicht grauen,	From frightful Pain and Evil,
Du sollt die Sonne schauen.	In spite of Hell and Devil.

Such alterations of the original, always with the idea of bringing a more terrible picture to the mind of the reader, can be justified on no ground whatever, and accounted for only by saying that the translator probably regarded this as one of the methods of

"resolving all the jarring Discords of Self-love into the heavenly Concords of Mutual Love and Affection. If this be not effected here below, we shall never be worthy to hear the glorious Anthems of the Seraphic *Quire* above."[48a]

The singularly inapt paraphrase of the couplet in stanza 3:

> Thy gracious Condescension,
> Has crossed his sore Intention

appears to slightly better advantage in stanza 7:

> In gracious Condescension
> Despise not my Intention;
> Nor Body, Soul, nor Spirit
> Can boast of any Merit.

---

[47] The other two are "Befiehl du deine Wege" and "Wie soll ich dich empfangen?"
[48] The *Psalmodia Germanica* is a collection of 60 hymns from the German.
[48a] Concluding lines of Jacobi's preface to his *Psalmodia Germanica*, 1722.

Another characteristic of the English versions of this period is the emphasizing of the tortures of Hell and the Devil. Just as in stanza 4 above, we are not surprised to read in stanza 8:

> From Satan's woeful doings,

although there is in the German no suggestion whatever of Satan or his deeds. Similarly, the concluding stanza, after the pleasing opening lines, causes something of a shock by its abrupt descent to the grotesque:

> Thy Bliss be my Salvation,
> My Heart thy Habitation;
> Thy Word my Food and Relish,
> Till thou destroy'st what's Hellish.

Except for the imperfect rhymes in most of his stanzas Kelly's version is unusually good both as a scrupulously faithful rendering and a successful attempt to keep the simple language and reproduce the characteristic touches of Gerhardt. The line:

> The sunlight shall delight thee,

takes on a new significance when compared with

> Du sollt die Sonne schauen,

and strophe 8 is particularly well done in that it has so large a predominance of Anglo-Saxon words:

So wollst du nun vollenden	Thou wilt, O Lord! be ending
Dein Werk an mir und senden	Thy work in me and sending
Der mich an diesem Tage	Who in his hands will take me,
Auf seinen Händen trage.	Today his care will make me.

Selected Stanzas:

J. C. Jacobi, in his *Psalmodia Germanica,* 1722.

I.

> My Soul awake, and tender
> To God, thy great Defender
> Thy Prayer and Thanksgiving,
> Because thou art still living.

II.

> Last Night, when lying senseless,
> And utterly defenceless,
> I was in greatest Danger
> From Darkness and its Ranger.

John Kelly, in his *Paul Gerhardt's Spiritual Songs,* 1867.

1. Awake, my heart! be singing,
   Praise to thy Maker bringing,
   Of every good the Giver,
   Who men protecteth ever.

2. As shades of night spread over
   Earth as a pall did cover,
   Then Satan sought to have me
   But God was near to save me.

Nun ruhen alle Wälder.—(*Goed.* 60.)
[*Evening.*]

First published in *Crü. Praxis,* 1648, no. 15, in 9 stanzas of 6 lines; thence in *Wackernagel:* no. 102; *Bachmann:* no. 2; *Unv. L. S.:* 1851, no. 529. Cf. *Koch,* IV, 607; VIII, 194.

This is one of the finest and one of the earliest of Gerhardt's hymns. In the time of Flat Rationalism in Germany the first stanza became the object of much derision.[49] But the shallow wit showed how little poetry was then understood, for Gerhardt followed in thus beginning his hymn a much admired passage of Virgil, *Æneid* IV, 522-528:

Nox erat, et placidum carpebant fessa soporem
Corpora per terras, silvaeque et saeva quierant
Aequora, cum medio volvuntur sidera lapsu,
Cum tacet omnis ager, pecudes pictaeque volucres,
Quaeque lacus late liquidos, quaeque aspera dumis
Rura tenent, somno positae sub nocte silenti
(Lenibant curas, et corda oblita laborum).

Among the common people the hymn became an exceeding favorite and was generally used as an evening prayer. Its childlike simplicity combined with its deep poetical charm has won the hearts of old and young to the present day. Frequently it has been sung on starry nights by men, women, or children in the fields on their homeward way, and many have laid themselves down for the long sleep of death with this hymn on their lips.

A troop of French soldiers entered Lisberg, a small town of Hesse, on the 14th of September, 1796, plundered and killed the inhabitants, and burned the whole town. A little way distant, at the foot of a mountain, was a small cottage in which a mother sat by the bedside of her sick child.

---

[49] Cf. "Jetzt schlafen weder Wälder," as no. 2338, in the final "Zugabe" to the *Herrnhut Gesangbuch,* 1735, dated "On Aug. 13, 1748, after Holy Communion at Herrnhut." This is a parody on the style of Gerhardt's stanzas I, II, III, VI, VII. It was translated and included in Part II of the *Moravian H. Book,* 1754, as "Tho' now no creature's sleeping."

Hearing the noise in the town and seeing the burning houses she locked the door and knelt by the bedside and prayed.   As the door burst open and a furious soldier rushed in, she spread her hands over the child and cried:

> Breit aus die Flügel beide,
> O Jesu, meine Freude, . . . (stanza VIII),

and lo! the wild soldier suddenly dropped his arm, stepped to the bed, and laid his rough hand gently on the child's head.   Then going outside he stood guard that none of his troop might harm the cottage.

Although in limited use in the English hymn books, the translations are numerous, as follows:

1. **Quietly rest the woods and dales.**
Omitting stanza VIII by Mrs. Findlater, in *H. L. L.*, 1st Series, 1854, p. 36 (1884, p. 38), included in *Cantate Domino*, Boston, U. S. A., 1859.

2. **Now all the woods are sleeping.**
A full and good translation by Miss Winkworth, in the 2d ed., 1856, of the 1st Series of her *Lyra Ger.*, 1855, p. 228.   Included in full in her *C. B. for England*, 1863, and the Ohio *Luth. Hyl.*, 1880.

3. **Now woods their rest are keeping.**
A translation of stanzas I, III, VIII, IX, by Edward Thring, as no. 18 in the *Uppingham and Sherborne School H. Bk.*, 1874.

4. **Jesu, our Joy and loving Friend.**
A translation of stanza VIII as no. 200 in the Appendix of 1743 to the *Moravian H. Bk.*, 1742.

5. **Now Woods and Fields are quiet.**
In the *Suppl. to Ger. Psal.*, ed. 1765, p. 73.

6. **Display thy both wings over.**
A translation of stanza VIII as no. 156 in pt. I of the *Moravian H. Bk.*, 1754.

7. **Jesus, our Guardian, Guide and Friend.**
A translation of stanza VIII as no. 765 in the *Moravian H. Bk.*, 1789 (1886, no. 1190).

8. **Lo! Man and Beast are sleeping.**
H. J. Buckoll, 1842, p. 76.

9. **Now rest beneath night's shadow.**
E. D. Yeomans, in Schaff's *Kirchenfreund*, 1853, p. 195.

10. **Now rest the woods again.**
Miss Winkworth, 1855, p. 226 (see no. 2 above).

11. **Rise, my soul, thy vigil keep.**
Miss Dunn, 1857, p. 9.

12. **Now resteth all creation.**
J. S. Stallybrass, in the *Tonic Solfa Reporter*, January, 1859, and Curwen's *Harmonium and Organ Book*, 1863, p. 58.

13. **Now every greenwood sleepeth.**
    Miss Manington, 1863, p. 133.

14. **Now hushed are woods and waters.**
    Miss Cox, 1864, p. 9.

15. **Now spread are evening's shadows.**
    J. Kelly, 1863, p. 285.

16. **The woods are hushed; o'er town and plain.**
    Dr. J. Guthrie, 1869.

17. **The duteous day now closeth.**
In the *Yattendon Hymnal*, 1899, thence in *Hymns of the Kingdom of God*, N. Y., 1910, 1916, and the *Hymnal of Praise*, N. Y., 1913.

Quaint and homely as it is, this hymn has done much to enkindle devotion and strengthen grace among Christian readers in Germany, and is now familiar to English-speaking peoples through the beautiful translations of Miss Winkworth and Mrs. Findlater. Both they and Dr. Guthrie have successfully imitated the sweetly domestic tone in poems that have soothed many a careworn spirit at the close of day.

In the version which appeared in her *Lyra Germanica* Miss Winkworth evidently overlooked the fact that line 3 of her first stanza had an extra foot:

O'er field and city, man, and beast.

In the version for church singing printed in her *Chorale Book* the line is changed to the normal six-syllable iambic measure to admit of its being set to the old German melody,[50] "O Welt, ich musz dich laszen."

Gerhardt's stanza VIII, "Breit aus die Flügel beide,"[51] has been a special favorite in Germany, and Lauxmann in *Koch* VIII, 194, says of it:

---

[50] In Mittenwalde, where Gerhardt had a pastoral charge from 1651-1657 (cf. p. 3 ff.), there prevailed the custom of playing an evening hymn from the tower. The one used up to that time was the old and then well-known lay, "Innsbruck, ich musz dich laszen." Gerhardt liked the air, but longed to see it associated with a better and more really evening hymn. For this end he composed "Nun ruhen alle Wälder." The melody was originally composed in 1488(?) by Heinrich Isaac, conductor of the choir of Maximilian I. The great masters Bach and Mozart are reported to have said that they would gladly give their best works for this single tune. In our hymnals it is usually called "Innsbruck," but in German hymn books it is given as "O Welt, ich musz dich laszen," from the first line of the hymn of Johann Hesse, 1855, which was set to it.

[51] Breit aus die Flügel beide
O Jesu, meine Freude,
Und nimm dein Küchlein ein!
Will Satan mich verschlingen,
So lasz die Englein singen:
Dies Kind soll unverletzet sein.

"How many a Christian soul, children mostly, but also God's children in general, does this verse serve as their last evening prayer.   It has often been the last prayer uttered on earth, and in many districts of Germany is used at the close of the baptismal service to commend the dear little ones to the protection of their Lord Jesus."

Miss Winkworth has successfully caught the truly childlike popular spirit of the stanza in the lines:

> My Jesus, stay Thou by me,
> And let no foe come nigh me,
> Safe shelter'd by Thy wing;
> But would the foe alarm me,
> O let him never harm me,
> But still Thine angels round me sing.

Interesting and amusing by its grotesqueness is the Moravian version of this stanza,[52] printed as a separate hymn in the edition of 1754:

> Matt. XXIII, 37.
> Breit aus die flugel beide.
>   *(sic!)*
> Display thy both Wings over
> Thy Chickens and them cover,
>   O Jesu, Savior mild!
> If devils would disturb 'em,
> Let holy angels curb 'em
> And bid them never touch thy Child.

In the rich language in which such hymns were conceived and expressed they possess a force that is not easily retained in a translation especially where as in the present instance there is such an abundance of double rhymes.   Dr. J. Guthrie's version has in England gained some popularity through the melodious rhythm he has given his lines by not restricting himself to Gerhardt's metre,[53] and certainly the iambic line is more suited to an English treatment of the theme of rest and repose.   Note this effect in Guthrie's lines:

> The woods are hushed o'er town and plain (1).
> Now hastes the body to repose (19).
> My laden eyes to slumber yield[54] (31).

---

[52] Founded on *St. Matthew* XXIII, 37.   "O Jerusalem . . . how often would I have gathered thy children together, even as a hen gathereth her chickens under her wings, and ye would not!"

[53] Line 3 in his stanza is the same length as Gerhardt's.

[54] Cf. the same effect in Adelaide Procter's hymn:

> The shadows of the evening hours
> Fall from the dark'ning sky
> Upon the fragrance of the flowers
> The dews of evening lie; etc.

The sound sequence in stanza VIII to which the lines owe some of their popularity Dr. Guthrie has obviously endeavored to imitate by the alliterative,

> My Savior, Shield and Sun!
> When Satan on my soul would spring,

which would indeed do justice to Gerhardt. However a less unpleasant sound than the repeated sibilant which he has used, would suit the English ear better.

As an attempt to translate with scrupulous faithfulness Kelly's version is of some interest. The difficulties in the double rhymes he overcomes by the device of inflectional endings and repetition of pronouns which although at first moderately satisfactory must eventually become monotonous:

declining	hasteth	tirèd
shining	divesteth	expirèd[55]
sing ye	make me	send you
bring ye	o'ertake me	defend you.

Mrs. Findlater has in her version changed the metre of the original for all lines except the third and sixth; in the closing couplet or even the concluding line of each stanza she has more than any other translator reproduced the idea of peaceful repose which was so evidently Gerhardt's intention.

Stanza 3, lines 5 and 6.   When I hear my Lord's command
To leave this earth and upward fly.

Stanza 8, lines 5 and 6.   Give to my beloved sleep,
And angels send to guard their home.

The omission of stanza VIII containing the figure of the hen gathering in her chicks is partially justifiable on the ground that the poem is complete without it, and that such similes while appropriately introduced into hymns of the seventeenth century are out of place in nineteenth century hymnody. On the other hand by this ruthless pruning the distinctive touch that Gerhardt gave the hymn is lost. It is interesting to note in the examination of the various English versions of Gerhardt's poetry the treatment which the "homely element" receives from the translator. The poem under consideration will form a good basis for discussion. Almost invariably the translator offers a paraphrase departing more or less widely from the original and effecting a colorless result: Gerhardt writes in stanza IV :

> Der Leib eilt nun zur Ruhe,
> Legt ab das Kleid und Schuhe.

---

[55] This rhyme occurs in two successive stanzas.

Miss Winkworth renders:

> The body hastes to slumber
> These garments now but cumber.

Mrs. Findlater:

> Now the body seeks for rest
> From its vestments all undrest.

Kelly:

> To rest the body hasteth
> Itself of clothes divesteth.

Guthrie, however, whose version as a whole would doubtless be considered the best literary production, is not content with what is in the German but takes the opportunity offered by the extra syllables in his longer line to describe the vestment more explicitly:

> Now hastes the body to repose
> Throws off its garments, shoes and hose.

Selected Stanzas:

Mrs. Findlater, 1854, in her *Hymns from the Land of Luther.*

> Stanza 1.   Quietly rest the woods and dales,
> Silence round the hearth prevails,
> The world is all asleep;
> Thou, my soul, in thought arise,
> Seek thy Father in the skies,
> And holy vigils with Him keep.

Miss Winkworth, 1863, in her *Chorale Book.*

> Stanza 1.   Now all the woods are sleeping,
> And night and stillness creeping
> O'er (field and) city, man and beast;
> But thou, my heart, awake thee,
> To prayer awhile betake thee,
> And praise thy Maker ere thou rest.

J. Kelly, 1863, in his *Paul Gerhardt's Spiritual Songs.*

> Stanza 1.   Now spread are evening's shadows,
> O'er forests, towns, and meadows,
> And sleepeth every eye;
> Awake my powers and sing ye,
> And pray'r and praises bring ye,
> That your Creator please on high!

J. Guthrie, 1869, in his *Sacred Lyrics.*

> Stanza 1.   The woods are hushed; o'er town and plain,
> O'er man and beast, soft slumbers reign:

The world has gone to rest.
But thou, my soul, my every sense,
Wake up, thy Maker's praise commence,
And be that praise thy best.

In the *Hymnal of Praise,* 1913 (translator's name not given).

Stanza 1.   The duteous day now closeth,
Each flow'r and tree reposeth,
Shade creeps o'er wild and wood.
Let us, as night is falling,
On God, our Maker calling,
Give thanks to Him, the Giver good.

Stanza 2.   Now all the heavenly splendor
Breaks forth in starlight tender
From myriad worlds unknown;
And man, Thy marvel seeing,
Forgets his selfish being
For joy of beauty not his own.

Ein Lämmlein geht und trägt die Schuld.—(*Goed.* 68.)

[*Passiontide.*]

Appeared in *Crü. Praxis,* 1648; thence in *Wackernagel:* no. 13; *Bachmann:* no. 7. Lauxmann in *Koch* VIII, 40, designates it as "the masterpiece of all Passion hymns." It is commonly sung in Germany and was included in the *Unv. L. S.:* 1851, no. 95, but because of the complexity and variety of figures it has not come into extensive English or American use.

English Versions:

1.   **A Lamb goes forth: the sins he bears**
Of every generation.

A translation of stanzas I and II and part of IV by A. T. Russell in his *Psalms and Hymns,* 1851.

2.   **A Lamb goes uncomplaining forth.**

Mrs. Charles' translation (combining Gerhardt's stanzas II and III as 2) appears in her *Voice of Christian Life in Song,* 1858, p. 232. The second part of her version, beginning, "Gate of my heart, fly open wide" (stanza VII), appears in the following: (a) Bishop Ryle's *Collection,* 1860; (b) Reid's *Praise Book,* 1872; (c) *Christian Hymns,* Adelaide, 1872.

3.   **A Lamb bears all its guilt away**
The world thus to deliver.

A full translation by *J. Kelly,* 1867, p. 49. The Ohio *Luth. Hymnal,* 1880, reduces it to 4 stanzas.

4.   **A Lamb goes forth and bears the Guilt**
Of all the world together.

J. Gambold, as no. 241 in part III, 1746, of the *Moravian H. Book.* In part II of the 1754 edition it begins "A Lamb goes forth and on him bears." In the ed. of 1801 it begins "A Lamb *went* forth," etc.   Stanzas V, IX, X, of this version, beginning, "Jesus, I never can forget," are included in E. P. Hood's *Our Hymn Book,* 1868.

**5. A Lamb goes forth and bears the Guilt
    Of Adam's Generations.**

A translation in the *Suppl. to Ger. Psal.,* ed. 1765, and also *Select Hymns from Ger. Psal.,* Tranquebar, 1754.

6. See, bowed beneath a fearful weight.

   Miss Dunn, 1857, p. 32.

7. A Holy, Pure and Spotless Lamb.

Miss Cox, in *Lyra Messianica,* 1864, p. 230, and also in her *Hymns from the German,* 1864, p. 107.

8. Forth goes a dear devoted Lamb.

   Dr. J. Guthrie, in his *Sacred Lyrics,* 1869, p. 82.

9. Behold a Lamb! so tired and faint.

Mrs. E. J. Carr, in *Songs of the Inner Life,* 1871. This version appeared also in Reid's *Praise Book,* 1872, with slight alterations.

10. A Lamb goes forth—for all the dues.

   Catharine Macrea, in Reid's *Praise Book,* 1872, no. 990.

The unusual figures in this Passion Hymn have prevented its receiving in English-speaking countries the wide popularity attained by "O Haupt voll Blut und Wunden."[56]   Yet because of its dealing with a theme that appealed so strongly to Gerhardt and its being so characteristic of his piety and simplicity, a glimpse into the treatment accorded it by English translators should not be without interest.   With hardly less depth of feeling than in "O Haupt voll Blut und Wunden" but with stranger imagery Gerhardt portrays the passion of Christ and reflects upon its significance, and the comfort the Christian derives from it.

The *Moravian Hymn Book* contains Gambold's translation in Gerhardt's metre of nine of the ten stanzas; the seventh, which abounds in metaphors, he has omitted.   Mention has elsewhere[57] been made of Gerhardt's familiarity of tone in addressing the Savior.   Gambold equals his master in this respect; witness stanza 5:

> Whilst I live here, I never shall
> Forget thy Grace amazing;
> Our love shall be reciprocal,
> I also Thee embracing.
> My heart's Light thou shalt be always,

---

[56] Cf. p. 86 ff.
[57] Cf. pp. 18 and 89.

> And when it breaks once (as one says)
> Thou'lt be my Heart thenceforward . . .

The figure in the concluding stanza of the bride clothed in purple is rather spoiled by Gambold by the baldness of the couplet:

> Thy Blood shall of my Weddingdress
> Be then the only splendor.

Nor have we in the German anything to suggest the final lines:

> Then will the Mother, who bore me,
> And nursed me up, my Lamb, for thee,
> Present me as thy Purchase.

Russell's short version of two stanzas presents an effective paraphrase of the last three lines of Gerhardt's stanza IV:

O süszes Lamm, was soll ich dir	O Lamb beloved! How shall I Thee
Erweisen dafür, dasz du mir	Requite for all, thus unto me
Erweisest so viel Gutes?	Such wondrous goodness showing?

Under the title "The sin-bearing Lamb" Dr. Guthrie gives in his *Sacred Lyrics* perhaps the most readable English translation, as it combines Gerhardt's beautiful piety and spiritual simplicity; it is also unique among translations from the German, in that it introduces more of the direct address than is usual, translators preferring as a rule to render quotations in the indirect form:

> "Give me," he says, "the wreath of thorn," etc.

Stanza 7, which Gambold omitted entirely, is the beginning of a hymn in Reid's *Praise Book*. It is a cento taken from Mrs. Charles' very free translation (1858) and is cited here to illustrate the liberties often taken by translators. Here, of course, the free paraphrase is reasonably justifiable:

STANZA 7.

Gerhardt.	Mrs. Charles.
Erweitre dich, mein Herzensschrein,	Gate of my heart, fly open wide—
Du sollt ein Schatzhaus werden	Shrine of my heart, spread forth;
Der Schätze, die viel gröszer sein	The treasure will in thee abide
Als Himmel, Meer und Erden.	Greater than heaven and earth:
Weg mit dem Gold Arabia!	Away with all this poor world's treasures,
Weg Calmus, Myrrhen, Casia!	And all this vain world's tasteless pleasures,
Ich hab ein Bessers funden.	My treasure is in heaven;
Mein groszer Schatz, Herr Jesu Christ	For I have found true riches now,
Ist dieses, was geflossen ist	My treasure, Christ, my Lord, art Thou,
Aus deines Leibes Wunden.	Thy blood so freely given!

Selected Stanzas:

In the *Moravian Hymn Book,* 1754 ed., part II (author's name not given).

Stanza 1.   A Lamb goes forth and on him bears
The Guilt and misdemeanour
Of all the World, and patient wears
The Likeness of a Sinner.

Stanza 2.   Great King! in ev'ry age confest,
Yet never more or greater,
Than when thou with thy Wounds wast drest,
Could I but praise thee better!

J. Gambold, in the 1754 edition of the *Moravian Hymn Book.*

Stanza 1.   A Lamb goes forth, and bears the guilt
Of all the world together,
Most patiently by his Blood spilt
To pay for ev'ry Debtor;
Sickness and toil he on him took,
Went freely to the Slaughter-block
All comfort he refused;
He underwent reproach and blame,
Death on the Cross, and Stripes and shame,
And said, I gladly chuse it.

A. T. Russell, in his *Psalms and Hymns,* 1851.

Stanza 1.   A Lamb goes forth: the sins He bears
Of every generation:
Himself with patience He prepares
To die for every nation.
All faint and weak, behold! He goes,
His life resigning to His foes:
No thought His grief can measure.
He yields to scorn, reproach, disdain,
Wounds, anguish, cross, and dying pain,
And saith, "It is my pleasure."

J. Guthrie, 1869, in his *Sacred Lyrics.*

Stanza 1.   Forth goes a dear devoted Lamb
And dies an expiation
For sinners all, of every name,
Of every age and nation.
Forlorn and faint, behold He gains
The scene of more than deadly pains,
No earthly good possessing:
"Give me," he says, "The wreath of thorn,
The stripes, the curse, the Cross of scorn,
That men may have the blessing."

Warum sollt ich mich denn[58] grämen?—(*Goed.* 122.)

[Cross and Consolation.]

Founded on *Psalm* LXXIII, 23.   Appeared in *Crü.—Runge,* 1653, no. 240, in 12 stanzas of 8 lines; thence in *Wackernagel:* no. 64; *Bachmann:* no. 29; *Crü. Praxis:* 1656, no. 320; *Unv. L. S.:* 1851, no. 784.   Cf. *Koch* IV, 525; VIII, 471-9.

This is a very beautiful hymn but difficult of translation.   It was a source of comfort to the Salzburg emigrants on their way through Swabia in 1732 (cf. Goethe's *Hermann und Dorothea*), and to Frederick William I. of Prussia on his deathbed, May 31, 1740.   The eighth stanza was the last utterance of Gerhardt on the day of his death, May 27, 1676.   It has since cheered and comforted many Christians, both in the season of trial and in the hour of death.   It was joyfully sung by the pious pastor Hosch of Gächingen in Württemberg, when on the 2d of July, 1800, French soldiers had plundered his house, leaving him almost nothing but his harp, with which he accompanied the cheering strains of this hymn.   The words of the seventh stanza:

> Unverzagt und ohne Grauen
> Soll ein Christ, Wo er ist,
> Stets sich laszen schauen. . . .

were spoken by the pious lawyer in Stuttgart, John Jacob Moser, when, in consequence of his fearless remonstrances against injustice, he was called before his sovereign, the Duke of Württemberg, to be sentenced to imprisonment.   The Queen of Poland and Electress of Saxony, Christiana Eberhardina, who died on the 5th of September, 1726, derived great consolation in her dying moments from the eighth stanza which was repeated to her by her chaplain.

English Versions:

1. **Why, my soul, thus trembling ever.**

A good translation of stanzas I, IV, VII, VIII, XI, XII, as no. 232 in the *Anglican H. Bk.,* 1868.   Translated by the Rev. Angelo A. Benson, 1862.

2. **Why should sorrow ever grieve me.**

In full by *J. Kelly,* 1867, p. 214.   His translation of stanzas I, V, X-XII, are repeated in the Ohio *Luth. Hymnal,* 1880, no. 420.

3. **Why should I continue grieving.**

In the *Suppl. to Ger. Psalmody,* ed. 1765, p. 58, in the *Moravian H. Bk.,* 1754, and in the *Supplement* of 1808 to the *Moravian H. Bk.* of 1801, but with stanzas VIII, X, altered and beginning "With undaunted resolution."

4. **Wherefore should I grieve and pine.**

Miss Winkworth in her *Lyra Ger.,* 1858, p. 198.

---

[58] "denn" is probably the authentic reading, although Goedeke prints "doch." Cf. p. 16.

5. **Wherefore, then, should I be gloomy.**
     N. L. Frothingham, 1870, p. 144.

This "Christliches Freudenlied" has an especial interest, for it seems to have been the hymn that was most comforting to Gerhardt. We know that in his last moments[59] he repeated stanza VIII:

> Kann uns doch kein Tod nicht tödten,
> Sondern reiszt Unsern Geist
> Aus viel tausend Nöten;
> Schleuszt das Thor der bittern Leiden
> Und macht Bahn, Da man kann
> Gehn zur Himmelsfreuden.

It was fitting that one whose hymns are so replete with expressions of earthly and the far greater heavenly joys should go to his final rest comforted by the full realization of their meaning.

The translator in the 1754 edition of the *Moravian Hymn Book* has with a few characteristic exceptions treated the peculiar rhythm and metre skillfully. Although the line

> Han't I still Christ my Hill,

(line 2) would not be acceptable to-day, still our attention is forcibly drawn to the rhythm and note of genuine fervor in the reproduction of our poet's last words:

> Conquered Death cannot destroy us,
> But cuts short grief and Smart
> That doth here annoy us;
> Shuts the door on sin and sadness
> And makes way for the Day
> Of eternal gladness.

John Kelly in his *Paul Gerhardt's Spiritual Songs* although he does not retain much of the lyric grace of the original translates the poem with scrupulous faithfulness. His stanza 8 suffers greatly by comparison with that of the Moravian version given above.

> Death can never kill us even,
>   But relief
>   From all grief
>   To us then is given.
> It does close life's mournful story
>   Make a way
>   That we may
>   Pass to heavenly glory.

---

[59] Cf. p. 5.

Selected Stanzas:

In the 1754 edition of the *Moravian Hymn Book* (author's name not given).

> Stanza 1.   Why should I continue grieving,
>   Han't I still Christ my Hill,
>   And my Savior living?
>   Who'll deprive me of Salvation
>   Which by Faith Jesus hath
>   Giv'n in expectation?

John Kelly in his *Paul Gerhardt's Spiritual Songs,* 1867.

> Stanza 1.   Why should sorrow ever grieve me?
>   Christ is near
>   What can here
>   E'er of Him deprive me?
>   Who can rob me of my heaven
>   That God's Son
>   As mine own
>   To my faith hath given?

Miss Winkworth in her *Lyra Germanica,* 1858.

> Stanza 1.   Wherefore should I grieve and pine?
>   Is not Christ the Lord still mine?
>   Who can sever me from Him?
>   Who can rob me of the heaven
>   Which the Son of God hath given
>   Unto faith though weak and dim?

Wir singen dir, Emanuel.—(*Goed.* 150.)
[*Christmas.*]

Included in *Crü. Praxis,* 1653, no. 100 in 16 stanzas of 4 lines. In *Ebeling,* 1667, 5, no. 52, four stanzas were added as IV, VIII, IX, XVII. The complete text in 20 stanzas is in *Wackernagel:* no. 10; *Bachmann:* no. 42; *Unv. L. S.:* 1851, no. 58. Cf. *Koch* IV, 136.

English Versions:

1. **Emmanuel, we sing Thy praise.**
This translation of stanzas I-III, V-VII, XVIII-XX, appeared in the *British Magazine,* January, 1838, p. 35. Repeated, omitting the translation of stanza XIX, and beginning "Emmanuel, Thy name we sing," in *Kennedy,* 1863.

2. **Immanuel, we sing to Thee.**
A translation of stanzas I-III, V, by A. T. Russell in the *Dalston Hospital H. Bk.,* 1848.

3. **Immanuel, we sing to Thee, Of life,** etc.

A translation of stanzas I-III, VI, XX, based on the earlier versions, in J. F. Thrupp's *Psalms and Hymns,* 1853, no. 35.

4. **Thee, O Immanuel, we praise.**

A good translation of stanzas I-III, V-VII, XVIII-XX, by Miss Winkworth, in her *Lyra Ger.,* First Series, 1855, p. 28. In her 2d ed., 1856, p. 24, she added a translation of stanza IX, and thus in her *C. B. for England,* 1863, no. 35. Repeated, abridged, in the *Hyl. for St. John's,* Aberdeen, 1870, and Flett's *Collection,* Paisley, 1871; and beginning "With all Thy saints, Thee, Lord, we sing" (stanza II), in Boardman's *Selections,* Philadelphia, 1861.

5. **We sing to Thee, Emmanuel, The Prince,** etc.

A good translation of stanzas I-III, V-VII, XVIII-XX, by Miss Cox, contributed to *Lyra Messianica,* 1864, p. 55, and in her own *Hymns from the German,* 1864, p. 35. In Schaff's *Christ in Song,* 1869, p. 56, it is in full, and in Jellicoe's *Collection,* 1867, omitting the translation of stanza V. In the Amer. *Bapt. Hy. & Tune Bk.,* 1871, it begins, 'All glory, worship, thanks and praise" (stanzas II, III, XIX, XX).

6. **We sing to Thee, Immanuel! Thou Prince of Life.**

A translation of stanzas I, II, XIX, XX, signed "F. C. C.," as no. 26 in Dr. Pagenstecher's *Collection,* 1864.

7. **We sing to Thee, Immanuel, Thou Prince of Life.**

As no. 109 in part III, 1748, of the *Moravian H. Bk.* (1754, part I, no. 436).

8. **Immanuel, to Thee we sing, Thou Prince,** etc.

L. E. Schlecht, in the *Moravian H. Bk.,* 1789, no. 45 (1886, no. 45).

9. **Immanuel! Thy praise we sing.**

Miss Fry, 1859, p. 163.

10. **To Thee, Immanuel, we sing, The Prince,** etc.

Miss Manington, 1864, p. 36.

11. **Immanuel! to Thee we sing, The Fount.**

J. Kelly, 1867, p. 37.

Few of the English versions of German hymns which appear in the old Moravian hymn books rise above a mediocre grade; many on account of their crudity deserve only passing mention, others are interesting merely by way of comparison with later renderings. The editions up to that of 1886 published no authors' names and it is now largely a matter of conjecture as to who may have written these earlier versions. Rarely did the translators succeed in giving even a fair impression of the original, and we suspect that imperfect knowledge of the exact meaning of the German or even indifference to the effect their versions produced may too often have been the cause of the crude and even grotesque language.

The translator of this Christmas hymn has, however, been a notable exception; choosing from Gerhardt's discursive strophes the most significant ideas, he has developed a poem of seven stanzas superior to most contemporary hymns from the German. The correspondence of strophes is as follows:

Gerhardt:	I	II	VII VI	VII VIII	VI IX	XI	XX
Mor. Hy. Bk.:	1	2	3	4	5	6	7

Especially happy are the epithets in lines 3 and 4:

Du Himmelsblum und Morgenstern, Thou Morning-star, thou Eden's Flow'r
Du Jungfrausohn Herr aller Herrn. The Lord of Lords, whom Mary bore!

The modern reader will enjoy the orthography in the lines:

Dost thou a stranger *chuse to be* (stanza 3),
and Thou *cloathest* all (stanza 3).

though he will recoil at the pronunciation of the first two lines of stanza 5:

Thou in a manger ly'st with beasts,
There thou a little Infant rest'st.

Stanza 6, a free paraphrase of stanza XI in the original, reproduces admirably the childlike confidence with which Gerhardt writes. The translator appreciates keenly the personal tone which pervades the poem when he sings:

I thank thee, loving Lamb! that thou
On my account didst stoop so low;
And as thy Spirit gives me grace,
I'll be thy Servant, if thou please.

In her *Chorale Book* and set to the old tune "Erschienen ist der herrlich Tag,"[60] Miss Winkworth gives the following arrangement of her ten-stanza version:

Gerhardt:	I	II	III	V	VI	IX	VII	XVIII	XIX	XX
Winkworth:	1	2	3	4	5	6	7	8	9	10

Stanza 9 shows how successfully she can imitate Gerhardt's simplicity and fervor; even the alliteration finds a partial correspondence in her third line:

Gerhardt (stanza XIX).	Winkworth (stanza 9).
Du bist mein Haupt; hinwiederum	Thou art my Head, my Lord Divine,
Bin ich dein Glied und Eigentum	I am Thy member, wholly Thine,
Und will, so viel dein Geist mir gibt,	And in Thy Spirit's strength would still
Stets dienen dir, wie dirs geliebt.	Serve Thee according to Thy will.

So also in stanza 10 (*Gerhardt* XX) for Gerhardt's favorite expression "für und für" we find a very happy equivalent, and also an exact rhyme which the German lacks:

---

[60] By Nicolaus Heermann (d. 1560).

Gerhardt (stanza XX).

Ich will dein Alleluja hier
Mit Freuden singen für und für,
Und dort in deinem Ehrensaal
Solls schallen ohne Zeit und Zahl.

Winkworth (stanza 10).

Thus will I sing Thy praises here
With joyful spirit *year by year;*
And they shall sound before thy throne,
Where time nor number more are known.

Miss Cox, whose translation of Gellert's Easter hymn

Jesus lives, thy terror now
Can no longer, Death, appal us,

is so well known, has given us one of the best modern versions of this Christmas hymn of Gerhardt's.   Her stanzas correspond as follows:

Gerhardt:	I	II	III	V	VI	VII	XVIII	XIX	XX
Cox:	1	2	3	4	5	6	7	8	9

Miss Cox makes a less personal appeal to the worshipper and thereby loses much that is so excellent and characteristic of Gerhardt; instead of keeping the pronoun in the singular, "So fasz *ich*" (stanza XVIII) "Du bist *mein* Haupt" (stanza XIX) and *"Ich* will dein Alleluja" (stanza XX), she has respectively *"Our* love grows bold," "Thou art *our* Head," and *"Our* hallelujahs."   If her poem is rather more polished, Gerhardt's is certainly the more direct, as witness these stanzas:

Gerhardt (stanza VII).

Du kehrst in fremder Hausung ein,
Und sind doch alle Himmel dein;
Trinkst Milch aus deiner Mutter Brust
Und bist doch selbst der Engel Lust.

Cox (stanza 6).

Thou who both heaven and earth dost sway,
In strangers' inn are fain to stay;
And though thy power makes angels blest,
Dost seek thy food from human breast.

The concluding stanza is inferior to the others and suffers by comparison with the excellent lines of Miss Winkworth cited above: it is a very free paraphrase and leaves the impression of having been hastily constructed:

As each short year goes quickly round,
Our hallelujahs shall resound;
And when we reckon years no more,
May we in heaven thy name adore!

Selected Stanzas:

From the *Moravian Hymn Book,* 1754.

Stanza 1.   We sing to thee Immanuel!
Thou Prince of life, salvation's well!
Thou Morning-star, thou Eden's Flow'r
The Lord of Lords whom Mary bore!
                              Hallelujah.

Stanza 2.   We sing thee 'midst thy chosen race
             With all our strength we give thee praise;
             That thou so long expected guest
             Didst come to visit us at last.

Frances Elizabeth Cox, 1864, in the Schaff-Gilman *Library of Religious Poetry*.

Stanza 1.   We sing to thee, Emmanuel,
             The Prince of life, salvation's well,
             The plant of heaven, the star of morn,
             The Lord of Lords, the virgin-born!

Stanza 2.   All glory, worship, thanks, and praise,
             That thou art come in these our days!
             Thou heavenly guest, expected long,
             We hail thee with a joyful song.

Miss Winkworth in her *Lyra Germanica*, 1865, p. 24.

1.   Thee, O Immanuel, we praise,
      The Prince of Life, and Fount of Grace,
      The Morning Star, the Heavenly Flower,
      The Virgin's Son, the Lord of Power!

      With all Thy saints, Thee, Lord, we sing,
      Praise, honour, thanks to Thee we bring,
      That Thou, O long-expected guest,
      Hast come at last to make us blest!

      E'er since the world began to be,
      How many a heart hath longed for Thee;
      Long years our fathers hoped of old
      Their eyes might yet Thy Light behold.

Befiehl du deine Wege.—(*Goed.* 185.)
[*Trust in God.*]

Appeared in *Crü. Praxis*, 1656, no. 333; *Wackernagel:* no. 66; *Bachmann:* no. 72 in 12 stanzas of 8 lines; *Unv. L. S.:* 1851, no. 620.

Lauxmann, in *Koch* VIII, 392, calls this hymn "the most comforting of all the hymns that have resounded on Paulus Gerhardt's golden lyre, sweeter to many souls than honey and the honey-comb." It is an acrostic on Luther's version of *Psalm* XXXVII, 5, "Befiehl dem Herren deine Wege und hoffe auf ihn, er wirds wohl machen," formed by the initial words of the stanzas, those of the *Wackernagel* edition being printed in blacker type. This acrostic form has been preserved by Jacobi and Stallybrass.

According to tradition Gerhardt wrote the hymn in a Saxon village to console his wife after they had been compelled to leave Berlin. But the hymn was printed as early as 1653, and although Gerhardt had to give up his position in 1666,[61] he did not leave Berlin until his appointment to Lübben in 1669, while his wife died in Berlin in 1668. Hence there appear to be two good reasons for discrediting this story. We must assume, therefore, that the hymn was written during the Mittenwalde period when as yet he could have had no thought of a position in Berlin. The perfection of the hymn is strikingly evinced by the fact that it soon spread through Germany, finding its way into all hymn books and ranking as one of the finest hymns of its class. Lauxmann relates that it was sung when the foundation stone of the first Lutheran church at Philadelphia was laid, May 2, 1743, and again on October 20, when Muhlenberg, the father of the American Lutheran Church, held the opening service.

English Versions:

1. Commit thou all thy griefs.

A very free but spirited rendering omitting stanzas V, IX-XI, by J. Wesley in his *Hymns and Sacred Poems,* 1739 (P. Works, 1869-72, vol. I, p. 125), in 8 stanzas of 8 lines. Wesley has here caught, far more successfully than any other, the real ring and spirit of Gerhardt. His translation has been included in many hymn books and collections, and has come into very extended use, but generally abridged. In the *United Presb. H. Bk.,* 1852, it began "To God commit thy griefs." It is also found under these headings:

(a) Thou on the Lord rely (stanza III).
(b) Thy everlasting truth (stanza V).
(c) Give to the winds thy fears (stanza IX). (This is the heading under which it appears in most American hymnals. Cf. p. 202.)
(d) O cast away thy fears (stanza IX altered).
(e) Through waves and clouds and storms (stanza X).
(f) Leave to his sovereign sway (stanza XIII).
(g) Thou seest our weakness, Lord (stanza XV).
(h) Put thou thy trust in God.

This last is a greatly altered cento with the stanza arrangement as follows:

Wesley:	III	I	III	V
Cento:	1	2	3	4

In this form also it has appeared in many hymnals.

2. Commit thy way, confiding.

A complete translation by Dr. H. Mills in the *Evang. Review,* Gettysburg, July, 1849, and his *Horae Ger.,* 1856, p. 172. His stanzas I, II, VI, XII, were included in the Lutheran General Synod's *Hymns,* 1852, and I, II, V, VI, XI, XII, in the Ohio *Luth Hymnal,* 1880.

3. Thy way and all thy sorrows,
Give thou into His hand.

A complete translation by Rev. A. T. Russell as no. 233 in his *Psalms and Hymns,* 1851, in 3 parts. Part II begins "In vain the powers of darkness / Thy will, O God,

---

[61] Cf. p. 4 f.

oppose": (Gerhardt's stanza V). Part III (Gerhardt's stanza IX) begins "Awhile his consolation / He will to thee deny."

4. Commit thy way to God.

A translation omitting stanzas IX, X, XII, by Mrs. Charles in her *Voice of Christian Life in Song*, 1858, p. 239. A cento of her version (Gerhardt's stanzas I, II, VI, VIII, XI) appears as no. 138 in Jellicoe's *Collection*, 1867, and another cento (Gerhardt's I, VI-VIII, XI) appears as no. 283 in Bishop Ryle's *Collection*, 1860.

5. Commit thy way, O weeper.

A free paraphrase in 6 stanzas of 4 lines by J. S. Stallybrass for the *Tonic-Solfa Reporter*, July, 1857, repeated in Curwen's *Child's Own H. Bk.*, 1862 and 1874.

6. Commit thou every sorrow, And care.

A translation of stanzas I-III, XII, by Miss Borthwick in Dr. Pagenstecher's *Collection*, 1864, no. 240.

7. Commit thy Ways and Goings.

J. C. Jacobi, 1720, 1722, 1732.

8. Commit thou thy each grievance.

In part I of the *Moravian H. Bk.*, 1754 and 1849.

9. Commit thy ways, thy sorrows.

Mrs. Stanley Carr in her translation of *Wildenhahn's Paul Gerhardt*, 1845 and 1856.

10. Commit thy secret grief.

Miss Dunn, 1857, p. 89.

11. Commend thy way, O mortal.

In Madame de Pontes's *Poets and Poetry of Germany*, 1858, vol. I, p. 424.

12. Commit thou all thy ways, and all.

Mrs. Bevan, 1859, p. 124.

13. Commit thy way unto the Lord, thy heavy.

Dr. R. P. Dunn in *Sacred Lyrics from the German*, Philadelphia, 1859, p. 85.

14. To God thy way commending.

Miss Cox, 1864, p. 161; and in the Gilman-Schaff *Lib. of Rel. Poetry*, 1883, p. 510.

15. Commit whatever grieves thee.

J. Kelly, 1867, p. 225.

16. Commit thy way, O weeping.

Dr. J. Guthrie in his *Sacred Lyrics*, 1869, p. 92.

17. Commit the way before thee,

N. L. Frothingham, 1870, p. 164.

18. Commit thy course and keeping.

Dr. John Cairns, c. 1850, but first published in Edinburgh, 1881, as an eight-page tract.

In the interesting and now very rare old *Psalmodia Germanica*[62] compiled and edited by J. C. Jacobi there are three of Gerhardt's hymns—"Wie
soll ich dich empfangen," "Wach auf, mein Herz, und singe," and "Befiehl
du deine Wege." The book is dedicated to

> "Their Royal Highnesses,
> Princess ANNE
> Pincess AMALIA,
> (*sic!*)
> AND
> Princess CAROLINA,"

and in one paragraph of this dedication we read:

"As a sincere Desire to promote Divine Psalmody has prompted me to
this Translation; so I presume to address the same, such as it is to YOUR
ROYAL HIGHNESSES, for no other End than to promote thereby
the Singing the Praises of our blessed Redeemer"; etc.

In most cases facing the beginning page of the hymns is an inserted leaf
(not numbered) containing the traditional melody unharmonized. It is a
reasonably safe conjecture that these books of Jacobi were among the very
first printed copies of anglicized German hymns, and the historical value
and interest of the books themselves as well as the versions they contain
cannot be overestimated.

The version of "Befiehl du deine Wege" is so free a paraphrase, combining, as it does, in the five stanzas ideas from the twelve of the original,
and introducing new elements altogether, that except for the first and fifth
strophes it is difficult to connect the themes definitely with any particular
lines in Gerhardt's poem. The correspondence seems, however, to be
approximately as follows:

Jacobi:	I	II	III	IV	V
Gerhardt:	1	2 5	7	7 3 4 8 10	12

Which line of Gerhardt suggests the injunction "Shake off that yoke of
Hell" (2, 6) is not clear: possibly here Jacobi had in mind the scriptural
passage (*Psalm* XXXVII, 5, ff.) where in verse 8 we read "Cease from
anger, and forsake wrath." Stanza 4:

> And he shall clear the Dullness
> That sits upon thy Mind

---

[62] 1st ed. 1720, later eds. in 1722 and 1732. Through the kindness of the Hartford
Theological Seminary Library it was the privilege of the writer to have access to the
1722 edition.

perhaps finds its basis in stanza VII:

> . . . was das Herze
> Betrübt und traurig macht!

or in stanza VIII:

> Wann Er   . . .
> Das Werk hinausgeführet,
> Das dich bekümmert hat.

To conclude his hymn, Jacobi again, as in strophe 2, dwells upon the punishment for sin, entirely an interpolation of his own, with no bearing on the original whatever:

> Redeem us all together
> From Sin, World, Death, and Hell.

Finally it must be said that for the modern reader this version must seem little more than a distorted paraphrase, made still further difficult of interpretation and appreciation through the use of words far more remote from our modern English than is the German vernacular of the seventeenth century from the modern German.   Phrases such as:

> His Fatherly Dilection
> is never at a stand (3, lines 7 and 8)

and

> Our Life and Conversation
> Lead by Thy Holy Hand (5, lines 5 and 6)

seem not well calculated to carry out the hope that the translator utters on the last page of his "dedication":

"If the Lover of Psalmody, can find in these Hymns an edifying Sunday's Entertainment, which, it seems, has hitherto been too much wanting in Abundance of Families, the Translator will think his Time well bestow'd, . . ."

In another chapter[63] mention has been made of the relation of John and Charles Wesley to the Moravians.   It is altogether probable that it was the singing of this hymn with its reference to winds and seas that first appealed to these Englishmen when on their voyage to America on the same vessel with a company of Moravians.   John Wesley's version (1739) is the second of the three earliest translations of this hymn which has come into such extensive use both in Germany and English-speaking lands.   A number of changes have been made by the translator, but in general the main features

---

[63] Cf. p. 31.

are quite faithfully reflected.   Firstly he has divided the 8-line strophes into quatrains, has disregarded the feminine rhymes of lines 1 and 3 and changed to iambic tetrameter the original iambic trimeter ending in a feminine rhyme.   These variations enable him often to introduce an additional thought, e. g. in line 3 "To his *sure truth* and tender care," where in Gerhardt there is only the idea of *"faithful care."*   Again he profits by being able better to express in English the more pithy German; for example, in stanza 14: "When fully he the work hath wrought" reproduces very acceptably the idea contained in the compound "hinausgeführt."

Omitting stanza V Wesley gives a free but spirited version of the stanza beginning

> Hoff, O du arme Seele
> Hoff und sei unverzagt . . .

as

> Give to the winds thy fears
> Hope and be undismayed
> God hears thy sighs and counts thy tears
> God shall lift up thy head.[64]

Omitting also stanzas IX-XI inclusive, in which the original emphasizes or repeats in sameness of strain the thoughts of the earlier part of the poem, Wesley offers in his final strophe a strong conclusion, though he departs from the idea of Gerhardt's theme of *distress* for which termination is besought, and dwells upon the *weakness* to which man is prone.   While Gerhardt asks to be guided to Heaven, to be *entrusted* ("empfohlen") to God's care, which one would expect for the appropriate conclusion of a poem beginning *"Befiehl* du deine Wege," Wesley prays only that God's children may *remember* His care:

> Let us, in life, in death,
> Thy steadfast truth declare
> And publish, with our latest breath,
> Thy love and guardian care!

The nearest date that can be set for the other early English translation of this most famous of Gerhardt's hymns is 1754 in the *Moravian Hymn Book* of that year where it appeared without the name of the author.   It is very likely the work of the editor himself, Dr. J. Gambold; for it has many of the characteristics of other hastily made translations in his collection of "German Hymns in the Seventeenth Century."   Many of the hymns of the early and exuberant development of Moravian hymnody seem at first sight like a highly-colored and almost morbid growth that had been grafted from without upon the stem of English church song.   If the immediate impres-

---

[64] Cf. p. 124.

sion this version makes is that of foreignness owing to its phraseology,[65] it must be remembered that in reality these efforts are part of a new development of a real spiritual life, at first perverted into fantastic forms, but certainly capable of culture and ultimately becoming a characteristic and permanent type of English hymn.   An unbiassed critic must concede that the whole atmosphere of this hymn in spite of its crudity is still that of childlike simplicity and tender devotion to Christ.

The author has rendered all stanzas but the fifth ("Und ob gleich alle Teufel," etc.), omitting this possibly because Wesley before him (1739) had omitted it.   The stanza is not far inferior to its prototype, stanza III[66] of Luther's "Ein' feste Burg," and would seem worthy of being included. The diction of the concluding lines shows evidently the influence of Wesley, who, as has been seen, departs here widely from the idea of Gerhardt. Wesley has:

> Let us, in life, in death,
> Thy steadfast truth declare,
> And publish, with our latest breath,
> Thy love and guardian care!

The Moravian version reads:

> Till, and beyond death's valley
> Let us thy *Truth declare*
> Yea then emphatically
> Boast of thy Guardian care.

Miss Cox preserves the eight-line form and the original metre in her complete translation of the twelve stanzas.   Taken as a whole her appeal is far less direct than Wesley's, her sentences and the ideas contained in them being much more involved.   On the other hand, in the very first quatrain her word "Trust" gives the keynote of the whole poem at once, a touch that the original certainly contains and which no other translator has successfully reproduced in the first stanza.   Strophe IX which is among those passed over by Wesley finds here a good English parallel in what appears to be a well-studied rendering:

> Gerhardt: Er wird zwar eine Weile
> Mit seinem Trost verziehen . . .

---

[65] Cf. Stanza 2.   Rely on God who good is
Fix on his work thy notice.
Stanza 8.   Sometimes he his Assistance
Does not directly show.
Stanza 9.   When least thou hop'st that Favour
He extricate thee will.

[66] Und wenn die Welt voll Teufel wär
Und wollt uns gar verschlingen, etc.

Cox: Awhile, perchance to try thee,
      He seems to hear thee not,
      All comfort to deny thee,
      As if thou wert forgot; . . .

But undeniably the closest parallel, showing too that she was at home
in both languages, is the concluding stanza.   Where others fail her translation here excels in that it follows the idea which Gerhardt emphasizes
throughout the poem, that of the heart *trusting*[67] in God:

End if thou wilt our sorrow,
And our probation close;
Till then we fain would borrow
Strength to support life's woes:
To thee *our way commending,*
Whose wisdom orders best,
We tread the pathway tending
To heaven's eternal rest.

Much of the native beauty and lyric grace of this charming hymn is to
be found in one of the less well known translations—that of Dr. John
Guthrie (1869).   He very appropriately designates the hymn "The Tri-
umph of Trust," and seems to have divined Gerhardt's meaning and use
of "Trost"[68] as being that comfort which has its source in Trust and Faith.
Note Guthrie's treatment of this theme in stanza 2:

Trust him and soon with wonder
His goodness shalt thou see
. . . Tis *faith* and prayer and waiting
That draw the blessing down.

or again in stanza 8 where the true "Stimmung" is present:

Trust Him to guard and guide thee,
And bid thy troubles flee
Trust Him, whate'er betide thee . . .

Not as successful in the concluding quatrain as Miss Cox, but nevertheless sensible of what Gerhardt intended to be the closing theme, as has been
noted already, Dr. Guthrie gives us this couplet:

That on thy care depending,
We heavenward still may go, . . .

Dr. John Kelly's version adheres more closely than any other to the metre
and language, but it would be impossible by this means to popularize for the

---

[67] Lasz . . . uns . . . deiner Pflege . . . empfohlen sein (stanza XII).
[68] For a discussion of Gerhardt's use of the word "Trost" cf. p. 22.

English reader Gerhardt's poetry.   The translator's effects are altogether too labored, as is apparent in stanza 2 where the only virtue is the very doubtful one of the retention of the feminine rhyme:

> The Lord thou must repose on
> If thou wouldst prosper sure,
> His work must ever gaze on
> If thine is to endure.

Throughout the poem occurs the same defect, a forcing of the rhyme:

evil	graciously	misery
cavil	early see	may we

In the last quatrain Kelly fails, as do the other translators, to bring out Gerhardt's strong repetition of the dominating theme, ending with the very inferior couplet

> So come we where prepar'd for
> Us is our bless'd abode.

Another translation that, like Kelly's is somewhat ultra-faithful to the original metres is that of Dr. A. T. Russell (1851).   He has divided the hymn into three separate poems:

> Part I, stanzas I, II, III, IV.
> Part II, stanzas V, VI, VII, VIII.
> Part III, stanzas IX, X, XI, XII.

In the very passage where others have made their poorest offering Russell has been unusually successful, namely in the last quatrain of stanza II ("Mit Sorgen und mit Grämen," etc.):

> God yieldeth nought to sorrow
> And self-tormenting care:
> Nought, nought with Him availeth;—
> No power save that of prayer.

He has obtained literality in a marked degree in the fourth stanza as a close examination will show:

Weg hast du allerwegen,	Thy way is ever open;
An Mitteln fehlt dirs nicht;	Thou dost on nought depend;
Dein Thun ist lauter Segen,	Thine act is only blessing;
Dein Gang ist lauter Licht,	Thy path light without end,
Dein Werk kann niemand hindern,	Thy work can no man hinder,
Dein Arbeit darf nicht ruhn,	Thy purpose none can stay,
Wann du, was deinen Kindern	Since Thou to bless Thy children
Ersprieszlich ist, willst thun.	Through all dost make a way.

The success is plainly due to the fortunate choice of Anglo-Saxon equivalents and the coincidence of verse accent and important words.   Contrast with this in Miss Cox's otherwise good translation her only poor stanza, all but unintelligible to modern readers through the use of the obsolete word "let" (line 6) for "hindrance."

> Stanza 4.   Resources rich possessing,
> That love still finds a way,
> Thy every act a blessing,
> Thy pathway cloudless day;
> In one unbroken tissue,
> Which no *let* e'er withstood,
> It brings to happy issue
> Plans for thy children's good.

It is unfortunate that a version so excellent in other respects should include this wide departure from the fervor and whole-heartedness of Gerhardt.

One final observation is interesting that in his last strophe Russell offers a compromise between Wesley's interpretation and that of Miss Cox:

> Thy truth and Thy protection
> Forevermore we pray:
> With these in heavenly glory
> Shall end our certain way.

This prayer for protection is closer to Gerhardt's lines and therefore better than Wesley's bold paraphrase, but it falls far short of the simple and forceful conclusion of Miss Cox:

> To Thee our way commending,
> Whose wisdom orders best,
> We tread the pathway tending
> To heaven's eternal rest.

Selected Stanzas:

J. C. Jacobi in *Psalmodia Germanica,* 1722.

I.

> Commit thy Ways and Goings,
> And all that grieves thy Soul.
> To him, whose wisest Doings
> Rule all without Controul:
> He makes the Times and Seasons
> Revolve from Year to Year
> And knows Ways, Means, and Reasons
> When Help shall best appear.

(Note: In the wording accompanying the musical score the second line reads "And all *what* grieves thy Soul.")

J. Wesley, 1739, in the Schaff-Gilman *Library of Religious Poetry.*

I.

Commit thou all thy griefs
And ways into his hands,
To his sure truth and tender care,
Who earth and heaven commands.

II.

Who points the clouds their course,
Whom winds and seas obey,
He shall direct thy wandering feet,
He shall prepare thy way.

The cento given in most American hymnals:

Stanza 1.   Give to the winds thy fears;
Hope, and be undismayed;
God hears thy sighs and counts thy tears;
God shall lift up thy Head.

Stanza 2.   Through waves and clouds and storms,
He gently clears thy way;
Wait thou His time, so shall this night
Soon end in joyous day.

Stanza 3.   What though thou rulest not,
Yet heaven and earth and hell
Proclaim, God sitteth on the throne,
And ruleth all things well.

Stanza 4.   Far, far above thy thought
His counsel shall appear,
When fully He the work hath wrought
That caused thy needless fear.

In the *Moravian Hymn Book,* 1754 (by Gambold, himself?).

Stanza 1.   Commit thou thy each grievance
And Case into his Hands,
To his sure Care and guidance,
Who heav'n and earth commands:
He who's the Clouds Director,
Whom Winds and seas obey,
He'll be thy feet's Protector,
He shall prepare thy Way.

(Note: the orthography of the *Moravian Hymn Book* has been retained.)

A. T. Russell, in his *Psalms and Hymns,* 1851.

Stanza 1.   Thy way and all thy sorrows,
Give thou into His hand,—

His gracious care unfailing,
Who doth the heavens command.
Their course and path He giveth
To clouds and air and wind:
A way thy feet may follow,
He too for Thee will find.

H. Mills, 1856, in his *Horae Germanicae.*

Stanza 1.   Commit Thy way, confiding,
When trials here arise,
To Him whose hand is guiding
The tumults of the skies:
There, clouds and tempests raging,
Have each its path assign'd,—
Will God for thee engaging,
No way of safety find?

Frances Elizabeth Cox, 1864, in the Schaff-Gilman *Library of Religious Poetry.*

I.

To God Thy way commending
Trust him whose arm of might,
The heavenly circles bending,
Guides every star aright:
The winds and clouds and lightning
By his sure hand are led;
And he will, dark shades brightening,
Show thee what path to tread.

J. Kelly, 1867, in his *Paul Gerhardt's Spiritual Songs.*

Stanza 1.   Commit whatever grieves thee
At heart, and all thy ways,
To Him who never leaves thee,
On whom creation stays.
Who freest courses maketh
For clouds, and air, and wind,
And care who ever taketh
A path for thee to find.

J. Guthrie, 1869, in his *Sacred Lyrics.*

Stanza 1.   Commit thy way, O weeping
And care-encumbered soul,
To His all-trusty keeping,
Who guides the glowing pole.
No cloud or wind fleets o'er thee
But God directs its flow;
That God will cleave before thee
A path wherein to go.

Mrs. Charles, 1858, in Bishop's Ryle's Collection of *Hymns and Spiritual Songs,* 1883.

Stanza 1.   Commit thy way to God;
The weight which makes thee faint—
Words are to Him no load!
To Him breathe thy complaint.
He who for winds and clouds
Maketh a pathway free,
Through wastes or hostile crowds
Can make a way for thee.

Ist Gott für mich, so trete.—(*Goed.* 229.)
[*Trust in God.*]

Based on *Romans,* VIII, 31-39. Cf. *Koch,* IV, 457. Included in *Crü. Praxis,* 1656, no. 330; thence in *Wackernagel:* no. 63; *Unv. L. S.:* no. 418. Lauxmann, in *Koch,* VIII, 408, quotes Langbecker: "This heroic hymn of Gerhardt's is worthy to be placed side by side with Luther's 'Ein' feste Burg.'"

The poem was written undoubtedly at the time when the Elector, Frederick William of Brandenburg, Gerhardt's sovereign, threatened with his severe displeasure those of the Lutheran clergy who would not sign a declaration[69] binding them not to say anything publicly against the Reformed party.   To this, most probably, the words of the thirteenth stanza refer,

Kein Zorn der groszen Fürsten
Soll mir ein Hindrung sein.

This hymn, springing from a heart full of faith and courage, has gone to the hearts of many, especially the tried and afflicted, cheering and encouraging them in the struggles of faith.   The third stanza in particular has often been made a blessing:

Der Grund, da ich mich gründe,
Ist Christus und sein Blut; . . .

A pious watchman in Berlin who, when calling the hours of the night, used to sing suitable verses, once sang these lines before the house of a shoemaker, who with some friends, just then assembled late at night, was in danger of leaving the Church and setting up a self-righteous sect.   The well-known words, coming so unexpectedly, had the desired effect, the shoemaker declaring to his friends, "As for me, I will rest upon that

---

[69] Cf. p. 4.

ground of Jesus and his blood, and not seek any other master." The final stanza:

> Mein Herze geht in Springen
> Und kann nicht traurig sein, . . .

has been the dying song of many a believing Christian.

English Versions:

1. If God be on my side.

A good translation omitting stanzas IV-VI, by Miss Winkworth in her *Lyra Ger.*, 1855, p. 130. Included, abridged, in *Holy Song*, 1869, and the *Evang. Hyl.*, 1880, N. Y.

Centos from this translation are:

(a) "If Jesus be my friend" (stanza I, line 5), in the *Andover Sabbath H. Bk.*, 1858; Hatfield's *Church Book*, 1872, etc.

(b) "Since Jesus is my friend" (stanza I, line 5 altered), in Robinson's *Songs for the Sanctuary*, N. Y., 1865; *Laudes Domini*, 1884, etc.

(c) "Here I can firmly rest" (stanza II), in the *Andover Sabbath H. Bk.*, 1858; Pennsylvanian Lutheran *Church Book*, 1868.

2. If God Himself be for me.

A good translation omitting stanzas IV-VI, X, by R. Massie in his *Lyra Domestica*, 1864, p. 110; from this are varying centos, e. g. *Laudes Domini*, 1884, no. 378 beginning: "I build on this foundation" (stanza III).

3. Is God for me? I fear not.

A free but spirited version, omitting stanzas V, XI, XII, by Mrs. Bevan in her *Songs of Eternal Life*, 1858, p. 39. This version was repeated and abridged in Snepp's *Songs of Grace and Glory*. In Reid's *Praise Book*, 1872, it appears as three hymns, the first as above; (2) "There is no condemnation" (stanza VI), and (3) "In heaven is mine inheritance" (stanza X).

4. Is God for me? t'oppose me.

In full, by J. Kelly, 1867, p. 208. The Ohio *Luth. Hyl.* includes a part of this version, i. e. the translation of stanzas III, XIV, XV, beginning "My Faith securely buildeth."

5. Is God for me? what is it.

J. C. Jacobi, 1725, p. 41 (1732, p. 139). Included in the *Moravian H. Book*, 1754, and altered in Bishop Ryle's *Collection*, 1883. In later editions it is abridged, beginning "Is God my strong salvation?"

6. The world may rise against me round.

Also "The world may fall beneath my feet," translations of stanzas I and XIII, by Mrs. Stanley Carr in her translation of Wildenhahn's *Paul Gerhardt*, 1845 (1856, p. 173).

7. If Christ is mine, then all is mine.

A hymn of three stanzas in M. W. Stryker's *Church Praise Book*, 1884, no. 485, marked "Benjamin Beddome 1776." Another cento is given in Bishop Ryle's *Hymns and Spiritual Songs*, 1883, p. 71.

"If God is mine, then present things."

The earliest accessible English version is that of Jacobi, 1725, printed in the 1754 *Moravian Hymn Book*.   The translations by this author are usually very crude and painfully laborious, but in the present case, with a few notable exceptions, he has very well caught the ring and spirit of Gerhardt.   Later compilers and publishers of hymns would of course omit the lines:

> "His Grace has cleansed and polished
> My humble Soul within."   (stanza 5.)

and

> "All this I have digested."   (stanza 12.)

Like many of the early translators of German hymns Jacobi is guilty of frequent imperfect rhymes:

| Merit | stanza 4 | spectre | stanza 14 | alone | stanza 15 |
| spirit | | conjecture | | begun | |

If we overlook these defects the version is one of the best that has appeared so far in English or American hymnals and considerably above the standard[70] of the Moravian hymns of the early eighteenth century.   The following lines offer a very true counterpart of the German:

> "All woes give way and flee," line 4.

> "And that in Change and Chances
> He stands at my right hand."   lines 13, 14.

> "The ground of my possession
> Is Jesus and his Blood."   lines 17, 18.

> "Should Earth lose its foundation
> Thou stand'st my lasting Rock."   lines 97, 98.

Bishop Ryle in taking over this version into his *Hymns and Spiritual Songs* has made a number of alterations, presenting a cento of four stanzas. His stanza 3, for example, is a combination of Jacobi's last quatrain of stanza 9 and first quatrain of stanza 10:

Ryle (stanza 3).	Jacobi (stanza 9).
For me there is provided	And how he hath provided
A city fair and new;	A city new and fair
To it I shall be guided,—	Where things, our Faith did credit
Jerusalem the true!	Shall to our eyes appear.
	(stanza 10.)
My portion there is lying,	My portion there is lying
A destined Canaan lot;	A destin'd Canaan-lot
Though I am daily dying,	Tho' I am daily dying,
My Canaan withers not.	My Heaven withers not.

---

[70] Cf. pp. 30 and 71.

American congregations are familiar with the hymn:

> Since Jesus is my friend
> (If)   (be)
> And I to him belong . . .

It is often called "The Rest of Faith," and is a cento of Miss Winkworth's very excellent version. Although she has not preserved the metre of the poem Miss Winkworth has thoroughly caught its spirit even imitating in the widely known last stanza[71] the sound sequence and alliteration:

> My heart for gladness springs,
> It cannot more be sad,
> For very joy it laughs and sings,
> Sees nought but sunshine glad.
>
> The sun that glads mine eyes
> Is Christ the Lord I love,
> I sing for joy of that which lies
> Stored up for us above.

For free adaptations from this hymn cf. pp. 139 and 136.

Selected Stanzas:

J. C. Jacobi (1725) in the *Moravian Hymn Book* (ed. 1754).

> Stanza 1. Is God for me, what is it
> That Men can do to me?
> Oft as my God I visit,
> All woes give way and flee.
> [72] If God my Head and Master
> Defend me from above,
> What pain or what disaster
> Can drive me from his Love?

B. Beddome, 1776, in Bishop Ryle's *Hymns and Spiritual Songs.*

> Stanza 1. If God is mine, then present things
> And things to come are mine;
> Yes Christ, His Word, and Spirit too,
> And glory all divine.
>
> 3. If He is mine, I need not fear
> The rage of earth and hell;

---

[71] Cf. p. 127.

[72] In Bishop Ryle's collection the quatrain reads:

> If God be my salvation,
> My refuge in distress
> What earthly tribulation
> Can shake my inward peace?

He will support my feeble power
And every foe repel.

Miss Winkworth in her *Lyra Germanica,* 1855, p. 130.

Stanza 1.   If God be on my side,
Then let who will oppose
For oft ere now to Him I cried
And He hath quelled my foes.
If Jesus be my Friend,
If God doth love me well,
What matters all my foes intend,
Though strong they be and fell?

Here I can firmly rest,
I dare to boast of this,
That God the Highest and the Best,
My Friend and Father is.
From dangerous snares He saves,
Where'er He bids me go
He checks the storms and calms the waves,
Nor lets aught work me woe.

I rest upon the ground
Of Jesus and His blood,
For 'tis through Him that I have found
The True Eternal God.
Nought have I of mine own,
Nought in the life I lead,
What Christ hath given me, that alone
Is worth all love indeed.

His spirit in me dwells,
O'er all my mind He reigns,
All care and sadness He dispels,
And soothes away all pains.
He prospers day by day
His work within my heart,
Till I have strength and faith to say,
Thou God my Father art!

When weakness on me lies,
And tempts me to despair,
He speaketh words and utters sighs
Of more than mortal prayer;
But what no tongue can tell,
Thou God canst hear and see,
Who readest in the heart full well
If aught there pleaseth Thee.   etc.

Mrs. Bevan, 1858, in Snepp's *Songs of Grace and Glory,* 1872 (abridged version).

Stanza 1.   Is God for me? I fear not, though all against me rise;
When I call on Christ my Savior, the host of evil flies;

My Friend—the Lord Almighty, and He who loves me—God,
What enemy shall harm me, though coming as a flood?
I know it, I believe it, I say it fearlessly,
That God, the Highest, Mightiest, forever loveth me!
At all times, in all places, He standeth by my side;
He rules the battle fury, the tempest and the tide.

J. Kelly, 1867, in his *Paul Gerhardt's Spiritual Songs.*

A SONG OF CHRISTIAN CONSOLATION AND JOY.

Stanza 1.   Is God for me? t'oppose me
             A thousand may uprise;
             When I to pray'r arouse me,
             He'll chase mine enemies.
             And doth the Head befriend me,
             Am I belov'd by God?
             Let foes then rise to rend me,
             The wild opposing brood!

Geh aus, mein Herz, und suche Freud.—(*Goed.* 239.)[73]

This beautiful poem of thanksgiving for the divine goodness in the gift of the delights of summer and of anticipation of the joys of Paradise appeared in the 1656 ed. of *Crü. Praxis,* no. 412, in 15 stanzas of 6 lines. It was also printed in H. Müller's *Geistliche Seelenmusik,* 1659, and included in *Wackernagel:* no. 103; *Bachmann:* no. 85; *Unv. L. S.:* 1851, no. 732. Cf. *Koch,* IV, 591; VIII, 141. Like Luther, who fondly loved nature and admired its beauties, Gerhardt showed himself in this inspiring poem a real lover of God's creation.

English Versions:

1. **Go forth, my heart, and seek delight.**

A good translation omitting stanza XIV, by Miss Winkworth, in the First Series of her *Lyra Ger.,* 1855, p. 136. Her translation of stanzas VIII-XI, beginning "Thy mighty working, mighty God," was included in the American *Sabbath Hymn Book,* 1858, and repeated in Boardman's *Collection,* Philadelphia, 1861.

2. **The golden corn now waxes strong.**

A good translation beginning with stanza VII, contributed by R. Massie to the 1857 ed. of Mercer's *C. P. and H. Bk.,* no. 463 (1864, no. 500). In the Appendix to the Second Series of *Lyra Domestica* Mr. Massie reprinted his translation at page 102, and prefixed a version of stanzas I-VI, beginning "Go forth, my heart, nor linger here." In this form it appeared in full in Reid's *Praise Book,* 1872.

3. **Come forth, my heart, and seek delight.**

   Miss Cox, 1841 and 1864.

---

[73] Cf. Friedrich von Spee's hymn: "Der trübe Winter ist vorbei"; also the Volkslied:
            "Herzlich tut mich erfreuen
             Die fröhlich Sommerzeit."
and B. Ringwald's
            "Gottlob, es ist vorhanden die frölich Sommerzeit."

4. Go forth, my heart, and revel in joy's flow.

Also "And oft I think, if e'en earth's sin-stained ground," a translation of stanzas I, IX, by Mrs. Stanley Carr in her translation of Wildenhahn's *Paul Gerhardt,* 1845 and 1856.

5. Go forth, my heart, and seek for praise.

Dr. J. W. Alexander, in Schaff's *Kirchenfreund,* 1849, p. 419; reprinted in his work *The Breaking Crucible,* N. Y., 1861, p. 15.

6. Go out, my heart, and pleasure seek.

    Miss Manington, 1863, p. 164.

7. Go forth, my Heart! the year's sweet prime.

    E. Massie, 1866, p. 36.

8. Go forth, my heart, and seek delight,
    In this summer.

    J. Kelly, 1867, p. 289.

9. Go forth, my heart, and seek the bliss.

    Mrs. E. L. Follen, in her *Lark and Linnet,* 1854, p. 30.

10. Go out, my heart, and seek delight.

A good translation omitting stanzas IV, V, VI, and XIV, by Miss Margarete Münsterberg, in her *Harvest of German Verse,* 1916.

None of Gerhardt's poetry has so well lent itself to English words as this hymn of praise for God's goodness and of contemplation of the joys in the next world, and the translators have without exception reproduced most successfully the exquisite feeling for nature which Gerhardt manifests, whether he be singing of forest and brook, or of flowers and fields.   Only Miss Winkworth and Dr. Alexander of the four or five prominent translators omit stanza XIV, and they do so apparently on the ground that it contains a complexity of figures.   Dr. Massie whose version except for the last stanza has more truly poetic lines than any other offers this paraphrase:

> Make for thy spirit ample room,
> That thus I may forever bloom.
> Like plants which root have taken:
> Oh let me in thy garden be
> A flourishing and righteous tree,
> Which never shall be shaken.

So well have all the translators succeeded that it would be perhaps merely a matter of individual taste as to which of the many excellent lines are deserving of highest praise.   Of stanza III Dr. Massie's verses are both more literal and harmonious than the others.   Gerhardt sings:

> Die Lerche schwingt sich in die Luft,
> Das Täublein fleugt aus seiner Kluft
> Und macht sich in die Wälder.

Dr. Massie interprets:

> The lark mounts singing to the skies:
> The dove forsakes her clefts, and flies
> To shady groves and alleys.

Miss Winkworth:

> The lark soars singing into space,
> The dove forsakes her hiding-place,
> And coos the woods among.

Dr. Kelly:

> The lark aspiring soars on high,
> Flies from her cleft the dove so shy,
> And seeks the woodland shadow.

Dr. Alexander:

> The lark floats high before the breeze,
> The dove toward the forest-trees
> From covert speeds along.

This last version is marred by the accent's falling on the unstressed syllable of "toward" in line 2. Several of our American hymnals contain the cento of four stanzas from Miss Winkworth's version (Gerhardt stanzas VIII-XI incl.) whose ring gives the freshness appropriate in an outdoor hymn of Spring and Summer.

Selected Stanzas:

C. Winkworth, 1855, in her *Lyra Germanica.*

> Stanza 1. Go forth my heart and seek delight
> In all the gifts of God's great might,
> These pleasant summer hours:
> Look how the plains for thee and me
> Have deck'd themselves most fair to see
> All bright and sweet with flowers.

> 8. Thy mighty working, mighty God,
> Wakes all my pow'rs; I look abroad,
> And can no longer rest;
> I, too, must sing when all things sing,
> And from my heart the praises ring,
> The Highest loveth best.

> 9. If Thou in Thy great love to us,
> Wilt scatter joy and beauty thus
> O'er this poor earth of ours;
> What nobler glories shall be given
> Hereafter in Thy shining heaven
> Set round with golden towers!

> 10. What thrilling joy, when on our sight
> Christ's garden beams in cloudless light
> And rings with God's high praise;

Where all the thousand seraphim
In one accordant voice and hymn
Their Alleluia raise!

11.   O, were I there! oh, that I now
Before Thy throne, my God, could bow,
And bear my heavenly palm!
Then, like the angels would I raise
My voice, and sing thine endless praise
In many a sweet-toned psalm.

J. W. Alexander, 1849, in the Schaff-Gilman *Library of Religious Poetry.*

Stanza 1.   Go forth, my heart, and seek for praise,
On these delightsome summer days,
In what thy God bestows!
How rich the garden's beauties be,
How lavishly for me and thee
It doth its charms disclose!

R. Massie, 1863, in the Schaff-Gilman *Library of Religious Poetry.*

Stanza 1.   Go forth, my heart, nor linger here
In this sweet season of the year,
When God his gifts dispenses;
See how the gardens in their best
For you and me are gayly drest,
And ravish all the senses!

J. Kelly, 1867, in his *Paul Gerhardt's Spiritual Songs.*

Stanza 1.   Go forth, my heart, and seek delight
In this summer time so bright,
The bounties God displayeth,
The garden's splendour go and see
Behold how God for me and thee
Them gorgeously arrayeth.

Miss Margarete Münsterberg, in her *Harvest of German Verse,* 1916.

Stanza 1.   Go out, my heart, and seek delight,
In this dear summer time so bright,
In God's abundance daily;
The beauty of these gardens see,
And look, how they for me and thee
Have decked themselves so gaily.

Many hymn writers since Gerhardt have drawn from the same scriptural sources as he, and it would be presumption to attempt to prove that all these had received any direct impulse from his verses; yet it must be realized that it is to a certain extent impossible that the conceptions of the hymn writers of one age should remain inseparable from the ideas of later poets. Bayard Taylor, in speaking about what he calls "intellectual genealogies in literature," says: "Most authors may be shown to be not imitators, but the spiritual descendants of others, inheriting more or less of their natures."[74] In the pages which follow are cited some hymns containing phrases thoroughly suggestive of Gerhardt's lines which will contribute evidence in addition to that already adduced to show the prominent place his works hold as influencing English hymn writing.

HYMNS SHOWING ADAPTATIONS OF IDEAS AND EXPRESSIONS FROM GERHARDT'S POEMS.

(a) C. Wesley in *Hymns and Sacred Poems,* 1742, p. 124. (Cf. Job. XIX, 25-27.)

[75] Gerhardt (*Goed.* 331).

Stanza 1.

			line
I know that my Redeemer lives:	I.	Ich weisz, dasz mein Erlöser lebt:	1
He lives, and on the Earth shall stand,		Er lebt . . .	3
		Er lebt fürwahr, der starke Held,	5
And tho' to Worms my Flesh he gives		Das Fleisch . . .	30
		Wird . . .	31
		zerbrochen . . .	32
My Dust lies numbered in His Hand.		von Maden . . .	33

Stanza 2.

In This Reanimated Clay	So wird er mich doch aus der Erd 17
I surely shall behold Him near,	Hernachmals auferwecken; 18
Shall see Him at the Latter Day	Ich selber werd in seinem Licht 50
	Ihn sehn und mich erquicken; 51
	Mein Auge wird sein Angesicht 52
In all His Majesty appear.	Mit groszer Lust erblicken; 53

Stanza 3.

I feel what then shall raise me up,	Er wird mich reiszen aus dem Grab 19
Th' Eternal Spirit lives in me,	Sein Geist wohnt mir im Herzen
	(no. 229, 49)
This is my Confidence of Hope	cf. above no. 331, 52, 53
That God I Face to Face shall see.	

(b) C. Wesley in *Hymns and Sacred Poems,* p. 180.

(*Goed.* 331.)

Stanza 1.

I know that my Redeemer lives	Ich weisz, dasz mein Erlöser lebt.
And ever prays for me	

Stanza 13.

With me, I know, Thy Spirit dwells,	Sein Geist wohnt mir im Herzen
(cf. *Wesley,* p. 124, stanza 3, line 2	(no. 229, 49)
above.)	

[74] *Studies in German Literature,* 1879.
[75] Cf. p. 81.

Stanza 15.
  Jesu, I hang upon Thy Word,   Das hab ich je und je gegläubt
                                  (no. 331, 43 ff.)
  I stedfastly believe   Und fasz ein fest Vertrauen,
  Thou wilt return, and claim me, Lord, Ich werde den, der ewig bleibt
  And to Thyself receive.   In meinem Fleische schauen;
Cf. also stanza 23.
  Lord, I believe, and rest secure
  In Confidence Divine, . . .

(c) C. Wesley, in *Hymns and Sacred*   (*Goed.* 263.)[76]
        Poems, p. 217.

1. Jesu, my Savior, Brother, Friend   1. Jesu, allerliebster Bruder,
   On whom I cast my every Care,   Ders am besten mit mir meint,
   On whom for all things I depend,   Du mein Anker, Mast und Ruder
   Inspire, and then accept my Prayer,   Und mein treuster Herzensfreund;

13. Here let my Soul's sure anchor be   Du mein Anker, Mast und Ruder.
    Here let me fix my wishful Eyes,   Cf. line 3 above.

(d) C. Wesley in *Hymns and Sacred*   (*Goed.* 229.)[77]
        Poems, p. 146.
Stanza 1.
  Jesu, my Strength, my Hope,   Ist Gott für mich, so trete   1
        (Cf. lines 1, 2.)   Gleich alles wider mich;   2
  On Thee I cast my Care,   Nun weisz und gläub ich feste 9
        (Cf. lines 51, 52.) Dasz Gott, der Höchst und Beste 11
  With humble Confidence look up   Mir gänzlich günstig sei,   12
        (Cf. line 9.)   (Sein Geist) Vertreibet Sorg und
                                Schmerzen 51
  And know Thou hearst my Prayer.   Nimmt allen Kummer hin 52

(e) C. Wesley in *Wesleyan Hymn Book,*   (*Goed.* 111.)[78]
     1780, no. 356.

  O come and dwell in me,   Zeuch ein zu deinen Thoren,
  Spirit of power within   Sei meines Herzens Gast,
  And bring thy glorious liberty   O hochgeliebter Geist.   5
  From sorrow, fear and sin!

  The inward, deep disease   Zeuch ein, lasz mich empfinden 9 ff.
  Spirit of health remove   Und schmecken deine Kraft,
  Spirit of perfect holiness   Die Kraft, die uns von Sünden
  Spirit of perfect love.   Hülf und Errettung schafft.
                         Entsündige meinen Sinn, . . .

---

[76] Cf. p. 72.
[77] Cf. p. 126.
[78] Cf. p. 52.

That blessed law of thine	Du bist ein Geist, der lehret 33
Father, to me, impart;	Wie man recht beten soll.
The Spirit's law of life divine,—	
O write it in my heart.	
Thy nature be my law	Erfülle die Gemüter 105
Thy spotless sanctity	Mit reiner Glaubenszier
	Gib Freudigkeit und Stärke
And sweetly every moment draw	zu stehen in dem Streit
	Richt unser ganzes Leben 121
	Allzeit nach deinem Sinn.
	So hilf uns Frölich sterben 126
My happy soul to Thee!	Und nach dem Tod ererben
	Des ewgen Lebens Haus.

(f) C. Wesley in *Pilgrim Hymnal*, no. 96.   (*Goed.* III.)

From our fears and sins release us	Entsündige meinen Sinn 13
Israel's strength and consolation	Du bist ein Geist der Freuden 41 ff.
. . . Joy of every loving heart.	. . . Erleuchtest uns in Leiden
	Mit deines Trostes Licht.
Born to reign in us forever	Du, Herr, hast selbst in Händen 56 ff.
Now thy gracious kingdom bring.	Die ganze weite Welt,
	. . . So gib doch deine Gnad;

In his *Psalms and Hymns*, 1851, Rev. A. T. Russell includes a group of hymns entitled "The Sufferings of Our Lord." One of them, no. 94, of three stanzas, bears such a striking resemblance to Gerhardt's "O Welt, sieh hier dein Leben"[79] that we should be inclined to trace its source to this hymn, though it is signed merely with the author's initials A. T. R. and is offered as original:

Russell (stanza 1).	Gerhardt (stanza 1).
O World, behold Him dying	O Welt, sich hier dein Leben
Who is thy life supplying;	Am Stamm des Kreuzes schweben!
Behold! He dies for Thee:	Dein Heil sinkt in den Tod!
He who in glory reigneth,	Der grosze Fürst der Ehren
No scorn, no shame disdaineth,	Läszt willig sich beschweren
From endless death my soul to free.	Mit Schlägen, Hohn und groszen Spott.

Stanza 2.	
Now from my Savior floweth	Tritt her und schau mit Fleisze:
The blood His love bestoweth	Sein Leib ist ganz mit Schweisze
On us that we may live!	Des Blutes überfüllt;
What grief His spirit rendeth!	Aus seinem edlen Herzen

---

[79] Cf. p. 42.

Whilst thus He condescendeth
His life for us His foes to give.

Vor unerschöpften Schmerzen
Ein Seufzer nach dem andern quillt.

Although its second and third lines are taken directly from the Bible, yet
stanza 3 as a whole appears to be influenced by the thoughts in Gerhardt's
stanzas VIII and III.   Line 5 might well be regarded as a condensation of
the repeated ideas of confession and repentance in Gerhardt's strophes.
(Cf. line 19 "ich und meine Sünden"; line 25 "ich sollte büszen").

Russell (stanza 3).	Gerhardt.
	(Lines 43-45.)
Of His own will He dieth,	Du springst ins Todes Rachen,
Who to His Father crieth,	Mich frei und los zu machen
"O Father! mercy show:"	Von solchem Ungeheur
	(Lines 16 and 17.)
Come, children of transgression	Du bist ja nicht ein Sünder
To Jesus make confession;	Wie wir und unsre Kinder
	(Line 48.)
Your all to His great love you owe.	O unerhörtes Liebesfeur!

A hymn by Dr. Maltbie D. Babcock which has been included in several
American hymnals would indicate that while the author may have had before
him only the scriptural passage from the Psalms[80] as he composed his verses,
yet because of the marked similarity of phraseology Gerhardt's hymn
"Befiehl du deine Wege" must have been more or less familiar to him
through the version of Wesley or another translator.

Rest in the Lord, my soul	Befiehl du deine Wege
Commit to him thy way	Und was dein Herze kränkt
What to thy sight seems dark as night	
To him is bright as day.	
	(Lines 9-12.)
Rest in the Lord, my soul	Dem Herren muszt du trauen,
He planned for thee thy life	Wenn dirs soll wolergehen;
Brings fruit from rain brings good from pain	Auf sein Werk muszt du schauen,
And peace and joy from strife.	Wenn dein Werk soll bestehn.
	(Lines 41-48.)
Rest in the Lord, my soul:	Hoff, o du arme Seele,
This fretting weakens Thee;	Hoff und sei unverzagt
	Gott wird dich aus der Höle,

[80] Cf. *Psalm* XXXVII, 5-7, "Commit thy way unto the Lord . . . Rest in the
Lord." Cf. p. 114 ff.

Why not be still? accept his will

Thou shalt his glory see.

> Maltbie D. Babcock, in the
> *Pilgrim Hymnal*, 1912.

Da dich der Kummer plagt,
Mit groszen Gnaden rücken:
Erwarte nur die Zeit,
So wirst du schon erblicken
Die Sonn der schönsten Freud.

Wesley's adaptation[81] of the thought in "Ist Gott für mich, so trete" is but one of many sacred poems that treat this theme of the Christian's Hope. A hymn now familiar to many congregations written by James Montgomery[82] in 1872 and avowedly based on *Psalm XXVII*[83] bears so strong a resemblance to this poem of Gerhardt's that two stanzas are here cited to show first the similarity of treatment of the general subject of Faith in the Power of God, and particularly the marked traces of Gerhardt's influence upon the English verses.

Gerhardt (*Goed.* 229).[84]

1. God is my strong salvation:	Ist Gott für mich, so trete	1
What foe have I to fear?	Gleich alles wider mich;	2
In darkness and temptation	Was kann mir tun der Feinde	7
	Und Widersacher Rott?	8
My light, my help, is near.	Mein Glanz und schönes Licht	26
Though hosts encamp around me	Ist Gott für mich, so trete	1
Firm to the fight I stand,	Gleich alles wider mich	2
What terror can confound me		
With God at my right hand?	Und bin geliebt bei Gott	6
2. Place on the Lord reliance	Nun weisz und gläub ich feste,	9
My soul with courage wait	. . . dasz ich finde	19
His truth be thine affiance.	Das ewge wahre Gut	20
When faint and desolate.	Wenn ich gleich fall und sterbe	75
His might thine heart shall strengthen	Sein Geist spricht meinem Geiste	
His love thy joy increase	Manch süszes Trostwort zu:	
Mercy thy days shall lengthen		
The Lord will give thee peace.		

> James Montgomery, in his
> *Songs of Zion*, 1822.

With less direct influence than appears in the hymns hitherto mentioned, yet showing much of the spirit of "Auf den Nebel folgt die Sonne"[85] is

---

[81] Cf. p. 136.
[82] Cf. p. 32.
[83] "The Lord is my light and my salvation; whom shall I fear?"
[84] Cf. p. 126.
[85] Cf. p. 68.

Sarah Flower Adams' hymn, "He sendeth sun, he sendeth shower." The final line of each stanza introducing the theme of Resignation to God's Will may well have been suggested by the refrain "Was Gott gefällt."[86]

He sendeth sun, he sendeth shower,	Auf den Nebel folgt die Sonne	1
Alike they're needful for the flower;	Auf das Trauren Freud und Wonne	2
And joys and tears alike are sent	Trost und Labsal, . . Meine Seele	
	. . . steigt	4, 5
To give the soul fit nourishment:	Hat mir meinen Geist erquickt,	9
As comes to me or cloud or sun,		
Father, thy will, not mine, be done!		
Can loving children e'er reprove	Gott läszt keinen traurig stehn	50
With murmurs whom they trust and	Der sich Ihm zu eigen schenkt	52
love?		
Creator, I would ever be	Und Ihn in sein Herze senkt;	53
A trusting, loving child to thee:	Wer auf Gott seine Hoffnung setzt	54
As comes to me or cloud or sun,		
Father, thy will, not mine, be done!		
Oh, ne'er will I at life repine;	Nu, so lang ich in der Welt	85
Enough that thou hast made it mine;	Haben werde Haus und Zelt	86
	. . . Ich will all mein Leben lang	89
When falls the shadow cold of death,	. . . Hiefür bringen Lob und	
	Dank.	91
I yet will sing with parting breath	Ich will gehn in Angst und Not	99
	Ich will gehn bis in den Tod	100
As comes to me or shade or sun,	Ich will gehn ins Grab hinein	101
Father, thy will, not mine, be done.	Und doch allzeit frölich sein	102

Sarah Flower Adams, 1841, in the
Schaff-Gilman *Lib. of Rel. Poetry.*

A very familiar hymn in English-speaking countries is Thomas Rawson Taylor's "I'm but a stranger here" written in 1834. It was published in 1836 in his *Memoirs and Select Remains,* and headed "Heaven is my home. Air—'Robin Adair.'" In America it is usually sung to Arthur S. Sullivan's "Saint's Rest." The hymn so closely resembles Gerhardt's lines in "Ich bin ein Gast auf Erden"[87] that the parallels are given below:

1. I'm but a stranger here;	Ich bin ein Gast auf Erden	1
Earth is a desert drear,		
Heaven is my home.	Was ist mein ganzes Wesen	9
Danger and sorrow stand	Als Müh und Not gewesen	11
Round me on every hand,		
Heaven is my fatherland,	Da ist mein Vaterland	4
Heaven is my home.		

---

[86] Cf. p. 56.
[87] Cf. p. 74.

2. What though the tempests rage,	Mich hat auf meinen Wegen	17
Short is my pilgrimage,	Manch harter Sturm erschreckt;	18
Heaven is my home.	Blitz, Donner, Wind und Regen	19
And time's wild wintry blast	Hat mir manch Angst erweckt;	20
Soon will be overpast,	So will ich swar nun treiben	57
I shall reach home at last	Mein Leben durch die Welt	58
	Doch denk ich nicht zu bleiben	59
Heaven is my home.	In diesem fremden Zelt.	60
3. There at my Savior's side,	Mein Heimat ist dort droben,	65
I shall be glorified,	Da aller Engel Schaar	66
	Den groszen Herrscher loben . .	67
Heaven is my home,	Die frommen heilgen Seelen	41
	Die giengen fort und fort	42
There with the good and blest	Da will ich immer wohnen,	105
Those I loved most and best,	Bei denen, die mit Kronen	107
I shall forever rest;	Du ausgeschmücket hast	108
	Da will ich . . .	109
Heaven is my home.	In meinem Erbteil ruhn.	112
4. Therefore I'll murmur not,	Hab ich doch müszen leiden	23
	Und tragen mit Geduld,	24
Whate'er my earthly lot,	Es musz ja durchgedrungen	53
	Es musz gelitten sein;	54
Heaven is my home.	So will ich zwar nun treiben	57
	Mein Leben durch die Welt.	58
For I shall surely stand		
There at my Lord's right hand;—	Cf. lines 105-112, above, quoted opp.	
Heaven is my fatherland,	stanza 3.	
Heaven is my home.		

Other similarities to "Ich bin ein Gast auf Erden" are:

(a) "The Pilgrim," by Sarah H. Palfrey, in the Schaff-Gilman *Lib. Rel. Poetry.*

> A Pilgrim am I on my way
> To seek and find the Holy Land . . .

This poem would perhaps bear but slight resemblance to Gerhardt's were it not for the final stanza where the element of Joy is introduced:

> While Joy shall spring
> with me through heaven's straight door.

These lines are certainly suggestive of Gerhardt's words in his stanza XIII:

> Du aber, meine Freude . . . du zeuchst mich . . .
> Ins Haus der ewgen Wonne.

(b) "The Pilgrim's song," by H. F. Lyte, in his *Poems chiefly Religious,* 1833 and 1845.

Stanza 1.   My rest is in heaven; my rest is not here;
Then why should I murmur when trials are near?
Be hushed, my dark spirit! the worst that can come
But shortens thy journey, and hastens thee home.

2.   It is not for me to be seeking my bliss
And building my hopes in a region like this:
I look for a city which hands have not piled;
I pant for a country by sin undefiled. . . .

4.   Afflictions may damp me, they cannot destroy;
One glimpse of thy love turns them all into joy: . . .

5.   Let doubt then, and danger, my progress oppose;
They only make heaven more sweet at the close. . . .

6.   A scrip on my back, and a staff in my hand,
I march on in haste through an enemy's land:
The road may be rough, but it cannot be long;
And I'll smooth it with *hope* and I'll *cheer it* with song.

Although Lyte based his hymn on Hebrews IV, 9, "There remaineth therefore a rest to the people of God," he treats in his concluding stanza the additional theme of hope and cheer which, as has been seen,[88] was a constant and favorite topic with Gerhardt. Since this chapter of Hebrews has no direct reference to this theme we have good reason to assume that from the striking similarity of language of the two hymns Lyte was influenced by Gerhardt's "Ich bin ein Gast auf Erden." Especially in stanza VII is the likeness most noticeable:

So will ich zwar nun treiben
Mein Leben durch die Welt,
Doch denk ich nicht zu bleiben
In diesem fremden Zelt. (Cf. Lyte stanza 6.)

Ich wandre meine Straszen,
Die zu der Heimat führt, (Cf. Lyte stanza 1.)
Da mich ohn alle Maszen
Mein Vater trösten wird. (Cf. Lyte stanza 5.)

(c) "In exile here we wander," by W. Cooke. [Septuagesima.] This hymn appeared in the *Hymnary*, 1872, under the signature "A. C. C." (i. e., "A Canon of Chester"), and is definitely known to have been suggested to Canon Cooke by Gerhardt's hymn. In Thring's *Collection*, 1882, stanza III, lines 4-8 is altered to:

And we shall rise in that great day
In bodies like to Thine
And with Thy saints in bright array, (Cf. lines 65, 66.)
Shall in Thy glory shine. (Cf. line 104.)

---

[88] Cf. p. 22.

There are of course numerous adaptations of Gerhardt's work which have less merit than those which have been mentioned, but it would be beyond the scope of this thesis to discuss them. From our consideration up to this point we may draw the following conclusions: many translators have taken the liberty of altering the original versions thereby injuring perhaps just those hymns possessed of the greatest warmth and vigor and have in this way prevented our poet from being more fully acknowledged; at the same time the best of his hymns as devotional lyrics with a pathos and sympathy which are exceptionally beautiful and powerful have become naturalized in English-speaking countries by the really good translations and will always serve to enkindle devotion and strengthen grace in the true Christian worshipper.

FINIS.

APPENDIX

SHORT BIOGRAPHICAL SKETCHES OF TRANSLATORS

Alexander, James Waddell, D.D., born 1804, graduated at Princeton, 1820, and was successively Professor of Rhetoric at Princeton, Pastor in New York, Professor of Church History, Princeton, and Pastor of the Fifth Avenue Presbyterian Church, New York. He died in 1859. His works include some translations published about two years after his death, under the title *The Breaking Crucible and other Translations.* Of these translations the most noted is "O Sacred Head now Wounded." He has translated nos. 25, 49, 239.[1]

Beddome, Benjamin, M.A. This prolific hymn writer was born at Henley-in-Arden, Warwickshire, January 23, 1717, where his father was at that time Baptist minister. He was apprenticed to a surgeon in Bristol, but removing to London, he joined in 1739 the Baptist Church, and became one of the most respected Baptist ministers in England. In 1770 he received the degree of M.A. from Rhode Island College,[2] Providence. He died September 3, 1795. It was his practice to prepare a hymn every week to be sung after his Sunday morning sermon. Many of these found their way into the *General Baptist Hymn Book* of 1793, and other collections. His popularity is now mainly in America. He has translated no. 64.

Bevan, Emma Frances, née Shuttleworth, born at Oxford, 1827. Mrs. Bevan published in 1858 a series of translations from the German as *Songs of Eternal Life* (London) which are above the average in merit. She has translated nos. 185 and 229.

Borthwick, Jane, born 1813 at Edinburgh. Together with her sister, Mrs. Findlater (q. v.), she translated from the German *Hymns from the Land of Luther* in four series. These translations have attained great success and hardly a hymnal in England or America has appeared without containing some of them. Under the signature of "H. L. L." Miss Borthwick has written various prose works and contributed many original poems to the *Family Treasury* and to other collections. She has translated nos. 185 and 284.

Buckoll, Henry James, M.A., born 1803. He was educated at Rugby and Queen's College, Oxford, graduating in 1826. He took Holy Orders in 1827 and died at Rugby in 1871. In 1839 he edited a *Collection of Hymns* for the Rugby Parish Church, and in 1850 compiled a new edition of the Collection for the Rugby School Chapel. That collection contains 14 of his hymns, a few of which were translations from the Latin and German. His *Hymns translated from the German* was published 1832. He has translated nos. 59, 60, 106.

Burns, James Drummond, M.A., born at Edinburgh, 1823, and educated at Edinburgh University. In 1855 he became minister of Hampstead Presbyterian Church, London. He died in 1864. Among his hymns which have become widely popular are 39 translations from the German which appeared in the *Family Treasury.* They are rendered exactly in the meters of the originals and many had not previously been translated. He has translated no. 71.

---

[1] The numbers refer to the page on which the poem begins in the Goedeke text.
[2] The early name of Brown University.

Charles, Elizabeth, née Rundle, born in Devonshire, the author of numerous and popular works on the early Christian life in Great Britain, of Luther and his times and of Wesley and his work. She has made some valuable contributions to hymnody, including original hymns and translations from the Latin and German. They appeared in *The Voice of Christian Life in Song*, 1858. She has translated nos. 68, 142, 185.

Cox, Frances Elizabeth, born at Oxford, well known as the translator of hymns from the German. Her translations were published as *Sacred Hymns from the German*, London, 1st ed., 1841, containing 49 translations printed with the original text together with biographical notes on the German authors. In the 2d ed., 1864, the number was increased to 56. She has translated nos. 60, 67, 68, 111, 118, 150, 185, 239, 293.

Dunn, Catherine Hannah, born at Nottingham, England, 1815, died 1863. In 1857 she published a little volume of 36 *Hymns from the German*. She has translated nos. 49, 60, 68, 89, 111, 139, 185, 293.

Findlater, Mrs. (Sarah Borthwick) born 1823, sister of Miss Jane Borthwick (q. v.). She has translated nos. 60, 89, 139.

Frothingham, Nathaniel Langdon, D.D., born at Boston, 1793, and graduated at Harvard, 1811, where he was also sometime Tutor. From 1815 to 1850 he was Pastor of the First Church (Unitarian), Boston. He died in 1870. His *Metrical Pieces* were published in 1855 and 1870. He has translated nos. 59, 74, 122, 155, 185, 274.

Gambold, John, M.A., was born 1711, graduated at Christ Church, Oxford, B.A. 1730, M.A. 1734. Taking Holy Orders, he became, about 1739, Vicar of Stanton Harcourt, Oxfordshire, but resigned 1742 and joined the United Brethren (Moravians) by whom he was chosen one of their bishops in 1754. He died in 1771. About 26 translations and 18 original hymns in the *Moravian Hymn Book* are assigned to him. One or two of his hymns, which were published by the Wesleys, have been claimed for them, but the evidence is in favor of Gambold. A collected edition of his works was published at Bath in 1789, and afterwards reprinted. He has translated nos. 49, 68, 71.

Guthrie, John, D.D., born 1814, graduated Edinburgh M.A. 1835. Sympathizing with the views of Dr. James Morison he was deposed from his pastorate and joined with Dr. Morison in forming the Evangelical Union, compiling in 1856 their hymn book. In 1869 he published *Sacred Lyrics; Hymns original and translated from the German, with versions of Psalms*. London, 1869. Many of these hymns have much beauty and sweetness. He has translated nos. 60, 68, 71, 100, 185.

Jackson, Samuel Macauley, from 1876 to 1880 pastor at Norwood, New Jersey, was born in 1851. He graduated from the College of the City of New York in 1870 and from Union Theological Seminary in 1873, after which he spent two years in travel, visiting Europe and the East. He was editor-in-chief of the New Schaff-Herzog *Encyclopaedia of Religious Knowledge*, and the author of *Huldreich Zwingli* (*Heroes of the Reformation* Series), 1901, 1903; *Zwingli Selections*, 1901. He has translated no. 49.

Jacobi, John Christian, a native of Germany, was born in 1670, and appointed Keeper of the Royal German Chapel, St. James's Palace, London, about 1708. He held that post for 42 years and died in 1750. Among his publications are *Psalmodia Germanica . . . translated from High Dutch.*[3] He has translated nos. 25, 59, 76, 111, 185, 229, 235.

---

[3] In the XVIIIth Century this term was current for "High German."

Kelly, John, educated at Glasgow University, studied theology at Bonn, New College, Edinburgh, and the Theological College of the English Presbyterian Church. His translations of Gerhardt's *Spiritual Songs* were published in 1867. His *Hymns of the Present Century from the German* was published in 1886. He has translated nos. 3, 7, 15, 17, 19, 23, 25, 28, 49, 59, 60, 62, 65, 67, 68, 71, 74, 78, 80, 81, 83, 89, 91, 93, 95, 100, 106, 108, 118, 120, 122, 124, 130, 135, 139, 142, 150, 153, 155, 158, 161, 171, 173, 176, 178, 185, 200, 205, 209, 212, 217, 220, 224, 226, 229, 232, 235, 239, 260, 263, 267, 271, 274, 284, 287, 289, 293, 296, 302, 304, 310, 312, 315, 319, 324.

Kennedy, Benjamin Hall, D.D., born 1804, and educated at St. John's College, Cambridge, B.A. 1827. He was later Professor of Greek in Cambridge University, and took Holy Orders in 1829. Besides several textbooks of the classics he published *The Psalter,* 1860, and also *Hymnologia Christiana,* 1863, which included numerous translations from the German.

Manington, Alice, born at Brighton, and later lived at Vienna. She published two sets of translations from the German, in 1863, and 1864. She has translated nos. 25, 60, 118, 150, 153, 158, 239, 312, 331.

Massie, Edward, M.A., was educated at Wadham College, Oxford; B.A. 1830, M.A. 1834. He took Holy Orders in 1830. He published in 1862 *A Few Hymns for Occasional Use in the Services of the Church,* and *Sacred Odes,* 1866 and 1867. The latter contain many translations from the German. He has translated nos. 19, 59, 118, 155, 239, 293 (2 versions).

Massie, Richard, born 1800. He published a translation of *Martin Luther's Spiritual Songs,* London, 1854, also *Lyra Domestica,* 1860. In 1864 he published vol. II which has an "Appendix" of translations of German hymns by various authors. He also contributed many translations of German hymns to Mercer's *Church Psalter and Hymn Book,* to Reid's *British Herald* and other periodicals. He has translated nos. 19, 25, 46, 47, 49, 108, 161, 176, 229, 235, 239, 293, 312.

Mills, Henry, D.D., born at Morristown, N. J., 1786, and graduated from Princeton in 1802. At the opening of the Auburn Theological Seminary in 1821 he was appointed Professor of Biblical Criticism and Oriental Languages from which he retired in 1854. He died at Auburn in 1867. In 1845 he published *Horae Germanicae; A Version of German Hymns.* This was enlarged in 1856. He has translated nos. 81, 161, 185, 235, 304.

Molther, Philipp Heinrich, born in Alsace, 1714. At Jena, where he studied theology, he joined the (Moravian) Brethren in 1737, and went to London 1739. He was minister of the Brethren's congregation at Neuwied from 1750 to 1761, and spent the rest of his life 1762-1780 in Dublin and Bedford. In 1775 he was consecrated as bishop of the Brethren's Unity. He has translated nos. 71, 155, 256.

Montgomery, James, born 1771. His early years covered a varied experience as bookseller, auctioneer, printer's assistant. He became editor of the *Sheffield Iris* and continued this work for thirty-one years. He was twice imprisoned in the next two years for items which appeared in the columns of the *Iris.* He edited many poetical works, among them *Original Hymns for Public, Private and Social Devotion,* 1853, *The Christian Psalmist,* 1825, and *Songs of Zion,* 1822. Cf. pp. 31, 32, 139.

Russell, Arthur Tozer, M.A., born 1806, educated at Manchester College, York, and St. John's College, Cambridge. In 1829 he was ordained by the bishop of Lincoln. He was the author of many works covering a wide range of subjects of a religious nature, and his original hymns and translations have found their way into many hymnals. In

1848 various of his own hymns, original and translated from the German, appeared in *Hymns for Public Worship*, and in 1851 appeared *Psalms and Hymns*. He died in 1874. He has translated nos. 25, 40, 68, 150, 155, 158, 185, 209, 312.

Stallybrass, James Steven, born in Siberia in 1826, the son of Rev. E. Stallybrass of the London Missionary Society. He died in London in 1888. He was well known as an educationist, and translated from the German a number of scientific works. He also contributed many translations of German hymns and poems to the various publications of Mr. Curwen, e. g. *The Sabbath Hymnbook*. He has translated nos. 60, 185.

Stryker, Melancthon Woolsey, D.D., born in 1851, graduated at Hamilton College 1872 and Auburn Theological Seminary 1876. He has held pastorates at Auburn, Ithaca, Holyoke and Chicago, and has edited six works on hymns, contributing many original hymns and several translations. He was President of Hamilton College 1892-1917. He has translated nos. 155, 235.

Thring, Edward, M.A., brother of Godfrey Thring, was born 1821, and educated at King's College, Cambridge, B.A. 1844. He became Head Master of Uppingham School in 1853 and held this position until his death in 1887. He was the author of several important works for schools and colleges and the joint editor of a hymn book to which he contributed some translations from the German. He has translated no. 60.

Warner, Anna, born near New York City about 1822. She is the author of the novel *Say and Seal*, 1859. She edited *Hymns of the Church Militant*, 1858; and published *Wayfaring Hymns, Original and Translated*, 1869. She has translated no. 89.

Wesley, Charles, the great hymn writer of the Wesley family, perhaps the great hymn writer of all ages, no less than 6500 hymns being ascribed to him. He was the youngest son and 18th child of Samuel and Susanna Wesley and was born at Epworth Rectory December 18, 1707, receiving his education at Westminster School and Christ Church, Oxford. He became one of the first band of Oxford Methodists, and went in 1735 with his brother John to Georgia as Secretary to Gen. Oglethorpe. His stay there was very short; he returned to England 1736 and shortly afterward came under the influence of Count Zinzendorf and the Moravians. His headquarters were at Bristol till 1771 when he moved to London devoting there much time to the spiritual care of the prisoners in Newgate. He died in 1788. Cf. p. 31.

Wesley, John, born at Epworth Rectory in 1703. He was educated at Christ Church, Oxford, and in 1729 became director of the little band of "Oxford Methodists." In 1735 he went as a missionary of the Society for the Propagation of the Gospel to Georgia where a new colony had been founded under the governorship of Gen. Oglethorpe. On his voyage he was deeply impressed with the piety and Christian courage of some German fellow travellers, Moravians. During his short ministry in Georgia he met with many discouragements and returned home much dissatisfied. In London he again fell in with the Moravians and from now on he labored to spread what he believed to be the everlasting gospel, travelling, preaching and making converts. He died at the age of 88 in the year 1791. The part which he actually took in writing the many hymns ascribed to the two brothers John and Charles is difficult to ascertain, but it is reasonably certain that more than thirty translations from the German, French, and Spanish, chiefly from the German, were exclusively his and although somewhat free they embody the fire and energy of the originals and have had a wide circulation. He has translated nos. 71, 185, 200.

Winkworth, Catherine, born in London in 1829. She took always a deep and active interest in the educational work in connection with the "Clifton Association for the Higher Education of Women" and kindred societies. She published (1) *Lyra Ger-*

manica, 1st Series 1855; (2) *Lyra Germanica,* 2d Series 1858; (3) *The Chorale Book for England* (containing translations from the German, together with music), 1863; and (4) *Christian Singers of Germany,* 1869. Although not the earliest of modern translators from the German into English, Miss Winkworth is surely the foremost in rank and popularity. Her translations are the most widely used of any from the German and have had more to do with the modern revival of the English use of German hymns than have the versions of any other writer. She has translated nos. 25 (2 versions), 49 (2 versions), 60 (2 versions), 62, 71, 76, 83, 95, 100, 108, 111 (2 versions), 122, 139, 150, 153, 155, 209, 217, 229, 232, 235, 239, 274, 284, 293, 298, 304.

TABULATIONS[4]

ALLITERATION (cf. p. 19)

Gerhardt clings to the traditional fondness of the German poet for alliterative phrases. If there be any virtue in the saw regarding "Apt alliteration's artful aid" our poet has found that virtue. The predominating sounds are the consonants; rarely is there alliteration of vowels. An enumeration shows the following results:[5]

Sequences of F, 12; of G, 36; of H, 20; of L, 27; of S, 30; of W, 20; of Z, 6. Of the other consonants there is an average of only two or three each.

B
beiszt und brennt 153, 47

D
Ohne dasz du, die du hier 28, 53
Ich will dein Diener bleiben 41, 42
. . . drang dich doch 47, 7
Entzünde mich durch dich 47, 40
dienen dir 150, 94

E (a) (i)
Und aller Erden Ecken 220, 44
Ist ihr erfüllet, ... 270, 12

F (V)
Fried und Freude 25, 22
Freund und Feinde 77, 47
für und für 93, 3
Fried- und Freudenswort 95, 2
Mit Freuden singen für und für 150, 97
Ist meiner Feinde Freude 178, 22
Trost, Friede, Freud und Leben 190, 7
Frisch und freudig 232, 98
Die vollkommene Freude 244, 120
Freuden Fülle 274, 3
Und fasz ein fest Vertrauen ... 331, 44

G
Gottes Gnad und Güt 7, 49
Gott gönnt ihm Guts 13, 80
ganz und gar 15, 6

Gottes Grimm 30, 112
Es grüszet dich mein ganzes
  Geist 44, 5
Dem Geber aller Güter 59, 3
Gegen Gott ....62, 68 & 69
Gnad und Gütigkeit 62, 90
Gift, Gall und Ungestüm 74, 20
Gut und Geld 80, 32
Gall und Gift 81, 23
Gut und Geld 86, 32
Dasz dir Gott Glück, Gut und
  Ehr 89, 3
Gnad und Güte 95, 11
Gottes Gnad und Gab 97, 13
güldne Gut und Geld 97, 38
Gottes Geist 105, 20
Gottes Grimm 111, 75
Gutes gönnen 115, 43
Geistes Gnad 135, 79
dein Geist mir giebt 150, 93
Gift und Gallen 153, 14
Gut und Geld 153, 57
Gottes Zorn und groszen Grimm 164, 61
ganz und gar 178, 8
Gold ist ihr Gott, Geld ist ihr
  Licht 190, 17
Geist und Glauben 226, 44
Hat er nicht Gold, so hat er Gott 226, 49
Hie ist Gott und Gottes Grund 232, 44
Gottes Gaben 239, 3
Des groszen Gottes groszes Thun 239, 44

---

[4] In these tabulations the poems are numbered according to the page on which they begin in the Goedeke text, thus: 153, 12 means poem no. 153, line 12.

[5] The tabulation is not exhaustive. A few somewhat forced cases are omitted.

Geld und Gut 242, 65
Gibt uns Gott dies einge Gut ... 244, 11
Gott und Gottes Gunst 248, 11
ganz und gar 253, 2
Dein Geberde, dein Gesicht 254, 9
ganz und gar 255, 41
Geduld ist Gottes Gabe
Und seines Geistes Gut ..... 267, 25 & 26
Gottes Grimm ..273, 7 (cf. 111, 75 above)
ganz und gar 284, 68
Güter und Gaben 293, 23
Gut und Gaben 298, 16
Gut und Gelde 319, 9
Gut und Gelde 321, 63

H

Mein Herrscher, mein Helfer .. 5, 61
Haus und Hof 7, 32
Himmels Haus 21, 26
Die Hände herzlich drücken ... 43, 14
Ihr Herz und Hand ist hoch
bemüht 51, 29
Ich mein Heil und Hülfe hab .. 93, 6
Meine Hülfe kömmt allein
Von des Höchsten Händen her 93, 7 & 8
Hiet und Hüter 120, 4
hoch und herrlich 139, 24
Weil heut der Herr der Herr-
lichkeit 171, 3
hartes Herze 200, 51
ich harr und hoff auf dich 212, 99
Wol halt und herrlich siege 217, 85
Haut und Hülle 220, 36
Sein Hoheit ist des Höchsten
Huld 226, 54
Häupt und Halse 232, 66
heilt und hielt 232, 72
Heil und Hort 267, 36
Herr im Haus 267, 56
Heilen im Herzen 293, 78

K

Knecht und Kind 86, 79

L

Lob und Liebe 17, 69
Lebens Leben 19, 58
Lieb und Lust 25, 54
Lieb und Leid 47, 56
Des Lebens Leben lebet noch ... 51, 5
Leben und Leiden 65, 40

Ich lechze wie ein Land 65, 46
liegt und legt 74, 19
Lebens Lauf 89, 85
lebt und lacht 139, 44
Lust und Lachen 149, 35
Alle Luft Laute ruft 155, 5
Leib und Seele laben 164, 64
Lebens Läng 164, 101
Im ewgen Leben labe 173, 96
Lebens Lauf 180, 72
Lieb und Leid 209, 41
Leib und Leben 229, 93
Kein Lieben und kein Leiden ...229, 107
Lob und lieb 235, 120
Ist viel mehr Lobs und Liebens
wert 242, 3
Sie thut ihm Liebes und kein
Leid 242, 9
Mein Leben lang 252, 47
Lieb und Lust 260, 89
Licht und Leben 271, 44
Lebens Licht 284, 98
Licht und Leben 313, 19
Luft und Leben 328, 50

M

Mich und mein armes Leben 47, 12
Entnehmen meinen Mut 74, 29
Mein Vater musz mich lieben ... 83, 10
Alle Menschen müszen leiden ... 274, 86

R

Regen, Reif, und Wind 10, 71
Ruh und Rast 46, 6
Reich und Rachen 62, 55
Ruh und Rast 328, 2

S

Ich stund in Spott und Schanden 25, 27
Springst und singst 28, 47
In Schlaf und süszer Stille 30, 48
schrickt und scheut 49, 10
So sorgten sie zur selben Zeit ... 51, 50
du sollt die Sonne schauen 59, 16
Die Sünden aller Sünder 68, 4
Schand und Sünden 76, 35
stiehlt und stellt 80, 31
Schand und Sünde 81, 13
Der Seelen Sitz mit Sinn und
Witz 83, 21

Der Schatten einen Schemen 86, 33
sanft und stille 86, 94
Spiesz und Schwerter 95, 4
. . . zerstörten Schlösser
Und Städte voller Schutt und
Stein ....95, 39 & 40
Stahl und Steine 111, 86
Zu stehen in dem Streit 111, 14
Dein Stab, Herr, und dein
Stecken 120, 27
sanft und still 139, 7
Ich steh im gewünschten Stande
. . . Scham und Schande
145, 109 & 110
Sammt, Seiden 158, 69
selig, süsz, und schön 200, 19
Stahl noch Stein 209, 61
Mit   Schimpf   und   groszer
Schande 212, 128
Ist voller Freud und Singen
Sieht lauter Sonnenschein
Die Sonne . . . .229, 115, 116 & 117
Seine Strafen, seine Schläge 235, 91
Hält sich selbst sauber; weisze
Seid 242, 43
Singt und springt 251, 17
schwache Schnur 254, 22
Schosz und Schutz 287, 76
Sind seine Sorgen
Segnen . . ..293, 32 & 33
Steht in steter voller Blüt 304, 68

T

Thun und Toben 108, 62
Tod und Teufel 312, 6

W

Wind und Wetter 10, 63
Gott weisz wol, was wir ver-
mögen 28, 25
Wirst du und wir mit dir gehn,
Wenn uns wird . . ..28, 62 & 63
Um welcher willen 30, 2

Aus welcher Wund 30, 307
Hast alles, was ich wünsch und
will 46, 26
Dich hat ein Weib der Welt ge-
bracht 47, 16
Mein Weirauch und mein Widder 59, 23
Wer dort wird mit verhöhnt,
Wird hier auch mit gekrönt;
Wer dort mit sterben geht,
Wird hier auch mit erhöht 74, 69-72
Werk und Worten 86, 46
Weisz alle Weisheit 100, 67
wertes Wort 104, 62
Wol und Weh 139, 37
Weg und Weisen 205, 33
Der Weizen wächset mit Gewalt 239, 37
Wol und Weh 263, 63
All deine Werk sind Wunder voll 287, 47
Weirauch und Widder
293, 29 (cf. 59, 23 above)
Wort und Willen 293, 75

Z

Durch Zittern und durch Zagen.. 19, 10
Mit Zittern und mit Zagen 30, 39
Zorn, Zank 111, 52
Zeit und Zahl 150, 99
Zur rechten Zeit zu zähmen 169, 11
Zu seinem Zweck und Ziel 185, 40

SPECIAL CASES OF ALLITERATION
Dein Schirm und Schild, dein
Hülf und Heil 118, 55
Wann Gottes Geist erhebt die
Hand 173, 41
Sein Herz ist voller Huld
Und gönnt uns lauter Guts.
Den Abend währt das Weinen,
Des Morgens macht das Scheinen
Der Sonn uns gutes Muts 180, 35-40
Ich liebe dich und leide Pein
Bin dein und doch betrübet ..190, 38 & 39
Lasset uns loben
Seliges Sterben ....270, 5 & 6

ASSONANCE

5, 58 grünen und blühn
19, 1 gehn und treten
   45 Sei der Verlasznen Vater
   46   . . . Berater
   47   . . . Gabe
   48 Der Armen Gut und Habe.

23, 69 Der Rat und That erfinden
       kann
28, 47 springst und singst
   62 Wirst du und wir mit dir gehn
   63 Wenn uns wird . . .

44,   2   Der herzlich . . .
      3   Wie schmerzlich . . .
46,   5   Du Träger aller Bürd und Last
      6   Du aller Müden Ruh und Rast
47,   7   Ach, wie bezwang und drang
          dich doch
     60   All seine Zeit vertreibe
60, 43   Breit aus die Flügel beide
     44   O Jesu, meine Freude
     45   Und nimm dein Küchlein ein!
65, 49   Saft und Kraft
68,   1   geht und trägt
      5   matt und krank
78, 12   selbst zum Helfer stellt
80, 40   Füll und Hüll
91, 58   schlecht und recht
100, 67   Weisz alle Weisheit
     70   Fleisz und Schweisz
111, 52   Neid und Streit
111, 82   Auf Reu der Freuden Blick
118, 49   sing und spring
122, 13   Gut und Blut
124, 27   . . . Spreu zerstreuet
132, 16   Gut und Blut (cf. 122, 13)
145, 47   Jagt und schlagt
    102   sing und klinge
    110   Scham und Schande
149, 15   Wunden unsrer Sünden
161, 88   Theil und Heil
164, 3   schlecht und recht (cf. 91, 58)
    131   weit und breit
171, 1   weit und breit (cf. 164, 131)
176, 12   So kennt, so nennt
193, 43   Tritt und Schritt
196, 4   Rat und That (cf. 23, 69)
200, 32   Tag und Nacht
     38   Not und Tod
209, 110 Da wird mein Weinen lauter
          Wein,
    111   Mein Ächzen lauter Jauchzen
          sein.

212, 11   Rat und That (cf. 23, 69 ; 196, 4)
217, 4   geht und steht
220, 45   Wer brachte Sonn und Mond
          herfür
     46   Wer machte Kräuter, Bäum
          und Thier
229, 45   Kein Urtheil mich erschrecket
     46   Kein Unheil mich betrübt
239, 28   Die Wiesen liegen
     44   Des groszen Gottes groszes
          Thun
242, 72   weit und breit (cf. 164, 131 ;
          169, 1)
244, 43   des roten Goldes Kot
251, 17   singt und springt (cf. 28, 47 ;
          118, 49)
253, 19   Kraft und Macht
254, 14   Gieng und hieng
260, 94   Rat und That (cf. 23, 69 ; 196, 4)
270.   In this poem note the unusual
          scheme of alliteration and
          sound sequence (regular
          except for one line) in
          the first four syllables of the
          concluding couplets of the
          first three stanzas :
   stanza 1
      5   lasset uns loben . . .
      6   Seliges Sterben . . .
   stanza 2
     11   Ihre Begierde . . .
     12   Ist ihr erfüllet . . .
   stanza 3
     17   Berkow, das feine, geschickte
          Gemüt
     18   Dessen Gedächtnisz . . .
271, 15   Tod und Sterbensnot
274, 87   webt und lebet
284, 71   hebt und leget
287, 53   Tag und Jahre Zahl
298, 125 webt und lebt (cf. 274, 87)
333, 54   Rat und That (cf. 23, 69 ;
          260, 94)

DOUBLETS OF EXACT OR APPROXIMATE SYNONYMS (cf. p. 19)

Ach und Weh . . . . 104, 8 ; 335, 10
Adern und Geblüte 158, 9
Angst und Not . . . 25, 55 ; 91, 66 ; 150, 89 ;
          193, 66 ; 209, 26 ; 232, 99 ; 325, 24
Angst und Nöten 185, 71
Angst, Furcht, Sorg und Schmerz 78, 19
Angst und Pein . . . . 122, 20 ; 224, 5

Angst und Plagen 19. 9
Angst und Qual . . 23, 10 ; 164, 97 ; 198, 8 ;
          271, 12
Angst und Schmerzen 220, 15
Angst und Trübsal 145, 30
Angst und Weh . . . 65, 64 ; 164, 53 ; 212, 37
ängstet und bemüht 78, 27

Arm und Kraft 284, 88

Bahn und Lauf 304, 16
Bahn und Steg ....83, 91 ; 248, 79
Berg und Spitzen 217, 22
betrübt und kränket 95, 31
Bett und Lager 313, 13
bewust und wolbekannt 139, 52
brechen und fallen 293, 67
Bund und Zeugnisz 91, 27
Bürd und Last 267, 32
Burg und Schlosz 190, 90

Dampf und Rauch 153, 12
Dieb und Räuber 106, 21
drück und quäle 108, 56

Ehr und Dank 324, 46
Ehr und Dienste 111, 15
Eilend und behend 315, 54
emsich und bemühet 328, 16
Ohn End und alle Masz 47, 41
Erb und Theil 190, 96
Erd und Kot 115, 20
Erd und Staub 324, 7
Erd und Thon 153, 7
Erkenntnisz und Verstand 260, 82
Ernst und Eifer 30, 246

fall und sterbe 229, 75
Fehl und Mängel 278, 23
Fels und Burg 145, 14
Fels und Stein ....30, 322 ; 127, 53
Feuer und Licht 242, 29
Fleisch und Blut ..30, 31 ; 217, 42 ; 324, 4 ;
                                      325, 12 ; 328, 30
Fleisz und Schweisz 100, 70
fliehn und haszen 81, 40
fleuch und haszt 229, 82
fliehn und laszen 71, 89
frech und geil 278, 108
sich freu und jubiliere 212, 102
Freud und Lust 97, 49
Freud und Seligkeit 209, 97
Freud und Singen 229, 115
Freud und Trost 51, 181
Freud und Wonne ....158, 25 ; 232, 2
Freuden und Lust 5, 33
Mein Freund und treuer Rat 217, 39
Fried- und Freudenswort 95, 2

Fried und Ruh ....95, 72 ; 205, 83
Frisch und freudig 232, 98
Füll und Hüll 80, 40
Furcht und Angst 120, 19
Furcht und Scheu 15, 43
Furcht und Schrecken ...51, 182 ; 229, 58
Furcht und Zagen 284, 39

Gall und Gift 81, 23
ganz und gar ....15, 6 ; 178, 8 ; 253, 2 ;
                                      254, 41 ; 284, 68
ganz und neu 251, 28
Geist und Gemüte 271, 2
Geist und Sinn ....78, 18 ; 158, 5
Geist und Sinnen 135, 78
Geld und Gut 242, 65
Gemüt und Seele 108, 55
gern und williglich 71, 84
getrost und unbetrübt 271, 1
getrost und unverzagt 125, 75
Gift und Gallen 153, 14
Glanz und Bild 46, 15
Glanz und Freudenlicht 118, 54
Mein Glanz und schönes Licht .. 229, 26
Glanz und Schein 103, 2
Glaub und Treu ....173, 28 ; 205, 40
Glück und Freude 10, 84
Glück, Gut und Ehr 89, 3
Glück und Heil 95, 30
Glück und Segen ....108, 88 ; 217, 3
Gnad und Gab 97, 13
Gnad und Gunst 304, 3
Gnad und Güte 95, 11
Gnad und Gütigkeit 62, 90
Gnad und Hulden 293, 84
Gott und Hort 253, 15
Gott und Retter 127, 16
Grab und Sarg 68, 29
Gram und Leid ....,.....135, 127
Gram und Schmerze 25, 43
Gras und Laub 324, 8
Gut und Geld(e) ..86, 32 ; 97, 38 ; 153, 57 ;
                                      319, 9 ; 321, 63
Gut und Heil 17, 56
Gut und Waaren 10, 60
Güt und Segen 21, 27

Hab und Gut 188, 19
Hasz und Neid 15, 19
Haus und Hof 7, 32

Haus und Zelt 173, 86; 232, 86
Heil und Gnaden 293, 76
Heil und Hülfe 93, 6
Herz und Mut 7, 62; 267, 16
Herz und Sinn ....83, 1 & 2; 205, 43
Heu und Stroh 158, 68
hoch und herrlich 139, 24
Hohn und Spott ...68, 8; 183, 17; 229, 86
Hohn und groszem Spott 71, 6
Huld und Gnaden 324, 23
Hülf und Errettung 111, 12
Hülf und Heil 118, 55
Hülf und Rat 188, 22
Hut und Güte 106, 29
Hut und Wach 287, 26

in Jammer und in Not 198, 10
Jauchzen und Freuden 5, 72

Kält und Frost 118, 17
kann und mag 239, 43; 274, 85
kann und weisz 25, 16
Klag und Sorge 226, 12
klar und rein 287, 39
Knecht und Kind 86, 79
Mein Können, mein Vermögen.. 235, 45
Kraft und Macht 253, 19

Last und Bürd 226, 22
Laster und Schande 293, 46
Leib und Leben 229, 93
Leib und Seel(e) ..7, 85; 25, 19; 30, 129;
  60, 39; 71, 52; 71, 59; 83, 20; 93, 29;
    127, 8; 164, 64; 248, 22; 325, 15
lenke und führe 293, 87
Lieb und Ehre 217, 45
Lieb und Gnad 278, 90
Lieb und Güt 78, 25
Lieb und Huld 3, 11; 7, 60; 25, 60;
    30, 329; 65, 24
Lieb und Lust 25, 54
Lieb und Treu 30, 229
List und Tück 91, 54
Lob und Preis 25, 14; 248, 5; 319, 13;
    324, 48
lobt und preist 10, 90
Lob und Dank 97, 22; 180, 7; 232, 91
Lohn und Sold 271, 33
Luft und Höh 15, 24

Lust und Freude 21, 54; 180, 88;
  193, 31; 226, 68; 244, 26
Lust und Freuden 124, 9

Macht und Kraft 108, 84
March und Bein 158, 42
Mark und Bein 328, 28
Masz und Zahl 15, 32
Masz und Ziel 10, 45; 183, 62; 232, 84

Neid und Hasz 321, 10
Neid und Streit 248, 60

Ort und Raum ......30, 344; 161, 39 & 40

Pein und Schmerz 328, 60
Pest und Gift 51, 240
Dein Pilgrim und dein Bürger .. 86, 81
Preis und Dank 106, 4
Preis und Ehr 150, 7

Ränk und List 80, 33
Rat und Hülfe 307, 4
Raub und Frasz 321, 12
rein und gerecht 65, 16
rein und hell 46, 14
rein und klar 278, 18
wir rennen, laufen 315, 50
Ruh und Rast 328, 2
Ruhm und Preis 302, 74
rühmt und preist 176, 12

Sanft und gelind 224, 37
sanft und still(e) 86, 94; 139, 7
Schand und Spott 103, 30
Schand und Sünde 81, 13
dein Schatz, dein Erb und Theil 119, 53
Schild und Hort 93, 39
Mit   Schimpf   und   groszer
  Schande 212, 128
Schirm und Schild 118, 55
schläft und ruht 335, 52
schlägt und drückt 325, 30
Schmerze und Sorgen ....185, 49 & 50
Schmerz und Weh 226, 9
schön und klar 158, 61
Das Schönste und Beste 293, 97
schrickt und scheut 49, 10
Schuld und Missethat 256, 109
Sclav und Knecht 325, 26
Seel und Geist 81, 44

Dein Seufzen und dein Stöhnen 71, 91
singen und loben 120, 48
sinken und fallen 212, 124
Sinn und Geiste 263, 69
       (cf. Geist und Sinn, q. v.)
Sitz und Ort 278, 176
Sitz und Raum 7, 35
Sonn und Zier 217, 47
Sorg und Schmerzen .....229, 51 ; 307, 46
Speis und Malzeit 244, 45
Spiesz und Schwerter 95, 4
Spott und Hohn ....100, 54 ; 135, 47
Spott und Schanden 25, 27
Dein Stab und dein Stecken 120, 27
Stadt und Land 7, 36
Stärk und Kraft ..28, 42 ; 271, 19 ; 239, 35
steif und fest ....161, 69 ; 178, 37 ; 226, 66
Stell und Ort ....220, 38 ; 310, 27
Straf und Last 30, 340
Straf und Zorn 224, 9
Stuhl und Thron(e) .....108, 70 ; 205, 84
Stund und Zeiten 60, 34
Sturm und Regen 267, 15
Sturm und Ungewitter 209, 84
Sturm und Wellen 229, 15
Sturm und Wetter ....7, 25 ; 93, 30
Sturm und Wind 253, 10

Thau und Regen 118, 16
Theil und Erbe 229, 73
Thun und Machen 19, 23
Thun und Toben 108, 62
Dein Tichten, dein Trachten, dein
    Thun 5, 17
Tief und See 15, 23

Tod und Ende 30, 192
trifft und schlägt 324, 17
Tritt und Schritt 193, 43
Trost und Freud(e) .....25, 18 ; 65, 22 ;
                196, 36 ; 302, 73
Aller Trost und alle Freude 108, 41
Trost und Labsal ....65, 57 ; 232, 4
Trost und Licht 328, 82
Trost und Schild 46, 16

Wall und Mauren 183, 15
Weg und Weisen 205, 33
Wege, Lauf und Bahn 185, 6
Weh und Klagen 97, 50
Weh und Schmerz(en) ..251, 3 ; 284, 38
Weis und Art 335, 62
Weisheit und Verstand ..139, 51 ; 158, 57
weit und breit ...164, 131 ; 171, 1 ; 242, 72
Werk und That ..217, 50 ; 220, 85 ; 304, 29
Werke und Thaten 293, 35
Wind und Wetter 10, 63
wirkt und schafft 139, 34
Witz und Sinn 220, 5
Wonn und Fröhlichkeit 310, 72
Wort und Reden 278, 20
Würd und Ehr 188, 88

ihre Zähren und Thränen ...142, 27 & 28
Zank und Geifer 321, 11
Zeit und Stund 244, 111
Zorn und Eifer 321, 9
Zorn und Fluch 103, 9
Zorn und Grimm 108, 14
Zorn und groszem Grimm 164, 61
Zweck und Ziel 185, 40

REPETITION[1]

Was ist doch gut ohn diesem Gut? 10, 96
Wenn dies Gut nicht im Herzen ruht 10, 97
Ist alles Gut verworfen 10, 98
O Häupt voll Blut und Wunden, ... 49, 1
Voll Schmerz und voller Hohn! 49, 2
O Häupt zu Spott gebunden 49, 3
O Häupt, sonst schön gezieret 49, 5
Auf, auf, ihr sollt beginnen 60, 5
Erdengut zerfällt und bricht 89, 35
Seelengut das schwindet nicht 89, 36
Aller Trost und alle Freude 108, 41
Dein Erfreuen ist die Weide 108, 43
Leuchte mir, o Freudenlicht 108, 45
Zeuch ein zu deinen Thoren 111, 1
Zeuch ein, lasz mich empfinden 111, 9
Und schmecken deine Kraft[2] 111, 10
Die Kraft die uns von Sünden 111, 11
Was Gott gefällt. .139, 5, 10, 15, 20, etc. (i. e. the concluding line of each of the 20 stanzas)
Wir singen dir, Emanuel 150, 1
Wir singen dir in deinem Heer 150, 6
Bist aller Haiden Trost und Licht, ... 150, 43
Suchst selber Trost und findst ihn nicht 150, 44
Du bist der süsze Menschenfreund 150, 46
Doch sind dir so viel Menschen feind 150, 47
Befiehl du deine Wege 185, 1
Gibt Wege, Lauf und Bahn 185, 6
Der wird auch Wege finden 185, 7
Sollt ich meinen Gott nicht singen? 235, 1
Sollt ich Ihm nicht dankbar sein? 235, 2
Alles Ding währt seine Zeit 235, 9
Gottes Lieb in Ewigkeit 235, 10
(This couplet concludes each of the twelve stanzas)

JUXTAPOSITION OF WORDS DERIVED FROM THE SAME ROOT, AND PLAYS ON WORDS (cf. p. 19)

Trotz sei dir, du trotzender Kot! 5, 65
Erbarm dich, o barmherzigs Herz 7, 76
Als das geliebte Lieben 25, 35
Zum Fluch dem, der Ihm flucht 25, 74
Das nennt der Lästrer Lästerwort 30, 106
Kein Wächter mag zu mächtig sein 39, 323
Drum, herzes Herze, bitt ich dich 47, 28
Wer dich recht liebt, ergibt sich frei, ... 47, 46
In deiner Lieb und süszen Treu 47, 47

---

[1] The complete tabulation of words and phrases used in repetition is too bulky for printing. These few selections will serve to illustrate this characteristic of Gerhardt's poetry. Cf. p. 19.

[2] Frequently, as here, the last word in the line is repeated as the first word in the next following line. Cf. 111, 69 & 70; 149, 44 & 45; 158, 23 & 24; 161, 117 & 118.

Der von unbeschnittnem Herzen 67, 3
. . . . mit Beschneidung 67, 5
Die Sünden aller Sünder 68, 4
O Wunderlieb! o Liebesmacht 68, 25
Die Trübsal trübt mir nicht 74, 45
Das Unglück ist mein Glück 74, 47
Gründst des tiefen Meeres Grund 76, 28
Und wo kein Mensch nicht helfen kann 78, 11
Sich selbst zum Helfer stellt 78, 12
Und Vater meines Lebens 81, 2
Wo du mein Leben nicht regierst 81, 3
So leb ich hier vergebens; 81, 4
Ja lebendig bin ich auch todt, ... 81, 5
. . . . Der hat das rechte Leben 81, 8
Der Wird zu Schanden, der dich schändt 91, 5
Und wie mich der so hoch erhöht, ... 97, 6
Der selbst so hoch erhoben 97, 7
Helfer in der rechten Zeit 108, 6
Hilf, o Heiland 108, 7
Ein Freund der Freundlichkeit 111, 50
Der Feindschaft bist du feind 111, 53
Zu rühmen seinen Ruhm! 115, 74
Kann uns doch kein Tod nicht tödten 122, 43
Auch tödte mich durch deinen Tod 132, 58
Lasz mich deinen Schutz beschützen 145, 11
Wenn mir Lebenskraft gebricht; 145, 76
Lasz mein Leben in dir leben 145, 77
Ich steh im gewünschten Stande 145, 109
Sein Licht und Heil macht alles heil 153, 21
Du bist meines Leben Leben 155, 70
. . . . . dasz ich mein End 161, 113
Auch also möchte enden 161, 114
Durch Adams Fall gefallen. 173, 15
Durch dieses Fallen ist die Macht 173, 16
Weg hast du allerwegen 185, 25
. . . . kein Sinnen 220, 79
Ihm hat ersinnen können! 220, 80
Der Grund, da ich mich gründe 229, 17
. . . . . mein Vermögen 235, 45
Nichts vermag, nichts helfen kann, ... 235, 46
Sein Vermögen beizulegen 235, 48
Wann andre löschen Feuer und Licht, ... 242, 29
Verlöscht doch ihre Leuchte nicht 242, 30
Ich lieb ihr liebes Angesicht 260, 41
Gütig dem, der Gutes thut. 307, 79
Nun, der sei mein schönstes Gut 307, 80

PLAYS ON WORDS

Herr Fromm ist fromm, das weisz man wol 13, 82
Der Frommen Lohn ....13, 124 (cf. 13, 82)
Sein Licht und Heil macht alles heil 153, 21
Da wird mein Weinen lauter Wein 209, 110
Wie seinem Mut zu Mute sei 223, 123
Steht in steter voller Blüt 304, 68

INDEX BY SUBJECTS*

HOLY TRINITY

Goedeke
Page Page

1. Was alle Weisheit in der Welt ....176.....62

ADVENT

1. Warum willst du drauszen stehen ....108.....51
2. Wie soll ich dich empfangen ....25.....82

CHRISTMAS

1. Frölich soll mein Herze springen ....155.....58
2. Ich steh an deiner Krippen hier ....158.....60
3. Kommt und laszt uns Christum ehren ....312.....79
4. O Jesu Christ, dein Kripplein ist ....153.....57
5. Schaut, Schaut, was ist für Wunder dar ....310.....79
6. Wir singen dir, Emanuel ....150....110

NEW YEAR

1. Nun laszt uns gehn und treten ....19.....38
2. Warum machet solche Schmerzen ....67.....42

GOOD FRIDAY (PASSIONTIDE)

1. Ein Lämmlein geht und trägt die Schuld ....68....104
2. Gegrüszet seist du, Gott, mein Heil ....46.....41
3. Hör an, mein Herz, die sieben Wort ....161.....60
4. O Haupt voll Blut und Wunden ....49.....86
5. O Herz des Königs aller Welt ....47.....41
6. O Welt, sieh hier dein Leben ....71.....42
7. Sei mir tausendmal gegrüszet ....40.....40

EASTER

1. Auf, auf, mein Herz, mit Freuden ....74.....44
2. Sei frölich alles weit und breit ....171.....61

WHITSUNTIDE

1. Gott, Vater, sende deinen Geist ....173.....62
2. O du allersüszste Freude ....76.....44
3. Zeuch ein zu deinen Thoren ....111.....52

CROSS AND CONSOLATION

1. Ach treuer Gott, barmherzigs Herz ....209.....65
2. Barmherziger Vater, höchster Gott ....212.....66
3. Befiehl du dein Wege ....185....114
4. Du bist ein Mensch, das weiszt du wol ....220.....67

---

* Only 76 of the 131 poems have been included in this index.

		Goedeke Page	Page
5.	Du liebe Unschuld du	3	36
6.	Geduld ist euch vonnöten	267	72
7.	Gib dich zufrieden und sei stille	274	74
8.	Ich hab in Gottes Herz und Sinn	83	48
9.	Ich hab oft bei mir selbst gedacht	226	68
10.	Ich habs verdient, was will ich doch	224	67
11.	Ist Gott für mich, so trete	229	126
12.	Nicht so traurig, nicht so sehr	89	48
13.	Noch dennoch muszt du drum nicht ganz	23	38
14.	Schwing dich auf zu deinem Gott	135	55
15.	Warum sollt ich mich denn grämen	122	108
16.	Was Gott gefällt, mein frommes Kind	139	56
17.	Wie lang, o Herr, wie lange soll	178	62

REPENTANCE

1.	Herr, höre, was mein Mund	65	41
2.	Nach dir, o Herr, verlanget mich	91	49
3.	Weg, mein Herz, mit den Gedanken	62	41

PRAISE AND THANKSGIVING

1.	Auf den Nebel folgt die Sonne	232	68
2.	Der Herr, der aller Enden	120	54
3.	Gott Lob! nun ist erschollen	95	50
4.	Ich singe dir mit Herz und Mund	118	53
5.	Nun danket all und bringet Ehr	78	46
6.	Sollt ich meinem Gott nicht singen	235	69
7.	Wie ist es müglich, höchstes Licht	324	81
8.	Wie ist so grosz und schwer die Last	7	36

PRAYER AND THE CHRISTIAN LIFE

1.	Herr, aller Weisheit Quell und Grund	260	71
2.	Herr, du erforschest meinen Sinn	287	75
3.	Ich danke dir demütiglich	205	65
4.	Ich erhebe, Herr, zu dir	93	49
5.	Ich weisz, mein Gott, dasz all mein Thun	217	66
6.	Jesu, allerliebster Bruder	263	72
7.	O Gott, mein Schöpfer, edler Fürst	81	48
8.	O Jesu Christ, mein schönstes Licht	200	63
9.	Wol dem, der den Herren scheuet	130	55
10.	Wol dem Menschen, der nicht wandelt	124	54
11.	Zweierlei bitt ich von dir	80	47

MORNING AND EVENING

1.	Der Tag mit seinem Lichte	296	77
2.	Die güldne Sonne	293	76
3.	Lobet den Herren, alle, die ihn fürchten	106	51
4.	Nun ist der Regen hin	17	37
5.	Nun ruhen alle Wälder	60	98
6.	Wach auf, mein Herz, und singe	59	95

DEATH AND ETERNAL LIFE

		Goedeke Page	Page
1.	Die Zeit ist nunmehr nah	142	57
2.	Du bist zwar mein und bleibest mein	100	50
3.	Herr Gott, du bist ja für und für	315	80
4.	Ich bin ein Gast auf Erden	284	74
5.	Johannes sahe durch Gesicht	319	80
6.	Nun, du lebest, unsre Krone	28	39
7.	Nun sei getrost und unbetrübt	271	73
8.	Was traurest du, mein Angesicht	289	76

INDEX OF ENGLISH VERSIONS

This index contains in general only the first lines of the translations and adaptations as they are given in Part II, Chapter II (pp. 35-143). The numbers refer to the pages on which the general discussions of the corresponding Gerhardt poems begin.

	Page
A Holy, Pure and Spotless Lamb	36
A Lamb bears all its guilt away	104
A Lamb goes forth and bears the Guilt	104
A Lamb goes forth—for all the dues	104
A Lamb goes forth: the sins he bears	104
A Lamb goes uncomplaining forth	104
A Pilgrim am I on my way	141
A pilgrim and a stranger	74
A pilgrim here I wander	74
A rest here have I never	74
After clouds we see the sun	68
Ah! faithful God, compassionate heart	65
Ah! Head, so pierced and wounded	86
Ah! Lord, how shall I meet thee	82
Ah! lovely innocence, how evil art thou deemed	36
Ah wounded Head! must thou	86
Ah wounded Head, that bearest	86
All hail! my Savior and my God	41
All hail to Thee, my Savior and my God	41
All my heart this night rejoices	58
All my heart with joy is springing	58
As pilgrims here we wander	74
Awake, my heart, be singing	95
Be glad, my heart! now fear no more	73
Be joyful all, both far and near	61
Be not dismay'd—in time of need	57
Be of good cheer in all your wants	71
Be thou content: be still before	74
Be thou contented! aye relying	74
Behold a Lamb! so tired and faint	104
Behold! Behold! what wonders here	79
Behold, O World, thy Life, thy Lord	42

Page

Bless'd is he the Lord who loveth 55
Bless'd is he who never taketh 54
Bring to Christ your best oblation 79
By John was seen a wondrous sight 80

Can I cease, my God, from singing 69
Can I fail my God to praise 69
Christians all, with one accord 38
Come, and Christ the Lord be praising 79
Come and let us Christ revere now 79
Come, enter Thine own portal 52
Come forth, my heart, and seek delight 131
Come now, my soul, thy thoughts engage 60
Come, O Thou Holy Dove 52
Come, Thou Source of sweetest gladness 44
Cometh sunshine after rain 68
Come to Thy temple here on earth 52
Come, unite in praise and singing 79
Commend thy way O mortal 114
Commit the way before thee 114
Commit thou all thy griefs 114
Commit thou all thy ways, and all 114
Commit thou every sorrow, And care 114
Commit thou thy each grievance 114
Commit thy course and keeping 114
Commit thy secret grief 114
Commit thy way, confiding 114
Commit thy way, O weeper 114
Commit thy way, O weeping 114
Commit thy Ways and Goings 114
Commit thy ways, thy sorrows 114
Commit thy way to God 114
Commit thy way unto the Lord, thy heavy 114
Commit whatever grieves thee 114
Creator, Father, Prince of might! 48

Display thy both wings over 98

Emmanuel, Thy name we sing 110
Emmanuel, we sing Thy praise 110
(See also "Immanuel.")
Evening and Morning 76
Ever by my love be owned 40
Extended on a cursed tree 42

Father of mercies! God most high 66
For Thee, Lord, pants my longing heart 49
Forth goes a dear devoted Lamb 104
From our fears and sins release us 137
Full often as I meditate 68
Full of wonder, full of art (2) 79
Full of wonder, full of skill (2) 79

Page

Give to the winds thy fears 114
God is my strong salvation 139
God, my Creator, and my Lord 48
Go forth my heart, and revel in joy's flow 131
Go forth, my heart, and seek delight (3) 131
Go forth, my heart, and seek for praise 131
Go forth, my heart, and seek the bliss 131
Go forth, my heart, nor linger here 131
Go forth, my Heart! the year's sweet prime 131
Go out, my heart, and pleasure seek 131
Go out, my heart, and seek delight 131

He never yet has made mistakes 53
He sendeth sun, he sendeth shower 140
Hence, my heart, with such a thought 41
Here I can firmly rest 126
Here, World, see thy Redeemer 42
Here, World, thy great Salvation see 42
Holy Ghost, dispel our sadness 44
Holy Spirit, Source of gladness 44
How can it be, my highest Light 81
How heavy is the burden made 36
How long, Lord, in forgetfullness 62
How shall I come to meet Thee 82
How shall I meet my Savior 82
How shall I meet Thee, How my heart 82

I build on this foundation 126
I give Thee thanks unfeigned 86
I have deserv'd it, cease t'oppose 67
I into God's own heart and mind 48
I know, my God, and I rejoice 66
I know that my Redeemer lives 81
I know that my Redeemer lives 135
I'll praise Thee with my heart and tongue 53
I'll sing to Thee with heart and mouth 53
I'll sing to Thee with mouth and heart 53
I'm but a stranger here 140
I sing to Thee with Heart and Tongue 53
I stand beside Thy manger-bed 60
I who so oft in deep distress 78
I will sing my Maker's praises 69
I yield Thee thanks unfeigned 86
If Christ is mine, then all is mine 126
If God be on my side 126
If God Himself be for me 126
If God is mine, then present things 126
If Jesus be my friend 126
Immanuel, Thy praise we sing 110
Immanuel! to Thee we sing, The Fount 110

Page

Immanuel, to Thee we sing, Thou Prince 110
Immanuel, we sing to Thee 110
(See also "Emmanuel.")
In exile here we wander 142
In grateful songs your voices raise 46
In heaven is mine inheritance 126
In me resume Thy dwelling 52
In prayer your voices raise ye 38
Is God for me? I fear not 126
Is God for me? t'oppose me 126
Is God for me? what is it 126
Is God my strong salvation 126
It is a time of joy today 79

Jesu, my Savior, Brother, Friend 136
Jesu, my Strength, my Hope 136
Jesu, our Joy and loving Friend 98
Jesus! Thou, my dearest Brother 72
Jesus, Thy boundless love to me 63
Joyful be my spirit singing 58
Joyful shall my heart, upspringing 58

Leave to his sovereign sway 114
Let not such a thought e'er pain thee 41
Let the voice of glad thanksgiving 58
Lightly bound my bosom, ringing 58
Lo! Man and Beast are sleeping 98
Look up to thy God again 55
Lord, be Thy Cross before our sight 42
Lord God! Thou art forevermore 80
Lord, how shall I be meeting 82
Lord, how shall I receive Thee 82
Lord, lend a gracious ear 41
Lord, Thou my heart dost search and try 75
Lord! to Thee alone I raise 49

May I when time is o'er 57
Mine art Thou still, and mine shalt be 50
Mortals, who have God offended 42
My face, why should'st thou troubled be 76
My Faith securely buildeth 126
My faith Thy lowly bed beholds 60
My God! my works and all I do 66
My heart's warm gush breaks forth in mirth 53
My heart! the seven words hear now 60
My rest is in heaven; my rest is not here 142
My Savior, how shall I proclaim 42
My soul awake and render 95
My Soul, awake and tender 95

Not so darkly, not so deep 48
Now all the woods are sleeping 98

Page

Now at the manger here I stand 60
Now every greenwood sleepeth 98
Now gone is all the rain 37
Now hushed are woods and waters 98
Now in His manger He so humbly lies 58
Now let each humble creature 38
Now rest beneath night's shadow 98
Now rest the woods again 98
Now resteth all creation 98
Now spread are evening's shadows 98
Now with joy my heart is bounding 58
Now woods and fields are quiet 98
Now woods their rest are keeping 98

O blessed Christ, once wounded 86
O blessed Jesus! This 57
O cast away thy fears 114
O Christ! how good and fair 57
O Christ, my Light, my gracious Savior 63
O Christ, my only Life and Light 63
O Christ, my sweetest Life and Light 63
O Christ! what consolation 86
O come and dwell in me 136
O Come, my soul with singing 53
O come with prayer and singing 38
O enter, Lord, Thy temple 52
O faithful God! O pitying heart 65
O Father! send Thy spirit down 62
O God! from Thee doth wisdom flow 71
O God! how many thankful songs 78
O God most true, most merciful! 65
O God, my Father! thanks to Thee 65
O God of mercy full and free 65
O God! who dost Heav'n's sceptre wield 37
O Head, blood-stained and wounded 86
O Head so full of bruises 86
O Head, so pierced and wounded 86
O Heart of Him who dwells on high 41
O Jesus Christ! my fairest Light 63
O Jesus Christ! Thy cradle is 57
O Lamb of God, once wounded 86
O Lord! I sing with mouth and heart 53
O my soul, why dost thou grieve 48
O Sacred Head! now wounded (varying centos) 86
O Sacred Head, surrounded 86
O Thou sweetest source of gladness 44
O World! attention lend it 42
O World, behold him dying 137
O, World! behold upon the tree 42
O World! see here suspended 42

                                                                    Page
O World! see thy Creator   42
O World! see thy life languish   42
Oh! bleeding head, and wounded   86
Oh, how shall I receive Thee   82
Oh Jesus Christ! how bright and fair   78
Oh, wounded head and bleeding   86
On earth I'm but a pilgrim   74
On thy bier how calm thou'rt sleeping   39
Our Lord be praising, All His glory raising   51

Praise God! for forth hath sounded   50
Praise God! revere Him! all ye men that fear Him   51
Praise ye Jehovah, all ye men who fear Him   51
Put thou thy trust in God   114

Quietly rest the woods and dales   98

Rest in the Lord, my soul   138
Retake thy own Possession   52
Rise, my soul, shake off all sadness   58
Rise, my soul, thy vigil keep   98

Say with what salutations   82
Scarce tongue can speak, ne'er human ken   62
See, bowed beneath a fearful weight   104
See the sun's glorious light   76
See World! thy Life assailed   42
See, World, upon the bloody tree   42
See, World, upon the shameful tree   42
Seven times the Savior spake—my heart   60
Shall I not his praise be singing   69
Shall I not my God be praising   69
Shall I not sing praise to Thee   69
Shan't I sing to my Creator   69
Should I not, in meek adoring   69
Since Jesus is my friend   126
Sunbeams all golden   76
Sweetest Fount of holy gladness   44
Sweetest joy the soul can know   44

Thank God it hath resounded   50
The daylight disappeareth   77
The duteous day now closeth   98
The golden corn now waxes strong   131
The golden morning   76
The golden sunbeams with their joyous gleams   76
The Lord, the earth who ruleth   54
The mystery hidden from the eyes   62
The sun's golden beams   76
The time is very near   57
The woods are hushed; o'er town and plain   98

Page

The world may rise against me round 126
Thee, O Immanuel, we praise 110
There is no condemnation 126
Thou art but man, to thee 'tis known 67
Thou art mine own, art still mine own 50
Thou must not altogether be 38
Thou on the Lord rely 114
Thou pierced and wounded brow 86
Thou seest our weakness, Lord 114
Thou'rt mine, yes, still thou art mine own 50
Thousand times by me be greeted 40
Through waves and clouds and storms 114
Thy everlasting truth 114
Thy manger is my paradise 57
Thy mighty working, mighty God 131
Thy Thanks, my Soul, be raising 95
Thy way and all thy sorrows 114
'Tis patience must support you 72
To God commit thy griefs 114
To God thy way commending 114
To God's all-gracious heart and mind 48
To Thee, Immanuel, we sing, the Prince 110
Tranquilly lead thee, peace possessing 74
Twofold, Father, is my pray'r 47

Up, my heart! rejoice with singing 58
Up, Up, my heart, with gladness, Receive 44
Up! up! my heart with gladness, See 44
Up! with gladness heavenward springing 58

Wake, my heart, and sing His praises 95
Wake up, my heart, elater 95
We go to meet Thee, Savior 82
We sing to Thee, Emmanuel, the Prince 110
We sing to Thee, Immanuel, Thou Prince of Life 110
What God decrees, child of His love 56
What God decrees, take patiently 56
What is our mortal race 76
What pleases God, O pious soul 56
What pleaseth God, my faithful child 56
What pleaseth God with joy receive 56
Wherefore dost Thou, blest of God 51
Wherefore dost thou longer tarry 51
Wherefore should I grieve and pine 108
Wherefore, then, should I be gloomy 108
Who is so full of tenderness 78
Why, my soul, thus trembling ever 108
Why should I continue grieving 108
Why should sorrow ever grieve me 108
Why should they such pain e'er give Thee 42

Page

Why this sad and mournful guise 48

Why, without, then, art Thou staying 51

With all Thy saints, Thee, Lord, we sing 110

With notes of joy and songs of praise 38

Yes, thou art mine, still mine, my son 50

INDEX OF GERHARDT'S HYMNS*

	Goedeke Page	Subject	No. of English versions	Page
Ach treuer Gott, barmherzigs Herz	209	Cross and Consolation	3	65
Also hat Gott die Welt geliebt	256	God's Love John III, 16	1	71
Auf, auf, mein Herz, mit Freuden	74	Easter	2	44
Auf den Nebel folgt die Sonne	232	Praise and Thanksgiving	2	68
Barmherziger Vater, höchster Gott	212	Cross and Consolation	1	66
Befiehl du deine Wege	185	Cross and Consolation	18	114
Der Herr, der aller Enden	120	Praise and Thanksgiving	1	54
Der Tag mit seinem Lichte	296	Evening	1	77
Die güldne Sonne	293	Morning	7	76
Die Zeit ist nunmehr nah	142	Eternal Life	3	57
Du bist ein Mensch, das weiszt du wol	220	Cross and Consolation	1	67
Du bist zwar mein und bleibest mein	100	Eternal Life	4	50
Du liebe Unschuld du	3	Cross and Consolation	1	36
Du meine Seele, singe	115	Psalm CXLVI	1	53
Ein Lämmlein geht und trägt die Schuld	68	Passiontide	10	104
Frölich soll mein Herze springen	155	Christmas	11	58
Geduld ist euch vonnöten	267	Cross and Consolation	1	72
Gegrüszet seist du, Gott, mein Heil	46	Passiontide	2	41
Geh aus mein Herz und suche Freud	239	Summer	10	131
Gib dich zufrieden und sei stille	274	Cross and Consolation	3	74
Gott Lob! nun ist erschollen	95	Praise and Thanksgiving	2	50
Gott, Vater, sende deinen Geist	173	Whitsuntide	1	62
Herr, aller Weisheit Quell und Grund	260	Prayer and the Christian Life	1	71
Herr, du erforschest meinen Sinn	287	Prayer and the Christian Life	1	75

* This index includes only those 84 poems for which English versions have been found.

	Goedeke Page	Subject	No. of English versions	Page
Herr Gott, du bist ja für und für	315	Eternal Life	1	80
Herr, höre was mein Mund	65	Repentance	1	41
Hör an, mein Herz, die sieben Wort	161	Passiontide	3	60
Ich bin ein Gast auf Erden	284	Eternal Life	4	74
Ich danke dir demütiglich	205	Prayer and the Christian Life	1	65
Ich, der ich oft in tiefes Leid	298	Psalm CXLV	2	78
Ich erhebe, Herr, zu dir	93	Prayer and the Christian Life	1	49
Ich hab in Gottes Herz und Sinn	83	Cross and Consolation	2	48
Ich hab oft bei mir selbst gedacht	226	Cross and Consolation	1	68
Ich habs verdient, was will ich doch	224	Cross and Consolation	1	67
Ich singe dir mit Herz und Mund	118	Praise and Thanksgiving	6	53
Ich steh an deiner Krippen hier	158	Christmas	3	60
Ich weisz, dasz mein Erlöser lebt	331	Job XIX, 25-27	2	81
Ich weisz, mein Gott, dasz all mein Thun	217	Prayer and the Christian Life	2	66
Ist Gott für mich, so trete	229	Trust in God; Cross and Consolation	7	126
Jesu, allerliebster Bruder	263	Prayer and the Christian Life	1	72
Johannes sahe durch Gesicht	319	Eternal Life	1	80
Kommt und laszt uns Christum ehren	312	Christmas	4	79
Lobet den Herren, alle, die ihn fürchten	106	Morning	3	51
Nach dir, o Herr, verlanget mich	91	Repentance	1	49
Nicht so traurig, nicht so sehr	89	Cross and Consolation	4	48
Noch dennoch muszt du drum nicht ganz	23	Cross and Consolation	1	38
Nun danket all und bringet Ehr	78	Praise and Thanksgiving	1	46
Nun, du lebest, unsre Krone	28	Eternal Life	1	39
Nun ist der Regen hin	17	Gratitude for Sunlight	1	37
Nun laszt uns gehn und treten	19	New Year	5	38
Nun ruhen alle Wälder	60	Evening	17	98
Nun sei getrost und unbetrübt	271	Eternal Life	1	73
O du allersüszste Freude	76	Whitsuntide	2	44
O Gott, mein Schöpfer, edler Fürst	81	Prayer and the Christian Life	2	48
O Haupt voll Blut und Wunden	49	Passiontide	10	86
O Herrscher in dem Himmelszelt	15	Petition during a storm	1	37
O Herz des Königs aller Welt	47	Passiontide	1	41
O Jesu Christ, dein Kripplein ist	153	Christmas	4	57
O Jesu Christ, mein schönstes Licht	200	Prayer and the Christian Life	2	63

	Goedeke Page	Subject	No. of English versions	Page
O Welt, sieh hier dein Leben	71	Passiontide	10	42
Schaut, schaut, was ist für Wunder dar	310	Christmas	1	79
Schwing dich auf zu deinem Gott	135	Cross and Consolation	1	55
Sei frölich alles weit und breit	171	Easter	1	61
Sei mir tausendmal gegrüszet	40	Passiontide	2	40
Sollt ich meinen Gott nicht singen	235	Praise and Thanksgiving	8	69
Voller Wunder, voller Kunst	304	Marriage	4	79
Wach auf, mein Herz, und singe	59	Morning	5	95
Warum machet solche Schmerzen	67	New Year	2	42
Warum sollt ich mich denn grämen	122	Cross and Consolation	5	108
Warum willst du drauszen stehen	108	Advent	3	51
Was alle Weisheit in der Welt	176	Holy Trinity	2	62
Was Gott gefällt, mein frommes Kind	139	Cross and Consolation	4	56
Was traurest du, mein Angesicht	289	Eternal Life	1	76
Weg, mein Herz, mit den Gedanken	62	Repentance	2	41
Wie ist es müglich, höchstes Licht	324	Praise and Thanksgiving	1	81
Wie ist so grosz und schwer die Last	7	Praise and Thanksgiving	1	36
Wie lang, o Herr, wie lange soll	178	Cross and Consolation	1	62
Wie schön ists doch, Herr Jesu Christ	302	Matrimony	1	78
Wie soll ich dich empfangen	25	Advent	8	82
Wir singen dir, Emanuel	150	Christmas	11	110
Wol dem, der den Herren scheuet	130	Prayer and the Christian Life	1	55
Wol dem Menschen, der nicht wandelt	124	Prayer and the Christian Life	1	54
Zeuch ein zu deinen Thoren	111	Whitsuntide	6	52
Zweierlei bitt ich von dir	80	Prayer and the Christian Life	1	47

84 Hymns.   Total number of English versions 271

AFTERWORD

In commemoration of the 300th anniversary of the death of Paul Gerhardt, June 7, 1676 (often referred to as the greatest hymn writer of the Lutheran church after Martin Luther), it is fitting that Concordia Publishing House make available again this book originally published by Yale University Press in 1918. Appreciation is hereby expressed to the original publisher for their cooperation and approval of this endeavor.

An updated bibliography is included following the Afterword, since the entries in the 1918 version do not go beyond 1913 (see footnote page XI). The updated entries are shown in two sections: German and English publications. The German listing also reflects a reorganization and revision of the German titles included in the original bibliography. Acknowledgment and appreciation is hereby expressed to Dr. Konrad Ameln, Posener, Germany, and Prof. Carl Schalk, River Forest, Ill., for supplying the updated bibliography.

BIBLIOGRAPHIE (Bibliography)

A. *Quellen* (Roots)

J. Crueger, Berlin 1647
PRAXIS PIETATIS MELICA. Das ist Vbung der Gottseligkeit in Christlichen und
Trostreichen Gesaengen/ Herrn D. Martini Lutheri fuernemlich/ und denn auch
anderer vornehmer und gelehrter Leute. Ordentlich zusammen gebracht/ und Mit
vielen schoenen ausserlesenen newen Gesaengen gezieret: Auch zu Befoderung des
KirchenGOttes dienstes mit beygesetzten Melodien/ Nebest dem Basso Continuo
verfertiget Von Johann Cruegern Gub: Lus: Direct. Mus. in Berlin ad D. N. Jn
Verlegung des Auctoris, und Christophori Runge/ Gedruckt zu Berlin Anno
1647.
Further Editions: 1653, 1657, 1661, 1664, 1666, 1667, 1670, 1671, 1672, 1674,
          1678, 1679, 1684, 1688, 1690, etc., till 1736.

J. Crueger, Frankfurt/M. 1656
PRAXIS PIETATIS MELICA. Das ist: Vbung der Gottseligkeit in Christlichen und
Trostreichen Gesaengen/ Herrn D. Martini Lutheri fuernemlich/ wie auch anderer
seiner getreuen Nachfolger/ und reiner Evangelischer Lehre Bekennerer [!].
Ordentlich zusammen gebracht/ und ueber vorige Edition mit noch gar vielen
schoenen Gesaengen de novo vermehret und verbessert. Auch zu Befoderung des so
wohl Kirchen- als Privat-Gottesdienstes mit beygesetztem bisshero
gebraeuchlichen/ und vielen schoenen neuen Melodien/ nebenst dazu gehoerigen
Fundament/ verfertiget Von Johan Cruegern/ Gub. Lusato. Direct. Musico in
Berlin. Jn Verlegung Balthasaris Mevii. Wittenb. Gedruckt zu Franckfurt/ bey Casp.
Roeteln Anno 1656.
Further Editions: 1662, 1666, 1668, 1674, 1676, 1678, 1679, 1680, 1683, 1693, and
          1700.

J. G. Ebeling 1666/67
PAULI GERHARDI Geistliche Andachten Bestehend in hundert und zwantzig
Liedern/ Auff Hoher und vornehmer Herren Anfoderung in ein Buch gebracht/
Der goettlichen Majestaet zu foderst Zu Ehren/ denn auch der werthen und
bedraengten Christenheit zu Trost/ und einer jedweden glaeubigen Seelen Zu
Vermehrung ihres Christenthums Also Dutzendweise mit neuen sechsstimmigen
Melodeyen gezieret. Hervor gegeben und verlegt Von JOHAN GEORG
EBELJNG/ Der Berlinischen Haupt-Kirchen Music: Director. BERLJN/ Gedruckt
bey Christoff Rungen/ ANNO M DC LXVII.
Further Editions: ca. 1669, 1670, 1671, 1672, 1682, 1683, and 1700.

Ch. Runge 1670
Neuvermehrete Geistliche Wasserquelle: Darinnen sich ein jedes frommes Hertz/ beydes auf der Reise und daheim/ bey guten kuehlen Tagen/ und in mancherley Hitze der Anfechtung/ leiblich und geistlich erquicken und erfrischen kan. Aus dem heylsamen Hauptbrunnen der Heiligen Schrifft/ und andern Christlichen Buechern zugerichtet: Sampt etlicher Koeniglichen/ Fuerstlichen und Graefflichen Personen Symbolis und Gedenkspruechen: Mit beygefuegeten schoenen neubekandten/ fuernemlich Herrn Pauli Gerhardi 120. Geist- und Trostreichen Liedern vermehret/ Jtzo aufs neue mit Fleiss uebersehen und an vielen Orten gebessert. Zu Berlin/ Gedruckt und verlegt von Christoff Runge. Anno M DC LXX.

J. H. Feustking 1707
PAULI GERHARDI Geistreiche Haus- und Kirchen-Lieder Zur Ubung und Gebrauch Des singenden Gottesdienstes vormahls zum Druck befoerdert; Jetzo aber Nach des sel. Autoris eigenhaendigen revidirten Exemplar mit Fleiss uebersehen/ Auch samt einem kurtzen/ doch Noethigen Vorbericht bey dieser ersten und gantz neuen Verbesserten und vermehrten Aufflage/ Ausgefertiget von Joh. Heinrich Feustking/ D. Hoch-Fuerstl. Consistorial-Rath/ Hof-Predigern und Beicht-Vater/ auch Superintendenten des Fuerstenthums Anhalt-Zerbst. ZERBST/ Zu finden bey Carl Anthon Davidis. Druckts Samuel Tietze/ 1707. Further Editions: 1717 and 1723.

B. *Neuausgaben* (New Editions)
   (in chronological order)

Leben und Lieder des Paulus Gerhardt, herausgegeben von E. C. G. *Langbecker,* Berlin 1841.

Paulus Gerhardts Geistliche Andachten in hundert und zwanzig Liedern. Nach der ersten durch Johann Georg *Ebeling* besorgten Ausgabe mit Anmerkungen, einer geschichtlichen Einleitung und Urkunden herausgegeben von O. *Schulze,* Berlin 1842, 2/1852, 3/1869.

Paulus Gerhardts Geistliche Lieder, herausgegeben von Ph. *Wackernagel,* Stuttgart 1843, 2/1849, 5/1869 (9. Aufl., von W. *Tuempel,* Guetersloh 1907).

Paulus Gerhardts Geistliche Lieder. Historisch-kritische Ausgabe von J. F. *Bachmann,* Berlin 1866, 2/1877.

Gedichte von Paul Gerhardt, herausgegeben von K. *Goedeke* (Deutsche Dichter des 17. Jahrhunderts, 12. Band), Leipzig 1877.

Paulus Gerhardts Geistliche Lieder. Mit Einleitung und Lebensabriss von K. *Gerok,* Stuttgart 1878; Leipzig 1890, 6/1907.

Paul Gerhardts Geistliche Lieder, herausgegeben von F. *von Schmidt,* Leipzig 1884.

Fischer, A. und *Tuempel,* W.: Das deutsche evangelische Kirchenlied des 17. Jahrhunderts. 3. Band, Guetersloh 1906, pp. 294—495.

Paul Gerhardts Lieder und Gedichte, herausgegeben von W. *Nelle,* Hamburg 1907.

Paul Gerhardt. Dichtungen und Schriften, herausgegeben und textkritisch durchgesehen von E. *von Cranach-Sichart,* Muenchen 1957.

Paul *Gerhardt,* Geistliche Andachten [1667]. Samt den uebrigen Liedern und den lateinischen Gedichten herausgegeben von F. *Kemp.* Mit einem Beitrag von W. *Blankenburg* (Deutsche Barock-Literatur), Bern u. Muenchen 1975. [Faksimile-Wiedergabe der "Geistliche Andachten" von J. G. *Ebeling,* Berlin 1666/67.]

C. *Biographien* (Biographies)

Hesselbacher, K.: Paul Gerhardt, der Saenger froehlichen Glaubens, Leipzig 1936.

Hiltsch, G.: Paul Gerhardt. Gesungenes Evangelium, Stuttgart 1951.

Ihlenfeld, K.: Huldigung fuer Paul Gerhardt (Edition Merseburger 1119), Berlin 1956.

Kaiser, P.: Paul Gerhardt. Ein Bild seines Lebens, Leipzig 1908.

Kochs, E.: Paul Gerhardt. Sein Leben und seine Lieder (Festschrift der Allg. ev.-luth. Konferenz), Leipzig 1907, 2/1926.

Nelle, W.: Paul Gerhardt. Der Dichter und seine Dichtung (Welt des Gesangbuchs, Heft 22), Leipzig u. Hamburg 1940.

Petrich, H.: Paul Gerhardt, seine Lieder und seine Zeit, Guetersloh 1907.

_____: Paul Gerhardt. Ein Beitrag zur Geschichte des deutschen Geistes. Auf Grund neuer Forschungen und Funde, Guetersloh 1914.

Trillhaas, W.: Paul Gerhardt (1607—1667). In: Die grossen Deutschen. 1. Band, Berlin 1956, pp. 533—546.

Wernle, P.: Paulus Gerhardt (Religionsgeschichtliche Volksbuecher IV, Heft 2), Tuebingen 1907. (Cf. *Guenther,* A.: Paul Gerhardt in religionsgeschichtlicher Beleuchtung. In MGkK 12. Jahrgang 1907, pp. 112—113.)

D. *Artikel in Nachschlagewerken* (Articles in encyclopedias and dictionaries)

Abbreviations: MGG=Die Musik in Geschichte und Gegenwart, Kassel und Basel 1949ff.
RGG=Die Religion in Geschichte und Gegenwart, Tuebingen 2/1927—1932, 3/1956—1965.

Blankenburg, W.: Johannes Crueger (1598—1662). In MGG II, columns 1799—1814.

_____: Johann Georg Ebeling (1637—1676). In MGG III, columns 1041—1045.

_____: Paul[us] Gerhardt (1607—1676). In MGG IV, columns 1790—1797.

Koch, E. E.: Geschichte des Kirchenlieds und Kirchengesangs der christlichen, insbesondere der deutschen evangelischen Kirche, 3. Band, Stuttgart 3/1867, pp. 297—327.

Matthias, W.: Paul(us) Gerhardt (1607—1676). In RGG 2. Band, Tuebingen 3/1958, columns 1413—1415.

Zscharnack, L.: Paulus Gerhardt. In RGG 2. Band, Tuebingen 2/1928, columns 1042—1044.

E. *Einzeluntersuchungen* (Special studies)

Abbreviations: JbLH=Jahrbuch fuer Liturgik und Hymnologie, Kassel 1955ff.
MGkK=Monatschrift fuer Gottesdienst und kirchliche Kunst,
Goettingen 1896—1941.

van Andel, C. P.: Paul Gerhardt, mysticus en barokmens. In: Kerk en Theologie,
April 1973, pp. 134—146.

Brodde, O.: Zur Typologie der Paul-Gerhardt-Lieder. In: Kerygma und Melos. Ch.
Mahrenholz 70 Jahre, Kassel u. Berlin 1970, pp. 333—341.

Fornacon, S.: Zu Paul Gerhardts Liedern. In JbLH 4. Band 1958/59, pp. 119—121.

Guenther, R.: Ueber Deutung und Aenderung einiger Stellen in Paul Gerhardts
Liedern. In MGkK 11. Jahrgang 1906, pp. 345—348.

Knipfer, J.: Paul Gerhardt. Gesammelte Aufsaetze. Leipzig 1906.

Mogensen, K.: Paul Gerhardts forsynstro (P. Gerhardts Vorsehungsglaube). In:
Dansk teologisk Tidsskrift, Kopenhagen 1969, pp. 118—134.

Nelle, W.: Gerhardt, Rist, Tersteegen, Gellert in unseren heutigen
Gesangbuechern. In MGkK 10. Jahrgang 1905, pp. 141—151; 189—191.

Nicolaisen, Lisbet J.: Die melodische Vorlage. In JbLH 13. Band 1968, pp. 156—160.

_____: Welche Vorlage hat Paul Gerhardt fuer sein Lied "O Welt, sieh hier dein
Leben" benutzt? In JbLH 17. Band 1972, pp. 235—239.

Roebbelen, I.: "Rechtfertigung" und "Gottvertrauen" in der Liederdichtung Paul
Gerhardts. In: Theologie und Froemmigkeit (Forschungen zur Kirchen- und
Dogmengeschichte, Band 6), Goettingen 1957, pp. 404—425.

Sauer-Geppert, W.-I.: Eine Vorlage zu Paul Gerhardts "O Welt, sieh hier dein
Leben." In JbLH 15. Band 1970, pp. 153—159.

_____: Noch einmal: Zur Quellenfrage von Paul Gerhardts Lied "O Welt, sieh hier
dein Leben." Eine Entgegnung an L. J. Nicolaisen. In JbLH 17. Band 1972, pp.
239—241.

Smend, J.: "Lobet den Herren alle, die ihn fuerchten." In MGkK 12. Jahrgang 1907,
pp. 105—107.

_____: "Wann ich einmal soll scheiden." In MGkK 7. Jahrgang 1902, pp. 75—78.

Spitta, F.: Paul Gerhardts Lieder und die Musik. In MGkK 12. Jahrgang 1907, pp.
84—90.

Zeller, W.: Paul Gerhardt. Zum 350. Geburtstag des evangelischen Kirchenlied-
dichters. In: Musik und Kirche, 27. Jahrgang, Kassel 1957, pp. 161—169.

_____: Zur Textueberlieferung der Lieder Paul Gerhardts. In JbLH 19. Band 1975,
pp. 225—228.

Zusammengestellt von (compiled by) Konrad Ameln
Nov. 1975

Collections

Kelly, John. *Paul Gerhardt's Spiritual Songs.* London: Alexander Strahan, 1867.
Pick, Bernhard. *Lyra Gerhardti or A Selection of Paul Gerhardt's Spiritual Songs.*
   Burlington, Iowa: The German Literary Board, 1906.
*Paulus Gerhardt Geistliche Lieder nach der bei seinen Lebzeiten erschienenen
   Ausgabe wieder abgedruckt.* Philadelphia, Pa., 1890.

Biographies

Dallmann, William. *Paul Gerhardt: His Life and His Hymns.* St. Louis: Concordia
   Publishing House, n.d.
Wenzel, G. A. *Pictures from the Life of Paul Gerhardt.* Easton, Pa.: Riegel, 1881.

*Biographical Sketches in Dictionaries
and Encyclopedias*

Ludolphy (tr.). "Paul Gerhardt." *Encyclopedia of the Lutheran Church.* Vol. II.
   Julius Bodensieck, ed. Minneapolis: Augsburg Publishing House, 1965, pp.
   906—908.
Mearns, James. "Paul Gerhardt." *A Dictionary of Hymnology.* John Julian, ed. 2nd
   ed. London: John Murray, 1915, pp. 409—412.
Polack, W. G. "Paul Gerhardt." *The Handbook to the Lutheran Hymnal.* St. Louis:
   Concordia Publishing House, 1942, pp. 510—511.
Spaeth, A. "Paul Gerhardt." *The Lutheran Cyclopedia.* Henry E. Jacobs, ed. New
   York: Charles Scribner's Sons, 1899, pp. 196—197.
   In addition brief unsigned biographical articles appear in: *Lutheran
   Cyclopedia.* Erwin Luecker, ed. St. Louis: Concordia Publishing House, 1954,
   p. 410; *Lutheran Cyclopedia,* rev. ed. Erwin Luecker, ed. St. Louis: Concordia
   Publishing House, 1975, pp. 329—330; *The Concordia Cyclopedia.* L.
   Fuerbringer, Th. Engelder, P. E. Kretzmann, eds. St. Louis: Concordia
   Publishing House, 1927, p. 288. See also E. E. Ryden, "Paul Gerhardt, Prince
   of Lutheran Hymnists," *The Story of Christian Hymnody,* Rock Island:
   Augustana Press, 1959, pp. 97—101.

Journal Article

Johansen, J. H. "Paul Gerhardt (1607—1676), poet of consolation." *The Hymn,* V,
   84—89 (July 1954).

Other Publications

Biarowsky, Wilhelm von. *Warum muss Paul Gerhardt unserer Kirche immer wert
   bleiben?* Reading, Pa.: Pilger-Buchhandlung, n.d.
Lindemann, Frederick. *Festbuechlein zur 300jaehrigen Geburtstagfeier Paulus
   Gerhardts, des Assaphs der lutherischen Kirche.* St. Louis: Concordia
   Publishing House, 1907.